LAN Operations

LAN
Operations

A Guide to
Daily Management

Peter D. Rhodes

Addison-Wesley Publishing Company, Inc.
Reading, Massachusetts · Menlo Park, California · New York Don Mills, Ontario · Wokingham, England · Amsterdam · Bonn · Sydney · Singapore · Tokyo · Madrid · San Juan

Many of the designations used by manufacturers and sellers to distinguish their products are claimed as trademarks. Where those designations appear in this book, and Addison-Wesley was aware of a trademark claim, the designations have been printed in initial caps or all caps.

The programs and applications presented in this book have been included for their instructional value. They have been tested with care but are not guaranteed for any particular purpose. The publisher does not offer any warranties or representations, nor does it accept any liabilities with respect to the programs or applications.

The publisher offers discounts on this book when ordered in quantity for special sales. For more information please contact:
Corporate & Professional Publishing Group
Addison-Wesley Publishing Company
Route 128
Reading, Massachusetts 01867

Library of Congress Cataloging-in-Publication Data

Rhodes, Peter D.
  LAN operations : a guide to daily management / Peter D. Rhodes.
    p. cm.
  Includes bibliographical references and index.
  ISBN 0-201-56301-0 (acid-free paper)
  1. Office practice—Automation.   2. Local area networks (Computer networks)   I. Title.
HF5548.2.R46 1991
658′.05468—dc20   90-883
                                                                    CIP

Copyright © 1991 by Addison-Wesley Publishing Company, Inc.

Sponsoring Editor, Ted Buswick
Production Supervisor, Perry McIntosh
Cover design by Absolute Design Services
Text design by Joyce C. Weston
Set in 10½ point Palatino by DEKR Corp.

ISBN 0-201-56301-0

Printed on recycled and acid-free paper
ABCDEFGHIJ—MA—943210
First Printing, October 1990

*Technical
Publishing
Advisory Board*

*Corporate and
Professional
Publishing Group*

Acknowledgment

To properly acknowledge all of those who have made this book possible would take an acknowledgment the size of a telephone directory for a small town. Therefore, I have selected one special group and one individual whom I wish to acknowledge. The group is my teachers, in academia and otherwise. I learned more from you than you will ever know. I also wish to acknowledge Scott Gant. You demonstrated that the value of integrity is far beyond any possible price.

*To my wife, Ann. For always;
in all ways.*

Contents

1. Introduction   1

   LAN Managers   1
      Responsibilities   2
      Abilities   3
      Challenge   4
   Supervisors of LAN Managers   4
      Performance of Hardware   4
      Budgets   5
      Other Activities   6
   Students of LAN Management   6
   Case Studies   6

2. An Overview of the What and the Why of Management for Local Area Networks (LAN)   8

   General Description of This Text   8
   History of Private Networks   9
      Remote Terminals   12
      Ring Networks   13
      Bus Networks   13
      The "Carterfone" Ruling   14
   LAN Topologies   15
      Star Networks   15

Ring Topology   17
Bus Topology   19
Access Methods   20
  Deterministic Access Methods   21
  Heuristic Access Methods   22
Connectivity   23
Impact of LANs on Corporate Culture   24
  Central Versus Distributed Computing   24
  MIS Viewpoint   26
  PC Users' Viewpoint   26
  LAN Manager's Viewpoint   27
  Information Movement Within the Organization   28
  Knowledge of the Organization   29
  Subscriber Satisfaction   32
Summary   33
Case Study   34

3. Accounting Management   35

Accounting Management Identifies Consumers of Resources   35
  History   36
  Methods   36
Positive Aspects of Accounting Management   39
  Identification of Bandwidth Consumers   39
  Improvement of Performance Management   40
  Allocation of Costs   40
  Reduction of G&A Expenses   40
  Separate Telecommunications Organization   40
  Review   42
Negative Aspects of Accounting Management   43
  Manpower Costs   43
  Hardware and Software Costs   43
  Internal Friction   44
  Separate Telecommunications Organization   45
  Review   46
Implementation of Accounting Management   46
  Measurement Methods   47
  Who Pays for Usage?   48
Growth of the Organization and Accounting Management   49
  Single LAN   50
  Multiple LANs   50

Interconnected LANs   51
Summary   52
Case Study   53

4. Configuration Management in Local Area Networks   56

Basic Knowledge of the LAN   56
  Topology   56
  Topography   57
  Inventory   57
  Functions   58
Knowledge Provides Control of LAN Assets   59
  Status   59
  Changes   60
  Updates   61
Positive Aspects of Configuration Management   62
  Records of LAN Conditions and History   62
  Commonality of Equipment and Functions   64
  Elimination of Unnecessary Expenses   66
  Manpower Savings   68
  Restoration of the LAN   68
  Repair Parts/TMDE   69
  Review   69
Negative Aspects of Configuration Management   70
  Development Is Frozen   70
  Dissension Within the Organization   72
  Prevention of Dissension   74
  Review   75
Implementing Configuration Management   75
  Organizational Goals   75
  Circuit Inventory   80
  Configuration Management Results   81
Summary   82
Case Study   83

5. Fault Management   85

Preventing and Correcting Defective LAN Conditions   85
  Proactive Fault Management   85
  Quality of Service   86
  Stress Points   86

Single Point of Failure   86
Alternative Routing   87
Monitoring   88
Reactive Fault Management   89
Rapidity in Restoration   89
Hot Sites   90
Contingency Planning   91
Prioritizing Efforts   92
Positive Aspects of Fault Management   93
Positive Aspects   93
Fault Versus Event   95
Negative Aspects of Fault Management   96
Personnel   96
Test, Measurement, and Diagnostic Equipment   97
Spares   98
Implementation of Fault Management   98
Technical Control   98
Contract Maintenance   101
Disaster Recovery   103
Growth of the Organization Supported by the LAN   104
Single Network Growth   104
Multiple Network Growth   106
Impact of Expert Systems on Fault Management   107
Summary   107
Case Study   108

6. Performance Management   111

Components of Performance Management   111
Objective Standards   112
Measurement by Subjective Standards   116
Positive Aspects of Performance Management   119
Resource Maximization   119
Performance Constraints   121
Complaint Prevention   123
Negative Aspects of Performance Management   123
Manpower   123
Specialized Equipment (TMDE)   124
Data Processing Equipment   124
Results   124
Changes   125

Implementation of Performance Management   126
   Throughput Evaluation   126
   File Transfer Time   128
   MTBF/MTTR   130
   Redesign   131
   Financial Impact of Redesign   132
   Recurring Performance Failures   133
Organizational Growth and Performance Management   134
   Subscriber Growth   134
   New Hardware   135
   Shrinking Organizations   135
   Relocation   135
   Automation and the LAN   138
Summary   139
Case Study   140

7. Network Security   142

Why Institute LAN Security?   142
   Preventing Loss of Corporate Resources   143
   Preventing Fraud and Theft   143
   Prevent Unauthorized Release of Information   143
   Methods of Denying Access   144
   Layered Security   149
Positive Aspects of Security Management   152
   Preventing Sabotage or Espionage   152
   Traffic Load Increase   153
   Preventing "Infection"   154
   Negative Aspects of Security Management   154
   Additional Subscriber Actions   154
   Audit Trails   154
   Random Number Devices   155
   Encryption Devices   155
   Biological Measuring Devices   156
   Dial Back   156
Implementing LAN Security Management   157
   Identify Threats   157
   Implement Security Plan   158
Summary   161

8. Measurements of the LAN   164

Why Measure the LAN?   164
  Performance Management   164
  Fault Management   165
  LAN Growth   165
  Usage/Budget Data   166
  WAN/VAN Vendor Billing   166
  Vendor Hardware Claims   167
Measuring Transmission Media   167
  Time Domain Reflectometer   167
  Signal-to-Noise Ratio   168
  Nonmetallic Transmission Media   168
Measure Throughput   169
Protocol Functions   171
Measure Response Time   173
Measurement Supports Several Management Functions   174
  Fault Management   174
  Accounting Management   175
  Performance Management   175
  TMDE Type and Applications   176
  Time Domain Reflectometer   176
  Oscilloscopes   176
  Meters   177
  Break Out Boxes   177
  Other TMDE   177
  Protocol Analyzers   177
Calibration   178
Summary   179
Case Study   179

9. Standards   182

Philosophy of Standards   182
Types of Standards   183
  International Standards   183
  Vendor-Specific Standards   184
The OSI Model   185
  Physical Layer (Layer 1)   185
  Data Link (Layer 2)   186
  Network Layer (Layer 3)   186
  Transport (Layer 4)   186

Session Layer (Layer 5)   186
Presentation Layer (Layer 6)   186
Application Layer (Layer 7)   186
Impact of Standards on the LAN Manager   187
LAN Management Standards   188
Accounting Management   189
Configuration Management   189
Fault Management   189
Performance Management   189
Security Management   189
Summary   190

10. Personnel in Network Management   191

Selection of Personnel   191
Selection   191
Costs of New Employees   192
Interviews   193
Legalities   193
Testing   194
References   195
Security   196
Bonding   197
Life Insurance   197
Training for LAN Staff   198
Engineer Training   198
Technician Training   199
Other Professional Training   200
Nonprofessional Training   200
Preventing Turnover   201
Challenging Work   201
Personal and Professional Growth   202
Evaluation   202
Promotions   204
Transfers   205
Other Activities to Prevent Turnover   205
Summary   206

11. Required Reports   208

Address   209
Add/Drop Subscribers   209

Alarm Conditions   211
Bandwidth Availability   213
Bandwidth Changes   213
Bandwidth Consumption   214
Circuit Status   216
Designed Capacity Limitations   217
Equipment Capacity   218
Equipment Status   219
Equipment Upgrade   220
Key Changes   222
LAN Access Count   222
Lease/Dial Circuit Cost   223
Lease/Dial Circuit Status   225
Loss/Slippage of Timing   225
Password Data   226
Private Branch Exchange (PBX) Data   227
Subscriber Authorization   228
Subscriber Location   228
Test, Measurement, and Diagnostic
Equipment (TMDE)   229
Trouble Ticket Data   230
Summary   231

Appendix: A Subscriber's Guide to the Corporate LAN   232

Introduction   232
  The LAN Manager   232
  The LAN Manager's Immediate Supervisor   232
  Training Department   233
  The Subscribers   233
  Required Subscriber Information   233
  Training Department   235
  Demarcation Point   235
  Review and Preview   235
The LAN Defined   236
  Definition   236
  Performance Objective   236
  Goals   236
  Makeup of the LAN   237
  The LAN in Concept   238
  How to Use the LAN   239

Who Pays for Use of the LAN? 241
  Usage Costs 242
  Cost Reduction 243
LAN Operation 244
  Physical Parameters 244
  Unauthorized Modifications 245
  Addresses 246
  Performance Objective 247
Telecommunications Failure 247
  Inform the Correct People 247
  Performance Objective 248
  Pay Attention to What Has Happened 248
  Performance Objective 249
  Assistance 249
  Accuracy in Reporting 249
  Performance Objective 250
Slow Response Time 250
  Subjective Evaluation 250
Performance Objective 250
Information Security 251
  Passwords 251
  Performance Objective 251
  Corporate Data 252
  Performance Objective 252
  Software 252
  Performance Objective 253

Glossary 254
Recommended Reading 258
Index 260

1 *Introduction*

This introduction discusses the types of people to whom this text will be useful and, in general terms, the relationship between Local Area Networks (LANs) and the organizations in which such LANs are installed.

While glancing through my library I noted several titles about some of the technical aspects of Local Area Networks (LANs); titles such as *Lord of the Token Rings, Zen and the Art of UNIX,* and *Tales of the Etherlan,* to name three. Nowhere did I see any work that could provide guidance to those who have been charged with the administrative management of LANs. This book provides help to those who have little technical background and little or no direct LAN management experience.

Three groups of people may find guidance within this text:

1 LAN Managers
2 Those to whom LAN Managers report
3 Students who study LAN management

LAN Managers

The key idea here is the function of management. The LAN Manager is charged with the operation and maintenance of a corporate asset. This asset is no different, in a managerial sense, from a lathe, a production line, or a personnel department. The LAN is composed of discrete items, each performing a definable function. Each is the responsibility of a technically, or soon to be technically, qualified person.

Because the LAN is a corporate asset, the standard management paradigm applies:

1 Define plans and goals.
2 Take action.
3 Measure results.
4 Correct deviations.
5 Revise plans and goals.
6 Repeat as required.

The *goal* of any LAN is to provide a means of information interchange between like and unlike data processing devices that are separated by a given distance. The *action* is the transport of that information through the LAN. The *measurement* is the evaluation of this information interchange for compliance with predetermined parameters. The *correction* involves taking one or more actions that remove temporary impediments to the information interchange. The *revision* includes modifying hardware or software such that information interchange does not degrade under LAN modifications or changes in corporate goals or missions.

Responsibilities

The LAN Manager has budgetary responsibilities:

- How much must be allocated for maintenance of current equipment?
- Will expansion of the plant require additional hardware, software, or people?
- How much will it cost to install that new equipment?
- What is the impact of new or expanded departments and divisions on the throughput of the LAN?

Technical people are required to design, install, operate, maintain, and modify the LAN:

- What skills must engineers, technicians, and operators have?
- What training will they require?
- Is turnover a problem?

Abilities

The LAN Manager must be able to:

- Write job descriptions.
- Set pay scales.
- Define performance objectives for training.
- Conduct formal periodic reviews of these people.

The LAN Manager must also know the organization that the LAN serves. The LAN Manager must create, evaluate, and promote new services for LAN users (subscribers). To be successful, these new services must have two major goals:

1 To be quicker, or provide more functionality, or be easier than the method now in use.
2 To be more cost effective than the present method.

For example, consider a branch of the organization that produces a daily report on the number of rejects from product line X. The report is mailed to corporate headquarters on the following Monday. All reports from other branches are summarized for a monthly statistics briefing. The cost of this information interchange is the cost of mailing the media on which it is recorded. A small report, two or three sheets of paper, or a single diskette, costs little more than first-class postage. Since this information interchange is already cost effective, it is not a good application for the LAN.

On the other hand, architectural or mechanical drawings are good candidates for LAN transmission based on three criteria:

1 *Size*—They are more expensive to mail than letters.

2 *Convenience*—It is easier to modify a drawing on a CRT (cathode ray tube) than to completely redraw it for every minor change.

3 *Speed*—A full-size (D or E) drawing sent through internal distribution may take a full day to get from the document repository to the engineer's desk. The same size drawing, sent via

the LAN, can be transmitted across the country and be available for use in less than five minutes.

Challenge

The greatest challenge to the LAN Manager is that of the periodic modifications of the LAN in response to changing corporate structures and goals. The term "periodic" can, in some organizations, mean daily. If the organization is large enough, some element of it will move, add, or delete subscribers to the LAN on a daily basis. Monitoring, evaluating, and recording these moves is a major effort. If the LAN is divided into subnetworks, the impact of these moves on the performance characteristics of the subnetworks must be evaluated before the move is made. Failure to perform this evaluation will require the LAN to be redesigned "on the fly" to support the move. During the redesign phase, subscriber satisfaction with LAN performance may well hit record lows.

Supervisors of LAN Managers

Those who supervise LAN Managers should benefit from this text by gaining a better knowledge of LAN management and learning how to support the neophyte LAN Manager. The LAN Manager's supervisor is, at times, the interface between the LAN Manager and senior management within the organization. The duties of the LAN Manager's supervisor do not require a great depth of technical knowledge, but they do require knowledge of how this technology can be integrated into the organization and how it can support the organization's goals.

Performance of Hardware

A LAN can pass only so much data (traffic) during a given time period. If more than the specified amount of data is offered to the LAN, throughput slows dramatically. Some types of LANs exhibit a logarithmic degradation when offered more traffic than they can handle. Whereas the design of subnetworks is technically difficult, such (re)design is a rather straightforward application of queueing theory, consuming more time than effort. Many types of simulation software are written with just this problem in mind.

The second greatest challenge to a LAN Manager's supervisor is that of providing a service to the organization as a whole. Any organization can be divided into two categories, production and production support. The LAN Manager's supervisor is in the second category. All decisions must be made with the idea that each dollar expended must be in support of the organization's product or service. Technology (the LAN) does not exist for its own sake.

Budgets

The LAN Manager's supervisor must evaluate LAN budgets, requests for unforeseen expenses, and modifications to the LAN in terms of maximum benefit to the organization for each dollar expended. In general, any expenditure for the LAN must increase the LAN's ability to perform information interchange. When evaluating the cost/benefit ratio for new purchases for the LAN, several criteria must be considered. Some of the more important ones are:

- Does this expenditure increase throughput?

- Can more data pass through the LAN faster, or are more subscribers allowed on the LAN without degrading performance?

- Does this expenditure help restore the LAN when it fails?

- Can it help isolate defective hardware or software faster or more accurately than the current method? Speed in restoration is all important. For as long as a subscriber is prevented from using the LAN, that subscriber may be loosing productivity. If no productivity is lost, satisfaction with the LAN is gained.

- Does this expenditure improve subscriber satisfaction?

- Does the subscriber find the modified LAN easier to use, or is that person more productive or more accurate in work completed?

- Does the hardware or software purchased integrate successfully with the hardware or software on hand?

- Will this expenditure pass "mahogany row?" Does senior management accept the fact that the LAN is a necessary part of the current corporate culture and must be treated as important in the production support function, as the personnel department, or the accounting department?

Other Activities

The LAN Manager's supervisor has other activities as the LAN is operated on a day-to-day basis. These activities are generally understood in other parts of this text, and they are addressed in more detail in the last section of Chapter 2, which discusses the impact of LANs on corporate culture.

Students of LAN Management

The management of a LAN is no different conceptually than the management of any other element of an organization. The LAN is a system that has several inputs: money, manpower, hardware, and software. It has one output: service to the user, which, in this case, is the subscriber. It is the LAN Manager's responsibility to ensure that these inputs are used in the most cost-effective manner, providing an economical, easy-to-use, and accurate means of interchange of information within and without the organization's boundaries. This text should give you a working knowledge of what must be done to achieve this goal.

Case Studies

Where appropriate throughout this text, a case study is appended at the end of the appropriate chapter. There is no case study in the chapter on security management. We see no reason to provide potential criminals with directions on how to break into LANs or the equipment connected to them. The case studies take the following format:

- Section 1 is directed toward certain factual data such as who, where, when, why, how much, and how many. Names of persons, organizations, and locations have been changed to protect the innocent (guilty?) parties.
- Section 2 addresses what was done, or what happened.
- Section 3 is concerned with losses, including time, money, product, or service to the customer.
- Section 4 is the lesson learned from this activity. It discusses

how to prevent these actions from recurring, corrective actions that must be taken, and, where applicable, the general costs involved.

Readers must realize that the cases discussed here may not directly apply to their organization. If the cause of the error was a loss of the token in a token-ring-based LAN, those using a bus topology LAN should not look to this particular case study as a panacea for their problems. Conversely, many cases can be applied to any type of LAN. Each case must be evaluated on its own merits for application to each LAN that is being managed. Finally readers must ask a very pointed question: What would be the single best way, other than the one discussed, to correct or prevent future recurrences of this problem?

An Overview of Local Area Network (LAN) Management

A beginning is the time for taking the most delicate care that the balances are correct.

—Dune, Frank Herbert

This chapter has several goals:

- To generally describe the text.
- To present a brief history of computer communications.
- To introduce LAN topologies.
- To provide a high-level overview of access methods.
- To discuss connectivity.
- To explore the impact of LANs on the corporate culture.

General Description of This Text

This text covers the administrative, not technical, aspects of LAN management. Chapters 3 through 7 cover the following specific areas of LAN management:

- Chapter 3—Accounting Management (AM) is concerned with allocating LAN usage among the subscribers for billing purposes.
- Chapter 4—Configuration Management (CM) is the control over the LAN's physical make-up. CM is concerned with the contents of the LAN.

- Chapter 5—Fault Management (FM) is directed to restoring the LAN when it fails to perform as required.
- Chapter 6—Performance Management (PM) addresses how well the LAN is doing the job of supporting the subscribers in terms of throughput quantity and quality.
- Chapter 7—Security Management (SM) is the function of protecting not only the LAN itself and its data, but also the data that is stored in resources to which the LAN is connected.

Chapter 8, perhaps the most crucial chapter of this book, explains, in some detail, the how and why of LAN measurement. Few people, particularly those in management, are fully aware of the necessity for obtaining true measures of performance of systems for which they are responsible. If you cannot measure a thing, you cannot manage it!

Chapter 9 addresses the roles played by standards bodies in regards to telecommunications, specifically LANs. Much of Chapter 9 has no direct bearing on the daily actions of the LAN Manager. These standards come into play when planning major new acquisitions, or integrating disparate networks.

Chapter 10 discusses how to manage the people who make up the LAN. Supervision of people is the subject of many texts by those learned in that area. Chapter 10 conveys a few observations of what to do and what to refrain from doing. These observations are based on actual field experience.

Chapter 11 covers in some detail the reports that LAN Managers must have available to understand the functioning of the corporate resource under their supervision.

History of Private Networks

A brief review of the subject and its history may lay the groundwork for the understanding of why LANs need management. Many acronyms and products appear in the discussion. Several of these technologies need explanation before much more discussion is presented. As you read this explanation, review Figures 2.1 and 2.2.

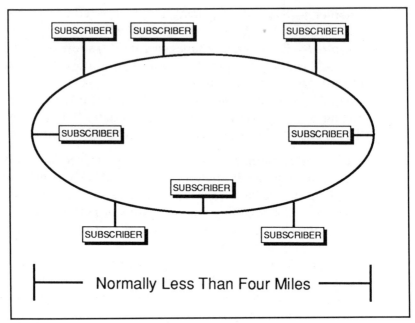

Normally Less Than Four Miles

FIGURE 2.1

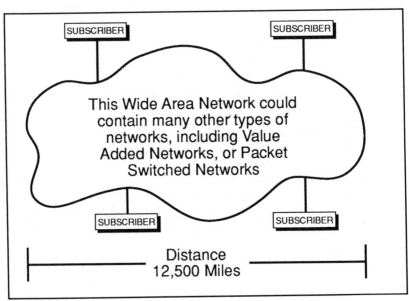

This Wide Area Network could contain many other types of networks, including Value Added Networks, or Packet Switched Networks

Distance
12,500 Miles

FIGURE 2.2

Local Area Network (LAN): A LAN usually consists of various data processing devices connected through one or more types of wire or cable. These devices include:

Bridges
Bus and network inter-
    face units
"Dumb" terminals (no
    processing power)
Facsimile machines
File servers/mainframe
    computers
Gateways
Personal computers
Print servers

Repeaters
Routers
Software
Tape drives
Text scanners
Terminal servers
Video teleconferencing
    equipment
Workstations, diskless or
    otherwise.

The types of wire and cable, sometimes known as transmission media, include thin and thick coaxial cable, twisted pair wiring, or fiber optic cable. Some LANs are connected via radio waves and some through light waves; however, these are not as common as wire and cable. (These terms are defined in the glossary.)

As a rule of thumb, LANs are confined to the immediate area of a building, or several buildings in a campus setting.

When trying to decide if a network is a LAN, remember these two key points:

1 A LAN is constrained by its topology. Some LANs cannot exceed 2800 meters in length.

2 The network must be *local*. Remember, we are talking about a *local* area network.

Wide Area Network (WAN): A WAN is normally not owned by the organization that uses it. A WAN is normally a communications capability provided by a common carrier such as AT&T, MCI, or other Regional Private Operating Agency (RPOA). The acronym RPOA derives from International Standards Organization terminology. Other terms meaning the same thing include the local telephone company or the Local Exchange Carrier (LEC). WAN users have minimal control over the transmission media and pay directly for using that media. Payment is computed based on bandwidth, that is, how many bits per second can transit the media; on the amount of time the user is connected to the transmission media; on the time of day in which the transmission takes place; and on the distance of the transmission. Exceptions to these rules exist. Sometimes WANs use leased lines.

When users buy leased lines, they buy a guarantee of some type of service from the vendor from one point to one or multiple points continually, for a fixed sum per time period, normally monthly. This provides the user with the same type of quality of service every time, with no chance of getting a "busy signal." This type of service is normally used when connecting two or more LANs across long distances on a continuous basis.

Packet Network: When using packet networks, the charge is based only on bandwidth and the number of packets sent. Bandwidth is measured in bits per second (bps), kilobits per second (Kbps), or megabits per second (Mbps).

Value Added Network (VAN): VANs are certain services provided to specialized customers. An entrepreneur purchases bandwidth in bulk from one or more of the major vendors such as AT&T or MCI. The entrepreneur modifies the bandwidth with extra benefits, creating extra value. The subscriber then pays for these extra benefits.

Commercial packet networks and VANs use the same technology and telecommunications infrastructure used by WANs. Conceptually, these two offerings are just another type of telecommunications service.

Remote Terminals

Remote terminals attached to a central processing unit (CPU) allegedly constituted the first LAN. This arrangement allowed the CPU user to be outside the same room where the computer was located. In this type of network, the emphasis was on the word "local." Normally the subscriber to the services was no more than 100 feet away from the CPU, and the connection was through thick, multipair cables. The remote terminals used during the earliest stages of data communications were teletype machines. The technology of the time allowed teletypes to be converted for communications via telephone lines. Soon subscribers could be very far away from the CPU that did the required computation. This same principle is in use today.

One of the prime examples of remote terminal networks is that of airline and hotel room reservation systems. The travel or booking agent enters the required information on a terminal at one location. This information is sent via transmission media to one or more computers located nearby or across the continent. The reservation information is then transferred to other locations as required through the same or different transmission media. According to the definitions just given, this approach is a WAN, not the LAN that is the subject of this text.

Ring Networks

The ring network was first proven functional in about 1969. This type of network was a closed loop, where stations could be added anywhere on the loop. The computer that was the shared resource was merely another station on the loop. This type of connection was like the old-time "party" telephone lines, where anyone could listen in on any other conversation, and could, if lacking in self-control, monopolize the entire network.

Several subtypes of this topology soon followed to eliminate monopolizing or at least to control access to the network. These are known as reservation services, or slotted rings. Another, and seemingly more prevalent type of ring LAN, is the token ring. These types of ring networks are discussed later in this chapter.

Bus Networks

The earliest proven bus LAN was the ALOHA network, which was created and tested in Hawaii, in about 1970. Instead of a connected ring, the ALOHA network was a series of subscriber stations connected to a central computer via radio. Each station could transmit to the central computer whenever it had data to transmit. Obviously this free-for-all approach did not work too well.

Once again several subtypes of this topology soon were made public. These were Carrier Sense Multiple Access with Collision Avoidance (CSMA/CA) and Carrier Sense Multiple Access with Collision Detection (CSMA/CD). The latter seems to be the more prevalent topology to date. The difference between these two types of topologies, ring and bus, are discussed later.

The "Carterfone" Ruling

Not all advances in technology derive solely from technology. Society often decides, through law or custom, what impact technology will have on its members. The Carterfone Company, a private manufacturing firm, created, marketed, and sold private telephone devices. Customers, once they bought these devices, found out that they were not allowed to attach them to the national telephone network. A lawsuit developed, and AT&T was ordered to allow non-AT&T devices to be attached to their networks.

The implications of this case are tremendous from a purely corporate point of view. The firm that had, for more than 50 years, monopolized the telephone communications in America, suddenly had competition. From this competition came vendors selling voice and data telecommunications equipment and circuits without the blessing of AT&T. Someone in every company in America had to be knowledgeable of the technical aspects of communications. If something went wrong, the one single solution of calling the "phone company" was no longer the answer. If new telephones were to be installed or moved or if new telephone lines were required, someone other than AT&T may have been the firm that did the work.

This change in source of telecommunications knowledge and ability soon influenced both data communications and voice communications. When this change in telecommunications methods was combined with the advent of the personal computer and the rapid decrease in the price of such devices, each organization needed one or more persons to accept responsibility for installing, operating, and maintaining this new organizational asset, the network. The organization's telecommunications "guru" was moved from a cubbyhole in the basement to at least a semi-private office, not far from those who needed him or her the most.

LANs, as we know them, could not exist today without the proliferation of various types of networks that combined with the technological advances of personal computers and the social changes inherent in the Carterfone and other similar rulings. Thus technical and social changes may have much greater impact on organizations than merely the sum of their parts.

The results of this synergy have caused institutions of higher learning to create new disciplines and courses of study. Business organizations have created job categories specifically for telecommunications support. Some organizations have combined both the telecommunications and computer functions, giving control of this combined support activity to a Chief Information Officer (CIO). The high salaries of these CIOs show just how important senior management regards this function. Additionally, a whole new branch of consulting has arisen from this technology, including the area of how technology of this type influences corporate culture.

LAN Topologies

LANs can be configured in three general types of topologies: star, ring, and bus. LANs are not required to be built in any specific topology. A ring LAN can be part of a star LAN. A bus LAN can be connected to a ring LAN as merely one station on the ring. The design of the LAN topology depends on what is available at the time of the design in terms of money, resources already installed, and the physical plant being served by the LAN.

Star Networks

As was mentioned earlier, this was the first form of LAN. A central computer or shared resource was connected locally to subscribers. The key point to remember is that each subscriber had a direct line to the resource and did not have to share the bandwidth available on that line.

As shown in Figure 2.3, the computer or shared resource is located at the logical center of the LAN. Each subscriber is connected to it. Let us evaluate some of the strengths and weaknesses of the star topology.

Strengths: Each subscriber has uninterrupted access to the resources of the LAN, which include the computer itself, applications resident on the computer, services provided by print and file servers, or other specialized hardware.

Communications between the resource and the subscriber are

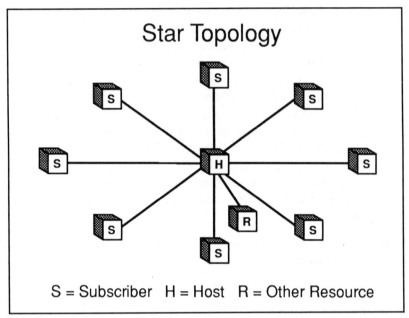

Star Topology

S = Subscriber   H = Host   R = Other Resource

FIGURE 2.3

simple. Normally only twisted pair wiring or thin coaxial cable are required. These types of transmission media are easy to install and fairly inexpensive.

Subscriber equipment is usually a "dumb" terminal, which is inexpensive compared to personal computers. Although dumb terminals provide little or no storage capacity, they provide some security because it is usually impossible to steal applications or data using these devices by themselves.

Maintenance on simple communications media and terminals does not require highly trained technicians and engineers. Facilities maintenance personnel can usually run the wiring through the physical plant and move or remove defective dumb terminals.

A malfunction of anything but the central shared resource eliminates only one subscriber from that resource.

Weaknesses: The central computer or shared resource is the single point of failure. If it fails, all subscribers connected to it are without access to its applications and data. Other topologies offer backup capabilities.

The star topology is the least flexible approach to LANs. Each subscriber must have a direct line to the central or shared resource. This means that wire or cable must be run every time a new subscriber is attached to the LAN. The length of the run is from the subscriber's location to the resource. This consumes a great deal of transmission media for just one subscriber. Under certain configurations, this topology can consume the most transmission media of the three topologies under discussion. The cost of removing transmission media is so great that unused wire and cable are not recovered. It is cheaper to replace unusable or unused transmission media with new wire and cable.

The intelligence for this topology LAN is in the central computer. This places a communications processing load as well as a computational processing load on the computer. Of course, twin loading on one processor will, at a minimum, slow down the processor.

Because there is no intelligence in this type of LAN, all LAN management information must reside on the central computer as well. This can place a third processing load on the central computer.

If more than one computer is installed in the organization, the subscriber must have a means of switching between two or more computers if required. If dumb terminals are installed, this could mean two terminals on each desk. Additionally, multiple runs of wire or cable are required.

Ring Topology

A ring topology LAN is just what its name suggests. All subscribers on the LAN are in a sequential series, with a closed loop being the result. There is no beginning or end point. (See Figure 2.4) As is the case of the star topology, there are strengths and weaknesses to the ring LAN.

Strengths: The amount of wire or cable needed to support such a topology may be less than that needed for a star topology.

Much of the electronic "intelligence" required to conduct communications is present in the hardware required for communications. This releases the computer's CPU for more computational functions, speeding up outputs from the application being used.

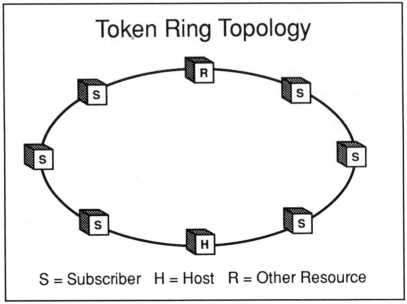

Token Ring Topology

S = Subscriber   H = Host   R = Other Resource

FIGURE 2.4

Installing new subscribers on the LAN is not as difficult as such installations using a star topology. Instead of running one complete set of transmission media for all new subscribers from the subscribers' location to the shared resource, transmission media must be run only to the nearest section of the ring.

Some subtypes of ring topologies provide slightly greater throughput than the other two types of topologies. This is particularly true under cases of heavy traffic loading.

Rings using fiber optic cable(s) provide throughput greater than 50 Mbps. Most wire or cable based rings have throughputs of less than 25 Mbps.

Weaknesses: A failure anywhere in the ring shuts down communications throughout the ring. Fail-safe mechanisms and counter rotating rings are installed to prevent this from happening. Fail-safe mechanisms automatically shunt a subscriber from the LAN if the subscriber interface to the ring fails. Counter rotating rings are duplicate sets of transmission media, installed in such a manner that a common disaster should not sever both sets simultaneously.

Of the three topologies, a ring topology is the most difficult to troubleshoot. If the transmission media fails, the technician must "walk the ring," examining every bit of the installed transmission media. Luckily there are devices that can be used to localize defective media to within a few meters.

Every time a new subscriber is connected to the LAN, every station on the LAN must be shut down for the duration of the connection.

Bus Topology

Figure 2.5 shows a bus topology LAN. Like the ring topology, all users share the transmission media.

Strengths: The bus topology requires the least amount of transmission media in most instances. Subscribers are connected via short "drop" cables to one backbone cable.

A break in the transmission media only isolates those who are on the "downstream" side of the break.

Additions and deletions of subscribers does not bring down the network as would be required with a ring topology.

Much of the electronic "intelligence" required to perform communications is present in the hardware required for communications. This releases the computer's CPU for more

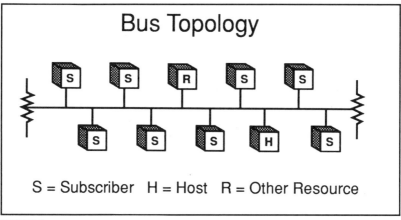

FIGURE 2.5

computational functions, speeding up outputs from the application being used.

Under certain conditions, the bus topology is the easiest to troubleshoot. Stations can be isolated one by one, without taking down the entire LAN.

Weaknesses: Most current bus topologies limit the number of subscribers that can be connected to the transmission media. As a result, bus topology LANs must be subdivided into segments and connected via specialized hardware and software.

Some types of bus topologies also limit the physical length of these segments, requiring additional hardware normally known as repeaters.

Some types of backbone transmission media (coaxial cable) used in bus topologies are thick, heavy, and expensive to install.

Review

It has not been the purpose of this section to provide an exhaustive summary of the positive and negative aspects of various topologies. A reader would have to have a very firm base of knowledge in electronics engineering and mathematics to be able to select the one single best topology for a given application. And, as was stated earlier, the aim of this text is to provide a nontechnical person with a knowledge of management of LANs, not LAN design engineering. The reader who wants to gain more knowledge in this area is directed to the list of suggested reading in Appendix A.

Access Methods

The previous section mentioned three topologies: the star, ring, and bus. In a star topology, the subscriber is connected to the resource from the time of logon to the time of logoff. The other two types are, in their most primitive arrangement, a free-for-all, with many subscribers trying to get on the LAN at one time. Selecting this free-for-all access method would certainly result in chaos.

This section addresses the two major methods of regulating access to the LAN: heuristic and deterministic. Usually heuristic methods are used with bus topologies, and deterministic methods are used with ring topologies.

Deterministic Access Methods

A deterministic access method guarantees each subscriber a certain amount of time on the LAN. This is done with either a "token" or a reservation.

In a token system, a special pattern of bits circulates through the LAN. A subscriber with traffic to pass over the LAN "captures" the token and transmits data for a given period of time. If this period of time is not sufficient to transmit all the traffic, the subscriber must wait for the token to return to his or her location. This process repeats until the subscriber has no more traffic to transmit or receive. If the subscriber has no traffic to transmit or receive, the token circulates past that location to the next location in the ring.

In a reservation system, a special message is inserted into the ring. Subscribers who intend to pass traffic on the LAN indicate whether or not they have their traffic ready to transmit. When the message has returned to the originating point, another message is generated giving subscribers the right to transmit the traffic for the period required for a complete transmission or reception. When the first subscriber's traffic has been transmitted, it's the next logical subscriber's "turn." This process is repeated until all subscribers in the ring have completed their individual turns.

Variations of both the token and reservation systems exist. Normally these variations are found only in very large, sophisticated networks associated with multiple subnetworks as are present, for instance, in the federal government or military departments. These variations can be based on the priority of traffic to be sent.

In the token passing ring, the token circulates once for the highest priority traffic, again for the next highest, and so forth. With the reservation system, the reservation is made first for the highest priority traffic, then for the next highest, and so forth.

The single most important positive aspect of the deterministic approach to traffic management in the LAN is that each subscriber has equal access to the transmission media in his or her turn. The single largest drawback to the deterministic approach is controlling the token or reservation mechanisms. Tokens and reservation messages transit the ring at a very high percentage of the speed of light. Therefore, these tokens and reservation messages must be controlled at equally high speed. A computer is needed to complete these tasks.

Heuristic Access Methods

The heuristic access method is most prevalent in bus networks. The previous discussion of the ALOHA LAN noted that CSMA/CD and CSMA/CA were subtypes of the bus topology. The "C" in CSMA stands for "carrier," a technical term from the radio engineering field. Carrier is a signal to which no intelligence has been applied. An example of a pure carrier signal is that of a radio transmitting no voice or music.

Essentially, in a CSMA/CD or CSMA/CA bus LAN, no station could transmit traffic as long as it could sense a carrier signal. Theoretically, this is a reasonable access method. However, because of the short distances involved in a bus topology LAN, one station might hear no carrier and start transmitting almost simultaneously with another station. The results of this almost simultaneous transmission would be a collision of data on the LAN, and neither station could communicate effectively.

The CSMA/CD or CSMA/CA access method functions as follows. One station listens to sense a carrier. If no carrier is present, it begins transmission, but still listens to the transmission media. If, during the listening process, another station transmitting data is detected (this is known as collision detection), the first station quits transmitting and waits a random interval before transmitting again. All stations repeat this process until no carrier is detected, and one station begins the transmitting cycle once again. The actual mechanisms involved in this process are somewhat complex, and further discussion would contribute nothing to this text.

The single major benefit of the heuristic access method is that it is much simpler than deterministic access methods. Because it is simpler, there is no need for additional electronic "intelligence" to control tokens or reservation mechanisms. Some "experts" state that heuristic access methods are better than deterministic because users with nothing to transmit are not polled to determine this fact.

The major drawback to popular heuristic access methods is the number of subscribers that can be connected to a single LAN.

LAN Operations

One of the more popular heuristic networks limits the length of one LAN segment to 500 meters, with subscriber connections separated by no less than 2.5 meters.

Neither the heuristic nor deterministic access method is the "best" way to create a LAN—no more than a bus topology or ring topology is the "best" method of wiring. Each approach has both its good and bad points. A token ring LAN has slightly higher throughput under heavy traffic loads at the cost of extra computational power to control the token passing mechanisms. The CSMA/CD bus LAN has greater throughput under comparably lighter loading without the added hardware and software. Each approach to LANs must be evaluated under the individual circumstances involved.

Connectivity

Basically two types of connectivity can be made within a LAN: connection-oriented LANs and connectionless LANs. Connection-oriented LANs are very much like the public telephone network. No connection is made until both parties are talking to one another. Connectionless LANs are those where a packet of data is injected into the LAN, and the intelligence within the LAN is responsible for routing the packet to its intended destination.

Connection-oriented LANs are those of the more common star, ring, or bus topologies. Connectionless LANs are those where more than one LAN exists such as a concatenation of stars, rings, or buses. True, there may be a wire-to-wire connection, but the addressing schemes of such hierarchical networks do not reflect this physical reality.

To compound these arbitrary differences, additional terminology is injected into the confusion. Several of the more common terms include "virtual circuits," "logical circuits," and "physical circuits." A physical circuit is the least arbitrary condition. In a physical circuit, the beginning and end points can be identified and the transmission media between the two traced. A logical circuit is the next step in abstraction. An observer may know that traffic is flowing between two defined points without really knowing for sure how it gets there. In a virtual circuit, abstraction has reached its limit. Once again, the two end points are definable.

However, there are so many paths that the traffic could cover that it is almost impossible to define them all.

Consider the following comparisons, which are given for illustration purposes only. A *physical circuit* can be compared to a pencil-and-paper, maze-type puzzle. A *logical circuit* could be compared to the question of how many angels can dance on the head of a pin. The answer is derivable. Determine the surface area of the head of the pin; measure the surface area of the angel's feet. Simply divide the smaller into the larger. In a *virtual circuit*, the closest comparison would be one of the more common questions in Zen philosophy: What is the sound of one hand clapping?

Impact of LANs on Corporate Culture

In an organization large enough to require a LAN Manager, obviously the LAN will affect the way in which the organization functions.

Central Versus Distributed Computing

Star topology networks are the oldest existing LANs. These originate from the use of a central computer, with multiple dumb terminals connected to it. One group of persons was charged with the responsibility for every function of the computer and LAN. Recently this group has been known as corporate Management Information Systems (MIS). Corporate MIS has multiple functions within their area of responsibility.

Operations included such tasks as basic as power for the computers and such ancillary devices as disk drives, printers, and telecommunications equipment. Also included in operations was the physical operation of the computer or shared resources. As a minimum, this included mounting tapes, loading operating systems, and performing general functions.

Maintenance included not only the hardware involved in MIS, but software revisions as well. As part of either operations or maintenance, studies were conducted by the MIS department to evaluate the quality of the support that the hardware and software provided.

Response to users covered such areas as managing memory, moving terminals, evaluating new software, or, in some cases, creating software for specific applications.

Historically, corporate MIS was an offshoot of the organization's finance and accounting functions. As computers became more flexible and new applications were available, other departments began to use the data processing capabilities inherent in these devices.

It was not unusual for several computers to be performing different functions within the same organization, yet requiring the same sets of data to perform these functions. Finance and accounting may have needed to know how many dollars' worth of raw material was on hand at a given time to compute taxes on inventory. Manufacturing needed to know the quantity of the same raw material for production runs. Why not link the two computers together to allow both groups access to the same data? This linkage of hardware and data was the forerunner of today's LANs.

Soon different types of computers became available. These specialized devices were used for such diverse functions as inventory management, engineering, bookkeeping, and document preparation. Yet, the users of these devices still required access to common sets of data.

Another example of widely separated computing power was in the larger colleges and universities. Here each department or discipline held one or more computers. These computers contained applications and data that many people outside of that department may have been able to use. When someone outside of the department required the interchange of data or applications, a tape or disk pack was physically carried from one location to another.

This physical transportation from one location to another proved to have drawbacks, including lost or delayed shipments, data corrupted in transport, or simply tapes sent to the wrong addresses. Someone must have finally said, "There's got to be a better way!"

One of the first true data communications networks of any size was the Advanced Research Project Agency (ARPA) network, or ARPAnet. Although it was not a LAN, ARPAnet linked the specialists working in various organizations in support of research projects for the federal government.

At this point, there were two groups of people who had access to computational facilities and the networks that linked such facilities. These were scholars and corporations. Enter the affordable personal computer (PC). It is the author's contention that PCs were required before LANs could reach their present state of functionality within the organization. The PC is the dog, the LAN is the tail. There is no question of who wags what.

Corporate MIS directors, or their counterparts in a college or university, were handed a problem when personal computers were introduced. Until the PC was generally available, the MIS department had total control of the data processing within the organization. With the presence of the PC, a user could do data processing without the bureaucratic blessing of the MIS department.

When an organization makes the transition to formal LAN management, a conflict may result between the MIS department and the PC user. In some organizations, the LAN Manager is a third party to this conflict. Problems are bound to arise as a result of these three groups' viewpoints.

MIS Viewpoint

The MIS department sees itself as a repository of technical skills. PC users are, in some perceptions, little better than weekend ball players attempting to play in the "pro" leagues. The MIS department also sees itself as the keeper of corporate secrets. Much of the data resident on tapes and disks is proprietary and should not be available without the approval of the MIS department, regardless of who the user is. The more enlightened MIS department understands that the users are the reason for the MIS department's continued existence. This is not always the case throughout every organization. Most MIS departments also view themselves as responsible for storing all data in uncorrupted forms.

PC Users' Viewpoint

This group perceives the personal computer as a means of being freed from the bureaucratic mire that is corporate MIS. The PC user is free to try new applications, not be charged for CPU cycles, to swap data and applications with peers without prior approval, and generally, to try to be more productive. A PC is a personal computer, normally set up for one person's perception of the way a task should be done. Some PC users are sloppy with data backups, some corrupt corporate data (intentionally or unintentionally), and a dishonest few are out to use the PC to steal what they can. An illegal copy of a software program leaves the organization open to charges of software piracy. Who controls the distribution of PC software? Is it the responsibility of the LAN Manager, or the purchasing department, or security? There is no textbook answer to this question.

LAN Manager's Viewpoint

The LAN Manager has no ax to grind with either the MIS department or the PC user. Rather, this person is the intermediary between these two groups. After all, the LAN is only the means of moving data, it is not the data itself. However, the LAN Manager has certain functions concerning the data that flows through the LAN—and LAN security is one of those functions. Backups of data on file servers are of prime importance. Maintenance and operation of hardware and software, including the part of the PC that connects to the LAN, are also the responsibility of the LAN Manager.

This can be viewed as either a win/win or lose/lose arrangement, depending on many variables. If corporate MIS personnel perceive the LAN Manager and his or her staff as usurping some of their functions, it is lose/lose. If corporate MIS personnel view the LAN Manager and his or her staff as their partners in supporting the data processing function, it is a win/win situation. The LAN Manager is usurping the MIS function when MIS personnel have no input into the tasks completed by the LAN Manager. Yet the MIS personnel cannot demand that the LAN Manager and his or her staff be totally subordinate to them unless the LAN Manager is part of the MIS department. The LAN Manager can support the MIS personnel by interacting with the users of the corporate MIS resources, freeing the MIS department personnel from some of the more trivial problems they face from LAN subscribers.

Between the PC user and the LAN Manager, the same range of conditions can exist. If the LAN Manager acts in an authoritarian manner, defining the configuration of hardware and software the PC user can select, the situation is lose/lose. If the LAN Manager can find some way to integrate the PC user's favorite hardware and software into the LAN, the situation is win/win.

These are not black and white situations; they are end points on a spectrum of possibilities. Many shades of gray exist, and the LAN Manager must find which shade fits best within the organization.

Information Movement Within the Organization

The introduction of the PC took data processing out of the hands of corporate MIS forever. The PC opened a Pandora's Box of problems and opportunities. The LAN offered the means of providing synergy between these two disparate approaches to the same goal, which is to manipulate data in support of the organization's goals or mission. The manipulation of data requires that data be moved within and without the organization. How, then, does the LAN support this movement of data?

A LAN tends to change the flow of information in the organization. The single most noticeable type of change is speed. Consider the following example. The division director goes to a department manager and says, "I need the sales figures for the widget sales for the past five fiscal years, and break them out by region." Even with a modern MIS department, it could take up to two days to obtain the basic data, plus another day to put it into some format that is not merely a printout from a database or spreadsheet. Using PCs, shared resources, and the LAN, the same report could be generated in less than one hour.

Another less obvious result is that of data interchange. If the East Coast office needs a written report on the most recent credit rating of a West Coast client, the data is exchanged at the lowest organizational level required to get the work done. A worker opens a connection to a commercial database through the LAN to the WAN, and then downloads the required data. The data is then electronically folded into the report outline. This eliminates, among other things, the need to retype data into the finished report.

Electronic Order Interchange (EOI) is another means of data interchange. With EOI, an organization can use the LAN and WAN to order supplies or raw materials. One of the clerks in the purchasing department opens a connection to a supplier's shipping department, types in the order for whatever is required, and gives authorization for the purchase at that time. The supplier sees this information come in, checks the authorization, and ships the required materials. This action has eliminated the sales function on routine purchases, the review process for minor repetitive purchases, and much of the paperwork involved.

These three examples pale when contrasted to some of the capabilities of the LAN. Much of today's middle management function is data gathering and analysis. Middle managers answer questions such as how much, where, when, and what are the trends involved. The middle manager's function is to digest raw data and present it in forms suitable to upper management. Almost all these functions can be replaced with PCs and LANs under certain conditions. Commercially available spreadsheets for PCs accept raw numbers, and with a little skill from the user, present textual and graphic representations of this data. A progressive organization can, with appropriate personal computers, hardware, software, and a LAN, eliminate one or more levels of management.

Knowledge of the Organization

The examples of information movement mentioned in the previous section would be the result of the actions of the LAN Manager only under certain very specific conditions. A decision made in regards to the corporate asset that is the LAN is no better than the data on which it is made. The LAN Manager must have access to two generic areas of organizational information: current needs and future activities.

Current Needs: Current needs are not always obvious by inspection. Supervisors or managers often do not reveal their workers' needs in the area of LANs for several reasons. The first reason may be ignorance. The manager does not know how a LAN can help workers accomplish their assigned tasks. The second reason may be fear of technology. Although it is somewhat of an exaggeration, some managers may still contend that quill pens and parchment are all that is needed to run a business.

The third and easiest reason to rebut is that PCs and LANs cost money that could be spent on other goods and services in support of the organization's mission or goal. Nothing could be further from the truth. PCs and the LANs that connect them to major computing resources may eliminate manpower requirements. Many studies have shown that manpower, with its associated expenses, is the single most expensive component of finished goods and services.

The fourth reason that managers do not recognize the usefulness of LANs is professional ego. No one knows better than the manager what his or her subordinates need. If a LAN is installed in the department, the manager loses control over the way the workers perform their assigned tasks. The manager perceives this as a loss of power.

A manager might ask, "If you don't know what my people are doing, how can you develop a LAN that will support their activities?" The obvious answer is that workers who use a LAN are involved in information interchange. Anything that makes this happen faster, easier, more accurately, or cheaper is a correct design. As to which topology and access method should be selected, that is merely an exercise in engineering. It can be solved with several matrices, which can be constructed with about two to three days' work for the average organization.

Future Activities: Future activities include many things, but the most important of these is the movement of the subscribers of LAN services. One study showed that every office in America, on a statistical basis, moves every 11 months. Evaluation of this study, along with personal experience, will show that the LAN Manager's single biggest task is controlling expenses in the movement of these subscribers. If costs are to be kept down, the LAN Manager must be able to plan for these relocations. To support the relocations in a cost-effective manner, the LAN Manager must be consulted very early in the planning stages.

If the organization plans either expansion or reduction in size, the LAN Manager must also be made aware of these activities. In a growing organization, the LAN Manager must be a project manager as well: arranging for the purchase of LAN hardware and software, if required; contracting for the installation of transmission media; identifying locations for connections to the subscriber; and staging the deliveries and installation in conjunction with the expansion. In a contracting organization, the LAN Manager must address several issues. What can be salvaged if a factory is closed? Can the transmission media be recovered? Are connections to the transmission media available and reusable if recovered? Does a market exist for second-hand LAN hardware and software? Questions like these must be answered in time to plan the contraction and recover as much of the installation expense as possible.

In the category of future activities looms the specter of mergers or corporate acquisitions. Assuming there is a requirement to integrate the computer resources of both organizations and to connect the LANs in both organizations, the LAN Manager faces an extremely difficult task not only in the organizational sense, but in the technical sense as well. The LAN Manager who is not very technically astute would be wise to bring in an external consultant for this project.

In all likelihood, the two separate organizations have two different types of computer resources, hardware, software, and LANs. Interconnecting these so that they have more than minimal functionality may well be so expensive that it may be better to throw away one set and put both organizations on one data processing standard. Before making this decision, the LAN Manager needs to determine the cost in terms of time and money to interconnect the two organizations. Do not forget to include the following factors:

- The expenses involved in training time for subscribers of the new services.
- The cost of the learning curve.
- The possibility of serious damage done through human error.

This decision must be made while the LAN Manager is integrating new people, policies, and programs. This type of decision requires thought and analysis. The analytical function cannot be performed too well while the analyzer is attempting to complete the action that he or she is analyzing. Or more succinctly, "It is hard to remember that the objective is to drain the swamp if you are up to your hips in alligators!"

Whether a consultant, or consulting team should be brought in to perform these tasks depends on such things as the quality and quantity of staff available, budgetary restraints, time constraints, organizational culture, and other real factors. This is the type of decision that causes the LAN Manager grey hair, and ulcers.

Subscriber Satisfaction

Although few LAN Managers argue with the description that theirs is a service function, many do not act as though they agree with this. Those who connect to the LAN and make use of its functionality are subscribers just as the owner of a telephone connection to the national telephone system is. If the LAN Managers approach their job in the same manner as any service provider, their subscribers will be satisfied and they themselves will earn praise.

As with any service function, the first rule is to listen to the subscriber.

- What functionality does the subscriber need?
- Is accuracy of response a foregone conclusion, and are subscribers concerned with speed of response?
- Do they need higher quality of printing, or can they get by with just draft quality?
- Is the device they use constrained by memory or other functionality?
- Do they need original or remedial training to wring the functionality out of the equipment they have been assigned?

The second rule of a service provider is to work with the subscriber and make sure the subscriber works with you. If a clerk says that an error occurs under such and such conditions, ensure that the clerk duplicates the conditions in front of a technician. A knowledgeable subscriber may be trying a short cut that does not quite work. The technician can determine where the subscriber is making the mistake.

If the subscriber is out of service completely, speed is of the essence, modified only by safety requirements. Ensure that defective equipment is either repaired or replaced as soon as possible. As a rule of thumb, the restoration function should be completed in less than 10 minutes for an operator-induced error and in 30 minutes if hardware or software must be replaced. Make sure the subscriber is satisfied when the technician leaves the site. Notify the subscriber's immediate supervisor when the restoration is complete. Above all, notify the subscriber when their connection to the LAN has been restored.

The LAN Manager is often the subject of abuse by dissatisfied subscribers. This abuse is just part of the job and the LAN Manager must learn to accept it. That is the lot of any service provider. Remember when the service station forgot to put your hubcaps back on after the brake job? Make sure that you replace the "hubcaps" when you provide service to the subscriber.

Summary

This chapter introduced the concept of LAN management by discussing the following points:

- A general overview of the content and format of this text.
- The history of data communications networks including
  — Remote terminals
  — Ring networks
  — Bus networks
  — Star networks
  — Carterfone ruling

- LAN topologies, including
  — Star
  — Ring
  — Bus

- LAN access methods, including
  — Deterministic
  — Heuristic

- Types of connectivity, including
  — Connectionless
  — Connection-oriented

- How the LAN impacts the corporate culture, including
  — Central versus distributed computing
  — Perceptions of the MIS department
  — Personal computer users
  — The LAN Manager's role
  — Information interchange within the organization
  — The need for knowledge of the organization
  — Subscriber satisfaction

Case Study

Section 1: Factual Data

The organization involved offers services to a varied group of clients. The firm has several locations connected to a centralized data processing facility in Washington, D.C. Connections are through the PSN (Public Switch Network) using modems at the remote locations. This study will concentrate on the Virginia location.

Section 2: What Happened

Managers in the Virginia location were under tremendous pressure to increase client satisfaction with its concomitant increase in revenues. They perceived the Washington headquarters MIS as being unresponsive to their needs based on this increased pressure from upper management. One person in the Virginia location was assigned the task of designing an automated system for the Virginia location. This system's "goal" was to off-load some of the work from the MIS department in Washington.

Section 3: Losses

Luckily for all concerned, no losses occurred with this new system. One of the managers in the Virginia location asked the obvious question, "Can these systems exchange data?" Once it became clear that the new system could not talk to the mainframes in the Washington headquarters without additional, expensive equipment, the plan was scrapped.

Section 4: Lessons Learned

This organization had two strikes against it from the beginning. First, it was struggling with uncontrolled growth. Second, its MIS department saw itself as a data processing organization, not a data communications organization. The MIS department almost totally ignored the telecommunications aspect of their activities. If more telecommunications were needed, they simply bought more modems and circuits. By hiring a person who was knowledgeable of both data processing and data communications, this firm was able to weather the increased growth without a severe loss of its customer base.

Accounting
Management

There ain't no such thing as a free lunch (TANSTAFL).
—*The Moon Is a Harsh Mistress*, R. A. Heinlien

Accounting management is interested in determining who will pay for using the LAN. Although we can say that the subscribers pay to use the LAN, how is this usage charged, and even more important, how is it computed? This chapter addresses:

- How accounting management is implemented.
- The positive aspects of accounting management, including a wholly owned telecommunications subsidiary.
- The negative aspects of accounting management, including a wholly owned telecommunications subsidiary.
- The impact of organizational change on accounting management.

Accounting Management Identifies Consumers of Resources

The LAN Manager provides a service to LAN subscribers. That service, at the most basic level of understanding, is information interchange. Subscriber accounting begins with accounting for the use of the hardware and software that facilitate this information interchange.

History of Accounting Management

The concept of accounting is not new, particularly in larger organizations. Each element of the organization is expected to account for telephone usage. Such usage falls into three general categories: within the organization, Inter-LATA, and Intra-LATA.

Telephone calls within the organization, particularly local offices, are not always charged to the originating party. Even midsized organizations see these as part of the "cost of doing business." Most organizations realize that internal telephone communication cannot be replaced with any other mode of person-to-person communications. Local calls may be treated differently by each organization.

One of the artificial boundaries established by Judge Greene in the AT&T break-up case was the Local Access Transport Area (LATA). Some LATA boundaries are the same as those of the area codes with which we are familiar. The geographical limitations of a given LATA should be ascertained from the servicing common carrier vendor. Whether or not a given organization wishes to charge users for intra-LATA calls is a policy decision for each organization. Intra-LATA calls are usually part of the "cost of doing business." Inter-LATA calls are almost always charged, in some way or another, to the originating subelement of the organization.

Methods

Accounting for telecommunications usage can take place in several ways. Assume, for the sake of discussion, that ABC Corporation had a telephone bill of $62,500.00 a month. If analysis of the bill showed that $23,456.78 of the calls originated in the marketing division, that amount would be deducted from the marketing division director's monthly operating budget through internal accounting. The information required to perform such internal accounting can come from one of two sources: the common carrier vendor selected by the organization or internally from the Station Message Detail Report (SMDR).

Each common carrier vendor's bill lists, as a minimum, two types of charges, intra- and inter-LATA calls. Additional charges may include rented or leased equipment, normally known as Customer Premise Equipment (CPE), as well as leased circuits. If maintenance contracts exist, such charges may also show up on the common carrier vendor's bill.

An internal source of such billing may be the Station Message Detail Report (SMDR) that is present on most modern Private Branch Exchanges (PBXs). The contents of an SMDR depends on many variables, the most common of which is the price of the PBX. However, as a minimum, such a report should list the following items for each call:

- Who initiates it
- Who receives it
- Beginning and ending times
- Total cost

More flexible PBXs also list:

- Route taken by the call
- Subscriber's name
- Geographical names of the locations called

The same type of information can be used to allocate charges to the LAN subscriber.

Information interchange is measured in four general ways:

1 Transmission media usage time
2 Number of bits transmitted
3 Host CPU cycles
4 Bandwidth consumption

One thing that is common to all LANs is the transmission media over which the signals flow. Subscribers should pay for whatever *time* their traffic is on the LAN. Such time can be computed either in time units or by the *number of bits* that are transmitted and received. The method by which these measurements are taken depends solely on the LAN topology. To count bits that pass over the LAN is a crude and somewhat expensive approach to the subject. There are better alternatives.

One of these alternatives is that of *host or server CPU cycle* accounting. If mainframes or file and print servers are attached to the LAN, they may have internal accounting functions. These functions identify who logged into such a device, and when. They also identify when that same subscriber logged out. From these accounting functions, the LAN Manager can identify how long each subscriber is attached to that device. The LAN Manager also knows the LAN's maximum throughput (in bits per second) and therefore can compute the maximum number of bits a subscriber could pass to the network resource or host. The "bill" for LAN usage (*bandwidth consumption*) is then based on the maximum number of bits that can be passed between a subscriber and a host.

Being charged the maximum fee motivates subscribers to reduce their internal billing by reducing the time they are connected to the network resource. This reduces traffic on the network, freeing bandwidth for other subscribers. Arguments as to whether or not this is a good idea are discussed later in this chapter.

Hosts attached to the LAN, or network resources that are part of the LAN, are not the only sources used for accounting management data. Intelligent devices such as bridges, routers, or gateways may also "capture" traffic data. Once this type of statistical information is gathered, it can be queried in various ways and analyzed. Then the resulting analysis can become part of the base of billing information.

Not all traffic can pass through the LAN. Some of it can pass over common carrier vendor circuits. Depending on the common carrier vendor's billing format, the LAN Manager may be able to identify the sink and source of all common carrier calls that are placed from the LAN to a non-LAN destination. With this information available, the LAN Manager can correlate a source telephone number with a particular user and "bill for services" as appropriate.

There is another method for determining non-LAN traffic. If the LAN is connected to a Private Branch Exchange (PBX), the LAN Manager can determine which calls were placed through the PBX. Most modern PBXs have what is known as a Station Message Detail Recording port, which provides a list of all traffic through that particular PBX. This list provides the sink and source of all calls, the duration of the call, and in some cases the cost of that particular call. This information tells the LAN Manager who placed the call and approximately how much to "bill" the user of the bandwidth consumed.

The key points to remember are that hardware and software usage must be accounted for, and whether or not the subscirber is to be charged for this usage is a corporate decision.

Positive Aspects of Accounting Management

No organization purchases and installs a LAN without intending to accomplish a positive result from the purchase. What this positive result is depends upon the organization itself, its mission, or its goals. Further, unless the LAN was purchased for the sake of having technology on hand or to soothe the corporate ego, the organization buying the LAN expects some rate of return on the investment. Without knowing the usage rate of such an investment, the return on investment cannot be ascertained.

Some of these positive aspects of accounting management include:

- Identification of bandwidth consumers
- Improvement of performance management
- More effective allocation of costs
- Reduction of general and administrative (G&A) expenses

Identification of Bandwidth Consumers

Earlier portions of this chapter indicated that bandwidth users could be identified by tracking the sink and source of all LAN traffic. This tracking of traffic by sinks and sources identifies the individual who is using the LAN. Usually, individuals are not "billed" for such LAN consumption unless they are contractors using organizational facilities to pursue their own tasks. Such tracking usually lists the sink and source of traffic by a department or division of the organization.

Typically, the result of such tracking is a report, on a recurring basis, showing traffic generated by elements such as the Marketing Department, the Personnel Office, or the R&D Section. LAN traffic billing is easier to compute than some may think. The maximum throughput on a segment of the LAN may be 10 Mbps. In a 10-hour period, the maximum traffic that could flow is 3.6×10^{11} bits. Assigning a cost of $0.00001 per 10,000 bits, the total "cost" of running the LAN for a 10-hour period is $3.60. If the R&D Section used 18 percent of the total available bandwidth during this period, they would be "billed" for 18 percent of $3.60. This works out to $0.65 for that particular day.

Improvement of Performance Management

Performance management (the subject of Chapter 6) tells the LAN Manager how well the LAN is performing as compared with the design criteria. Part of the requirements to make this comparison is to measure how much traffic flows through the LAN at any given time. This same information is required for accounting management. Therefore, one measurement can be used for two purposes.

More Effective Allocation of Costs

Many software packages currently available allow subscribers to log on with their name, account number, and the job the LAN is being used to support. With this information in hand, the LAN Manager can identify who used the LAN, for how long, and why the traffic was required. This analysis allows costs to be assigned to either a specific product or project, or to a specific customer account. Such detailed assignment of costs aids in forecasting future budgets. The ability to assign costs also helps managers of current operations identify the need for additional bandwidth if required.

Reduction of G&A Expenses

Many organizations assign telecommunications costs to General and Administrative (G&A) accounts. Normally G&A expenses are subtracted from profits as overhead and are accepted as part of the cost of doing business. By allocating LAN usage to a specific product, project, or customer, G&A expenses are reduced. Reduction of G&A expenses can, under some conditions, make the firm that much more profitable. Reduction of G&A expenses results in lower overhead expenses, freeing up more capital for additional expansion of, among other things, the LAN.

Separate Telecommunications Organization

If the organization the LAN Manager works for is large enough or if multiple LANs are connected through WANs, the supported organization may wish to create a captive telecommunications corporation. This text is not a vehicle to weigh the pros and cons of such a decision. We will address three major positive points of such a subordinate organization here, and in the next section we will discuss three major negative points that have a bearing on this decision.

An internal telecommunications organization is autonomous. Normal organizational channels are not required to manage the captive corporation. Yet the corporation provides telecommunications support under the direct supervision of the senior organization. This autonomy within the supporting telecommunications organization frees the supported organization from tasks involved with finance and accounting, personnel, payroll, training, and other administrative functions that increase overhead.

The danger involved with this approach is lack of oversight through traditional reporting channels. Normally, when a wholly owned telecommunications subsidiary is created, the senior person in the subsidiary reports directly to the chief executive officer or other highly placed officer in the supported organization. The person charged with the directing of the subsidiary organization must have all the skills and abilities of an entrepreneur, yet be amenable to directions from the director's "customers." These same customers are also this director's financial backers. It is a difficult position, and people with this combination of skills may be hard to find.

The creation of an autonomous telecommunications organization can create another important facet to explore. What are the financial ramifications of creating such an organization? Who benefits from the sale of the supported organization's hardware and software? What are the channels for transfer of funds between the supported and supporting organizations? How does the supported organization maintain control over the supporting? A simple majority of the stock may be enough, but is the supporting organization publicly or privately held? In theory, the supporting telecommunications organization could grow large enough to swallow the supported organization. It may not be a question of whether the dog wags the tail or vice versa. Under these circumstances, it may just be that the tail and the dog can no longer be told apart.

The current regulatory environment allows any person or organization with specific physical and financial assets to become established as a telecommunications common carrier. Assume that the supported organization was national in scope, and the links between various local elements were not fully utilized. What is to prevent the autonomous telecommunications organization from selling its underutilized bandwidth to all comers? This question can be answered in one word—nothing! There are no laws or regulations that prevent a firm as large as General Motors or as small as the corner grocery store from setting themselves up as a telecommunications utility. (A curious reader may want to find out who "owns" GEISCO or TYMENET.)

Another benefit from an internal telecommunications organization is that of captive expertise. If the supported organization has created a subordinate telecommunications organization, the senior organization can draw on the expertise in the supporting organization for reasons other than telecommunications. With the advent of software-driven voice and data telecommunications equipment, programmers have become a necessity. Those who design, install, and maintain such networks are, in all likelihood, degreed electronic engineers. What skills do these people have that the supported organization could use? Can the supported organization draw on the people in the internal telecommunications organization for consulting purposes? Consider the following example.

A major national manufacturing firm has a telecommunications network consisting of multiple LANs linked together through WAN/VAN networks. The firm has created a captive telecommunications organization to manage this large network. Can the firm use the people who manage this network in a consulting firm? (A curious reader may want to investigate how some of the larger consulting firms got started.)

Review

The implementation of accounting management offers several potential benefits. It identifies bandwidth consumption, which shows who is using what portion of the LAN and helps evaluate performance management. Accounting management allows the allocation of charges for a particular product, project, or customer. This allocation reduces G&A expenses. If the organization has a network of sufficient scope and flexibility, an internal autonomous telecommunications organization is created, providing a profit center in place of a cost center.

Negative Aspects of Accounting Management

There are drawbacks to the implementation of accounting management:

- Manpower costs
- Hardware and software costs
- Internal friction

Manpower Costs

Even if the network is sufficiently "intelligent" to be able to provide the LAN Manager with raw usage data, this data must be evaluated and then manipulated in such a manner so as to provide "bills" for those who use the LAN. Each bill must identify the part of the organization to be charged, the source of the traffic, the quantity of the traffic, the beginning and ending time of each connection, the total number of bits sent over the LAN, and if possible, the identity of the subscriber who used the LAN for this purpose. If the subscriber can identify the product, project, or customer account when logging into or out of the LAN, or the host attached to the LAN, so much the better.

Hardware and Software Costs

Many software products, for example, databases and spreadsheets, can store and manipulate LAN usage data. However, because of the overwhelming bulk of information available, manual entry is much too slow. Specialized types of hardware and software can be used to capture the flow of traffic through the LAN and provide a written history and database of such traffic. Such traffic flow information is available in bridges, routers, gateways, terminal servers, file servers, print servers, hosts, and network analyzers, as shown in Figure 3.1.

The LAN Manager can open a connection to a file server and find out who logged on to that file server, for how long, and what happened during that session. In a large LAN, the LAN Manager is faced with an overwhelming amount of data. This data is required to create the bills, but in the large LAN there is just too much information be manipulated manually. Therefore, besides

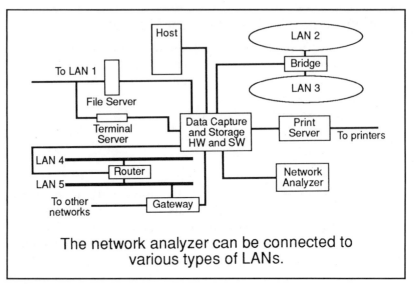

The network analyzer can be connected to various types of LANs.

FIGURE 3.1

the intelligent hardware in the LAN, additional software is required to manipulate the mass of data and provide useful results.

Various vendors provide specialized software to perform such analysis and billing. Aside from the expense of such software, there is another major shortfall. Such software may not provide the types of information needed by a specific organization. Custom software is even more expensive and may require many weeks of usage to eliminate bugs and glitches.

Because of the large amounts of data involved and the lack of software that can be directly applied to the process of billing, LAN usage data must be manipulated through one or more software programs. This requires human intervention and many CPU cycles. The computer used for this data manipulation and the printers used to produce the final bill are, in all likelihood, part of the LAN. Creating bills by using the LAN creates more LAN usage, thereby creating more bills. Has perpetual motion finally been created?

Internal Friction

Another negative aspect of accounting management is the friction created within the supported organization. Many departments may wish to create and install a LAN that suits their particular function within the organization. Historically, those who deal with money matters, or administrative functions, prefer IBM or IBM-compatible computers. Those who deal with scientific functions, that is, R&D, have found that DEC computers are more suited for their efforts. Both of these use different operating systems and do not communicate well with each other without some type of data translation activities.

The LAN within an organization that uses accounting management is, in effect, a monopoly. Subscribers cannot install their own equipment or software. They are forced to rely on services provided by others. This same condition holds true with the corporate telephone network. Because these are monopolies, the subscribers cannot control the costs incurred from using the LAN. This creates ill will if the LAN Manager's service is less than excellent.

When accounting management is begun, additional duties are performed by someone within the corporate telecommunications department. These duties include data collection, manipulation, and bill preparation. As this is a lower level type of administrative function, one or more additional clerical workers may be required to perform such billing functions.

Separate Telecommunications Organization

As was stated in the previous section, creation of accounting management can be the starting point of the creation of an autonomous, but wholly owned telecommunications subsidiary. This type of organization has several negative aspects.

In such an autonomous telecommunications subsidiary, there must exist a support infrastructure of personnel functions, payroll functions, training, and all the other administrative functions that in the past had been provided by the supported organization. Certain finance and accounting functions must be split off to support the telecommunications organization. What is the status of forecasted return on investment in network hardware and software? Who must approve such massive changes in the organization?

In addition to the increase in administrative overhead for the autonomous telecommunications subsidiary, new managers must be brought on board to supervise the support functions. This provides an even smaller profit margin if the autonomous tele-communications subsidiary is viewed as a profit center, not a cost center. What is the impact on corporate culture of such a division? Will the people who work for the telecommunications organization still feel as if they are part of the older, supported organization? Does this pose a problem considering the present attitudes of employees? How does the creation of such an autonomous organization impact on the organizational development plans of the supported organization? Such a move can create more problems than it solves.

Problems created by such an autonomous telecommunications subsidiary can be external as well as internal. When an organization sells bandwidth on the open market, the sale is controlled by both the federal government in the Federal Communications Commission, and also by state governments in the Public Utilities Commission or other similar body.

Such a bandwidth vendor must meet other requirements. Each state has its own laws and regulations concerning these requirements. Certain decisions must be made in regards to whether the subsidiary is privately held or publicly held. Should it be incorporated or not? What are the impacts of incorporating in a publicly held mode, only to go bankrupt? Such bankruptcy proceedings could strip the supported organization of all its external telecommunications capability.

Review

The implementation of accounting management has several negative points. Accounting management requires additional hardware, software, and manpower expenditures. It can also bring about a monopoly, creating friction among those who have no choice but to use it. A byproduct of accounting management may be an autonomous telecommunications subsidiary. This brings about the problems involved in any new organization.

Implementation of Accounting Management

Once the decision to implement accounting management has been approved, the LAN Manager has several steps and decisions to make.

Measurement Methods

Before anyone can be billed for LAN usage, the traffic on the network must be measured and recorded. How is the measurement to be performed?

Assume for the sake of discussion that there is a method to measure each bit that flows through the network. Most modern LANs use a packet format for data transmission and reception. Each of these packets contain data bits and overhead bits. The overhead bits are required to ensure that the packet carrying the data gets to the intended destination and that the data within the packet is not corrupted. Some types of LANs use more overhead bits than others.

Should the subscribers be forced to pay for these packets that are "fat" with overhead bits? Consider, too, that the subscriber is not allowed to modify the packet structure. This question becomes even more distressful, but still moot, when it becomes obvious that the subscribers who are paying for the use of the LAN have no say in the type of LAN over which their traffic flows.

Computation of Usage: Consider the quantity of data that flows through a LAN in a given 8-hour period. Let us assume that a CSMA-based LAN has an average throughput of about 24 percent of specified bandwidth. That means that 2,400,000 bits of traffic are passing through the LAN every second. There must be some device that will count each of these bits, identify the sink and source of these bits, and then store this information in a file that humans or computers can access to create bills. Let us assume that in this same LAN, a packet contains an average of 120 bits. This means that, at any given second, 20,000 packets are in existence on the network.

Each packet contains an address for the sink and source of that packet. This address, in a CSMA LAN, requires 8 bits for the transmit address and 8 bits for the receive address, for a total of 16 address bits. Multiply these 16 address bits—remember, we must know who to send the bill to—by the 20,000 packets, and we find that a file of 320,000 bits accumulates each second. Because the record does not include the total number of bits, we cannot bill the user by bit usage, but by packet usage. If we want to bill by bit usage, we must add another file to our billing information record. Every hardware and software vendor has developed a means of overcoming this type of data buildup.

Billing subscribers can be done on either a bit or packet basis. Much depends on the topography in use and internal organization policies. This decision is in the LAN Manager's lap. However, this decision is not as clear cut as it may appear.

Computation Errors: Billing on a bit transmission basis does not account for all traffic on the LAN. In the CSMA LAN under discussion, certain types of equipment send out "beacon" messages. These messages include the address of the device and a specific signal that shows it is ready to pass traffic. Who pays for these beacon messages? The same general type of overhead traffic exists in token ring LANs. Even if no subscriber has traffic on the network, the token circulates through the network. By circulating as it does, it takes up bandwidth. Who pays for the bandwidth consumed by the token?

Still another problem exists when billing LAN users. Assume a technician is testing a portion of the LAN. As part of the procedures, the technician loads the LAN with a burst of test traffic. This burst contains thousands of packets. The loading is so heavy that other subscribers experience long delays in their traffic. Who pays for the technician's bandwidth consumption?

All of the foregoing scenarios were based on the assumption that everything in the LAN was working correctly. What would have happened if a bridge, a router, or some other device started a constant broadcast of gibberish packets? There may not be any way to identify the source of such packets, yet the packets do consume bandwidth. Who pays for this unproductive bandwidth consumption?

Who Pays for Usage?

Does the transmitter (source) or receiver (sink) of the traffic pay for use of the LAN? The answer is not as obvious as it appears. Assume that a subscriber with a personal computer wants to upload a file from a file server. The subscriber does not own the file server; he or she is just storing files there. The LAN Manager may own the file server. If the subscriber is billed for traffic sent to the file server, who pays for traffic received by the subscriber? Is it fair that the subscriber pay for traffic both ways?

Let us examine this problem from another viewpoint. Assume that a subscriber is connected to the LAN through a dumb terminal and the intelligence is in a large mainframe over a thousand miles away. The subscriber is entering data into a database on the mainframe. If she is a member of most organizations, she will be charged for CPU time and disk storage space. She or her department will also probably be charged for using the WAN vendor's long distance line. The subscriber finishes her data entry and breaks for lunch. After lunch she opens another connection to the same mainframe to print out her database entries. The printed documents show up in a print server near her desk. Who pays for the WAN and LAN usage of the bandwidth required for the printout? The manager of the mainframe would not be pleased to be billed for those charges.

There is no easy answer to any of these questions. Previous sections of this chapter discussed some of the pros and cons involved in setting up the accounting management function. Is the gain of such a function worth the time, money, and manpower invested? The answer to that question can only be found in organizational policies and procedures.

There is one other idea to consider before we leave this particular subject area. Assume the R&D department incurred a LAN usage "bill" of $2345.60 during the last billing cycle. Does this mean that the department manager must write a check for this amount to the organization? The obvious answer is no. Yet, these funds must be transferred somewhere. This is, of course, an internal accounting function. This requires ledger entries. These ledger entries require time, money, and manpower. And, by the way, if the accounting department is on the LAN, this creates another entry on the accounting department's bill.

Growth of the Organization and Accounting Management

Organizational growth, in respect to the LAN, can show up in one of two ways: increased size of the LAN in use or the creation of more LANs. What follows is a discussion of these two methods and their impact on Accounting Management.

Single LAN

No new hardware or software is required to perform the additional accounting management functions when only one LAN is involved. Many LANs have upper limits to the number of subscribers that can be attached to them. Most modern computers and their associated software can handle such a limited number of subscriber accounts with little or no problem. No new manpower should be required to handle the increased accounting load. Most of this accounting should be done automatically.

With a single LAN, no great amount of preplanning is required within accounting management to support organizational growth. The database that stores accounting management information should be large enough to accommodate all possible subscribers.

Multiple LANs

When more than one LAN is in use, certain technical problems exist concerning accounting management. One of the major problems is addressing. If one LAN is in use, no addresses can be duplicated. However, if two LANs are joined through a bridge, duplicate addresses are possible. Even if these duplicate addresses are identified and corrected by those charged with configuration management, the possibility still exists. If addresses are duplicated on two subLANs, more than one person or department can be billed for consumption of LAN resources.

When more than one LAN is in use, a bridge or router must be used to filter traffic between the LANs. (See Figure 3.2.) Let us assume that LAN A has addresses ranging from 1 through 999. LAN B has addresses ranging from 1,000 through 1,999. Traffic from address 50 on LAN A to address 1351 on LAN B will be counted twice. The same for traffic from address 1351 on LAN B to address 50 on LAN A. Therefore, the accounting management functions must eliminate double billing for single transmissions.

Keeping the two LAN situation in mind, consider this problem. Each subLAN has traffic within it that will never reach the other subLAN. How does the hardware and software on one subLAN count the traffic on the other subLAN? The answer is that such actions cannot be performed successfully. Bridges and routers prevent such information from being known. Therefore,

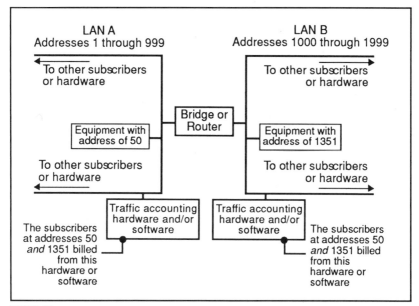

LAN A
Addresses 1 through 999

LAN B
Addresses 1000 through 1999

To other subscribers or hardware

To other subscribers or hardware

Bridge or Router

Equipment with address of 50

Equipment with address of 1351

To other subscribers or hardware

To other subscribers or hardware

Traffic accounting hardware and/or software

Traffic accounting hardware and/or software

The subscribers at addresses 50 *and* 1351 billed from this hardware or software

The subscribers at addresses 50 *and* 1351 billed from this hardware or software

FIGURE 3.2

the LAN Manager must have a data-gathering device on each LAN for counting traffic. At certain intervals, each traffic counting device "dumps" its statistics in a central device for billing purposes.

Interconnected LANs

When LANs are connected via WANs or VANs, other types of billing problems arise. This is perhaps the traditional method of LAN growth. A subelement of an organization, the R&D branch for instance, is located in one city. The personnel and manufacturing departments are located in another. Each subelement has its own LAN. Corporate policy requires that the two groups interconnect the LANs. If the distance is far enough, one cost-effective way to connect is through a common carrier vendor. Billing for such usage can cause several problems.

Traffic flow within the LAN can be easy to count. It is more difficult to count packets that flow through the WAN or VAN circuit connecting the two LANs. This is not to say that such traffic counts cannot be made. When using public packet-switched networks, VAN vendors, for instance, can bill subscribers on the number of packets that transit their network. The supported organization pays for such traffic. But which one of the subelements of that organization is to be charged for the traffic?

Both subelements are charged for traffic on their respective LANs. Are they to be charged for traffic on the other subelement's LAN? If so, at whose rate of usage? The two LANs may be different, with different expenses for using the LAN. Let us assume that an equitable agreement can be worked out for traffic charges on each subLAN. What about the cost of the WAN or VAN transmission media? Who is to pay for those charges?

The easy way out of this dilemma is to say the supported organization pays the bill, and then apportions the charges out to each subelement within the organization. Yet this is not fair. One subelement may use the LAN more than the sum of two or three other subelements telephone companies usually charge the party placing the call. This is not an unfair method. Yet with LANs, a "call" can be placed at one time, the recipient can be forced to reply at another. This puts the bill on the shoulders of those who reply to the original caller.

Depending on the WAN/VAN vendor's billing capabilities, the source and sink of the data passing through the public network may be identifiable. If so, the subscriber can be billed accordingly. There is no "textbook" solution to this problem.

When subLANs are connected through a VAN or WAN, the same billing problems exist as were experienced by interconnecting LANs. Double billing and duplication of hardware/software requirements are two of the problems we discussed earlier.

Summary

This chapter has raised many questions about some of the problems existing in the accounting management function. The chapter is not designed to provide "textbook" answers to these problems, but to make the reader aware of the potential traps involved in performing the accounting management function.

This chapter addressed the following areas involved with accounting management for LAN usage:

- How accounting management is to be implemented, including
  - Who uses the LAN
  - Where usage information is derived
  - How to measure usage

- The positive aspects of accounting management, including
  - What aids performance management
  - Tracking subscriber changes
  - Billing users
  - Reducing G&A costs

- The negative aspects of accounting management, including
  - Increased costs
  - Friction among various subscribers
  - Increased manpower requirements

- The procedures required to implement accounting management, including
  - Who is billed
  - How to avoid duplication of billing
  - Who pays for testing procedures that use the LAN

- The growth of the LAN and how it affects the accounting management function, including
  - The impact of one large LAN
  - The impact of multiple, interconnected LANs

Case Study

Section 1: Factual Data

The organization involved is a manufacturing firm, Widgets Inc. Players involved include J. Wilson, an engineer; M. Smith, a secretary; and C. Black, the secretary's immediate supervisor. This action took place within the firm's single location in New England.

Section 2: What Happened

J. Wilson was involved with one of the firm's more remote customers in southern Texas. He was required to transmit certain digital data between Widgets Inc. and the customer's location via the internal LAN and a common carrier vendor's WAN. Wilson was directed by his supervisor to keep this project's costs to a minimum. Wilson realized that the constant interchange of data between New England and Texas would increase his department's telecommunications costs, thereby increasing the cost of the product. Relying on his friendship with M. Smith, he used Smith's personal computer and connection to the LAN to transmit this data to the customer's location. WAN telecommunications expenses could then be charged against C. Black's department where Smith worked. Wilson's department would not show any increases in telecommunications costs related to this project. This improper use of the LAN was discovered when Smith requested assistance from the telecommunications staff when a file transfer was not completed and Smith thought the LAN was at fault.

Section 3: Losses

Who lost what in this matter? The cost of the transmission must be borne by the originating caller, Widgets Inc. Wilson's department was not billed directly by the WAN common carrier vendor. The bill received by Widgets only showed a certain number of minutes of usage between the locations involved, southern Texas and a state in New England. Widgets Inc. did not lose any money, they did not lose a contract, and the customer was satisfied with the product received. What was lost was control over internal assets. Such loss of control, in this instance, was poor management of a resource. If Wilson had been sending proprietary or secret data to an unauthorized recipient, the theft could not have been traced to him until it was much too late.

Section 4: Lesson Learned

A properly implemented Accounting Management effort would have provided the LAN Manager with tabular or graphic indications of increased traffic flowing to or from Smith's LAN address. Occasional spikes of traffic are to be expected. Long-term duration of the increase in traffic loading would have alerted the LAN Manager to changes in LAN subscriber operating procedures. Such long-term increases may also be an indication of multiple retransmissions, indicating a hardware or software fault that needs investigation. Without the Accounting Management effort, Wilson was able to continue his subterfuge for over three months.

The implementation of accounting management to identify

LAN Operations

and correct this single problem would not be cost effective. But what if Wilson's improper procedures had involved the transmission of proprietary or secret data? Accounting management would only catch this problem after it happened. This is *reactive* management, rather than *proactive* management. Reactive management is locking the door after the horse has been stolen. Yes, it may prevent future losses, but it is too late now. How else could this loss have been prevented?

Configuration Management in Local Area Networks

For knowledge, too, is itself a power.
—*Meditationes Sacre. De Hoeresibus,* Bacon

Configuration management is formalized knowledge of what components are part of the LAN, where they are located, and their status. This chapter discusses:

- Configuration management activities.
- The positive and negative aspects of configuration management.
- Some of the key procedures to be used when configuration management is implemented.

Basic Knowledge of the LAN

Configuration management begins with a knowledge of the LAN, which answers the question: What type of LAN is in use?

Topology

Configuration management is, at its core, the procedure for obtaining and recording knowledge of the LAN. The foundation for this knowledge is an in-depth understanding of the topology of the LAN. This knowledge helps us determine the type of LAN that is in use. Is it a ring, bus, or star? Is it token passing, CSMA/CD, or some other method? What is the capacity of the LAN in throughput? Throughput is a measure of the ability of the LAN to pass traffic. Normally, throughput is measured in bits per second (bps), kilobits per second (Kbps), or Megabits per second (Mbps). One of the more common types of bus topology LANs is an Ethernet. A pure Ethernet LAN has a specified throughput of 10 Mbps. However, under heavy traffic load, the response times degrade to the point where they are noticeable when traffic reaches the 2.5 Mbps level. When traffic reaches the 5–6 Mbps level, response time slows to a crawl and many subscriber complaints are heard. The same can be said about token ring networks, except that the larger, noticeable increase in response time takes place at the 6–7 Mbps level.

Many nonsophisticated users do not realize that the advertised throughput is not the throughput that can be expected in the "real world." The advertised throughputs were achieved under strict laboratory conditions and are normally not available in the workplace.

Topography

After gaining knowledge of the topology of the LAN, the next general grouping of knowledge is the topography of the LAN. The topography is concerned with the actual physical layout of the transmission media. What types of wire and cable are located where? Where are taps, the connections to the transmission media, located? What type of connections are made, and where are they? Connections are not the same as taps. A tap is the point where a subscriber connects to the LAN. A connection is a joining of another LAN or nonsubscriber device to the transmission media.

Inventory

Once the type of LAN is determined and its topography identified, the next step in obtaining the required basic knowledge is to inventory the LAN contents by location. If the reason for this inventory is not immediately apparent, it should become so in the latter part of this chapter. The result of this inventory is a complete list of all hardware and software in the LAN. The inventory can answer various questions: How many terminal servers connect to the LAN? How many drops are located in what room(s) or area(s)? How many taps are on a given cable segment?

Which taps are or are not in use? The result of this effort is a series of lists of hardware and software, by serial number wherever possible, giving the locations of these LAN components.

Functions

The last act in acquiring the basic knowledge of the network is to understand the functions of each piece of hardware and software in the LAN. It is all well and good to know that such and such a device is labeled as a "terminal server," but what does it do? How many subscribers connect to this device? Can printers or modems be connected to a terminal server? The same comments can be made concerning the LAN software. If a PC needs a particular type of software to accomplish file transfers, what else does that software do? How did the user obtain that particular copy of that software? Has the organization been placed in jeopardy by "pirated" software?

We now need to separate this equipment by function. All data telecommunications hardware is placed into either of two distinct subsets, DTE (Data Termination Equipment) and DCE (Data Communications Equipment). DTE is the always the source or sink of data communications. A computer or terminal is normally thought of as DTE. A multiplexer or terminal server is normally thought of as DCE.

One possible format for this inventory is shown in Table 4.1. Note that the "Component ID" field in this figure is a locally generated number, the first four digits indicating the year of purchase, the next two digits indicating the month of purchase, and the last digits indicating the sequence of purchase. For example, 1989–12–2 indicates that this was the second device of this type purchased during December 1989.

Obtaining this raw information about the LAN is, in and of itself, a time-consuming process. Under normal conditions, an organization that is large enough to require a LAN Manager already has one or more technicians or LAN analysts on its payroll. It should be the responsibility of these persons to obtain the required information. The LAN Manager should not merely accept, at face value, the findings of these persons. If they report that copy number 14 of the terminal emulation software is on PC number 4 in the accounting department, the LAN Manager should check a representative number of these identifications and loca-

Table 4.1: Format for Inventory

Component Type	Serial Number	DTE/ DCE	Component ID	Building or Campus	Floor	Room
Terminal	A12C45	DTE	1989-12-12	Rose Hall	3	28
File Serv	1223-87	DTE	1989-12-44	Fredrick	B	1
Modem	890254	DCE	1988-1-22	Friar Hall	1	18
PC-AT	4452122	DTE	1990-2-2	Jones Lib	2	21

tions. As was stated earlier, the information gleaned now is the foundation for the entire configuration management effort. Any errors made now will return to inflict damage on future LAN management efforts.

Suppose, for example, that three new people are to be connected to the LAN segment in the personnel office. The LAN Manager reviews her own records and notes that no taps exist where the new people are going. She concludes that she must purchase new material and expend manpower in order to connect these new people to the LAN. If the taps and their associated drop cables in fact were already in place, the LAN Manager would have to justify the expense of duplicating existing capabilities, which is not easy to do.

Knowledge Provides Control Of LAN Assets

How this basic knowledge of the LAN helps the LAN Manager involves three general areas of the LAN management function: status, changes, and updates. See also Chapter 11.

Status

Status means the operating conditions of the hardware, software, and circuits that make up the LAN. The operating status of hardware includes whether it is defective, in use, operational, or standby. If the LAN is large enough or the LAN Manager is meticulous enough, the defective category of "awaiting repair" can be further subdivided into "waiting for repair parts" or "manpower."

The status of software may include an inventory of a

particular version or release of an application by serial number and known bugs. Release 1.3 of a file transfer application cannot work with files over 63,999 bits. Release 2.0 can work with files of any size. Who should get the earlier or later release? Can Release 1.3 be traded up to Release 2.0 at minimal cost? Should it be done?

When evaluating the status of circuits, you should consider two areas. The first area is the operational capability of the circuit. Will it pass traffic? If the circuit is down, every effort should be expended to restore it now. If it is operational, does it meet the design specifications? The term "design specifications" includes throughput. If a circuit is designed to pass traffic at a given number of Kbps and does not, someone should be trying to find the reason(s) why it does not. Does the circuit under consideration see any use at all? If it does not, why not? Someone installed it at some time for a purpose.

The second area of consideration of circuit status is that of circuits that are part of the LAN, but are also part of a WAN or VAN. The organization that uses these non-LAN circuits pays for them. If they are not being used or if the usage is incorrect, the organization is paying for something it does not need or use. One of a manager's responsibilities is ensuring proper usage of corporate assets and resources. The LAN Manager is not exempt from this responsibility. By being aware of circuit usage, the LAN Manager can identify circuits that are not being used but are being paid for. Eliminating these circuits saves money for the company.

One of the more common mistakes in connecting VAN and WAN circuits to a LAN is that of duplication of effort. The headquarters of an organization may have circuits going from the local personnel office to the personnel office of an activity in another town or state. The marketing office may have another circuit to the same location. The LAN Manager must ascertain whether the traffic between the two locations is sufficient to warrant the duplication of transmission media.

Changes

The LAN Manager needs knowledge of the LAN in the areas of installation/termination of service, movement of subscribers, and modification of service. No organization is totally static for a long period of time. Combine this state of flux with the new offerings of technology and the LAN Manager is kept busy indeed. In any organization people voluntarily resign, new hires come on board, and promotions cause moves within the organization. As an element of an organization grows or shrinks, subscribers may be assigned or removed from that element. Growth or shrinkage of the element may cause it to move to larger or smaller office space. In any of the above conditions, the LAN Manager is responsible for providing service in support of these moves.

These moves are not cost free. The LAN Manager must decide where taps and connections can be made to the transmission media, when subscribers can be serviced, and when unused taps and connections can be removed or salvaged. Usually, when one group moves out of an area, another moves in shortly thereafter. If possible, the LAN Manager must juggle the requirements of both groups to ensure the move is made with a minimum of expense and a maximum of connectivity.

New installations can be treated differently than moves, reinstallations, and terminations. The latter requires very little new hardware and software; the former requires much more planning. This planning for new installations must be based on knowledge of what is currently on hand. If the number of new connections is large enough, formal project management techniques may be required. Each new installation must be handled on a case-by-case basis, and the LAN Manager must use whatever management tools proved successful in the past.

Updates

As vendors of hardware and software receive feedback from users, they modify the products that are in the field to provide a better, faster, or more flexible means for accomplishing the task for which the hardware and software was designed. By maintaining up-to-date records of what hardware and software is in the LAN, the LAN Manager can identify which of these parts of the LAN have been updated and which are to be updated in the future. Care should be taken at this point. Usually, most modifications do not prevent the modified product from working with an unmodified product. Further, it is not normally required to update all like components of a LAN simultaneously. However, check with each specific vendor first.

Positive Aspects Of Configuration Management

No effort is made without some type of gain being foreseen. This section addresses the following gains derived from configuration management:

- A formally recorded history of the LAN
- Commonality benefits
- Reduced costs
- More rapid restoration of service
- Lowered inventory of spare equipment

Records of LAN Conditions and History

Readers who are following this text sequentially know that the LAN Manager has certain data already on hand. Certain types of knowledge of the LAN are available. This data and knowledge should be codified into formal records. Some of the more important formal records that the LAN Manager must maintain are described here.

Network Topography: The single most important record is an up-to-date blueprint, sketch, or schematic of the topography of the network. As a minimum, such a blueprint should show

- The route taken by the transmission media.
- The location of taps.
- The location of connections.
- The terminating point of drop cables.
- The location of all nonsubscriber equipment.

An archive copy and a working copy are the minimum required. As a change is made on the working copy and final approvals granted, the working copy is redrawn and becomes the archive copy. Another working copy is made frcm it, and the process begins again.

Equipment Inventory: The next most important record is that of equipment inventory. Whereas the location of nonsubscriber equipment may be shown on the network blueprint, such a record usually does not contain all of the required information on all equipment. The LAN Manager must know the equipment location by serial number, by model or revision, by capacity, and if possible by age and cost of procurement. (See Table 4.1.)

Maintenance History: Maintenance history of the equipment that makes up the LAN is another useful set of records to keep. Maintenance history records answer such questions as:

- At what point have maintenance costs made a device uneconomical to repair?
- Has this piece of hardware or software been updated in accordance with the vendor's specifications?
- How many of the model "X" modems are still within warranty or guarantee periods?

One possible format for such history is shown in Table 4.2.

The maintenance history of the LAN is different from the history of the equipment that makes up the LAN. Maintenance history of the LAN is directed toward subscriber-reported problems. If a clerk in the personnel department cannot access the LAN, the problem is investigated and corrected. The symptoms and corrective actions taken to eliminate the problems should be recorded for future restorative activities. Such types of information are particularly useful when documenting failures in new equipment or when settling claims against vendors who refuse to back their products. Such records are also useful when determining man-hours expended for maintenance functions.

Table 4.2: Equipment Maintenance History

Equipment Type:	Personal Computer	
Purchase Date:	February 1990	
Serial Number:	4452122	
Warranty Expires:	February 1991	

Date	Cost	Repair Performed
3/90	33.42	Replaced defective cable from CPU to monitor
6/90	432.20	Replaced hard drive (parity errors)
7/90	−00.00	Replaced hard drive. Repair under warranty

Commonality of Equipment and Functions

When, and if possible, a common source of LAN hardware and software should be used. It is easy to say, and just as easy to prove, that vendor A's modem is 10 percent less than vendor B's modem which offers the same functionality. Yet this 10 percent difference will soon be eaten up in the cost of outages for one or more subscribers if vendor B's product is not as reliable as the slightly more expensive model. Consider the following arguments in favor of commonality of hardware and software.

Common Specifications: When modifications are made to the LAN, "build to" specifications for the interoperability of new hardware and software are immediately known from existing records. If an outside agency is to perform the modifications, the LAN Manager saves on fees by being able to provide the outside agency with complete LAN performance specifications very rapidly. This means less time, with its concomitant expenses, expended in determining the makeup and functions of the LAN. In very large LANs, particularly those LANs interconnected via WANs and VANs, this could save up to 30 percent of the expenses involved in finding out exactly which piece of equipment does what and, more importantly, how.

Support Equipment: Each LAN requires what is euphemistically known as support equipment. Support equipment is usually lumped into the category of Test, Measurement, and Diagnostic Equipment (TMDE). TMDE is further subdivided into two areas, common and specialized. Common TMDE includes devices such as multimeters and oscilloscopes. Specialized TMDE includes such devices as network analyzers used to determine operational characteristics, or special test jigs for other test and evaluation purposes. A modern digital multimeter can be used in almost every type of LAN available. However, a network analyzer that is designed to work with a CSMA/CD LAN provides no functionality when working with a token ring LAN.

If both types of LANs are part of an organization, both types of network analyzers are required. Network analyzers normally can cost as much as half of an engineer's yearly salary. This is a strong reason to ensure commonality of LAN types. The additional benefit should also be obvious. If a major extension to the current LAN is required, it is easy to specify the additional TMDE required to support this major extension. No new types of equipment are required, just more of the same type.

Training: Part of the function of the LAN Manager is to provide technical assistance to the department that trains new users of the LAN. If the same types of hardware and software are used throughout the LAN, only one set of performance objectives are required. This eliminates multiple training sessions, lesson plans, and periods of practical exercise. What is even more important, the commonality of LAN equipment eliminates the time and manpower required to create many different training programs to achieve the same objective, a knowledgeable subscriber of LAN services.

Another benefit flows from commonality of LAN equipment vis-à-vis training: those who are charged with maintaining the LAN need to be trained on fewer types of equipment. Normally this training is provided by the technician's employer in an on-the-job training program or by the vendor. In the former case, the trainee must learn the idiosyncrasies of fewer types of equipment. In the latter case, money is saved because the trainee does not have to attend as many of the equipment vendor's formal classes.

Budgeting: Commonality of equipment within the LAN has budgetary advantages. The LAN Manager is responsible for forecasting, for planning purposes, the amount that is to be set aside for maintenance for the next budgetary cycle. If the LAN did not change in the past year, the forecasting is simple. It is reasonably safe to assume that the next year's maintenance costs will be close to last year's. But what happens if the size or configuration of the LAN changes? With the knowledge that one out of every ten modems will fail in any given 90-day period, it is easy to compute the financial results of an increased number of modems on the maintenance budget—as long as the new modems are the same make and model as the ones now in use!

Amortization costs can also be computed much more easily if all equipment within the LAN is common. Once again, using the modems for example, it is easy to see. If the accounting department decrees that amortization will be straight line over four years, it is simpler to compute the amortization for one modem and multiply that amount by the number of like modems than it is to compute the amortization for many types of modems and then sum all the computations.

Elimination of Unnecessary Expenses

One of the immediate benefits of configuration management is cost savings in several areas. Some of these were discussed earlier in regard to commonality of the devices that make up the LAN. This section addresses additional cost savings that can be achieved through configuration management. Each organization must evaluate its internal requirements and select whatever parts of configuration management are most applicable to those needs.

Leased Circuits: Cost savings can be realized by reducing the number of leased circuits. As a rule of thumb, leased circuits (from VANs and WANs) are used to link elements of the LAN that are too expensive to connect in any other way. Traditionally gateways and bridges are used for this function. Historically, users have committed to leased circuits on an ad hoc basis with no central control over expenses involved. It was not unheard of for separate departments within an organization to have multiple leased lines in parallel from one location to another location. These leased lines were used at the 10 to 15 percent level. Significant cost savings could be achieved by multiplexing these subscribers over one leased line. Placing the LAN Manager in charge of procuring leased lines reduces this expense.

When an organization purchases a LAN, it is purchasing a method of information interchange. Manufacturing organizations create profit by changing raw materials into finished products. Service organizations create profit by turning manpower into required services. The LAN Manager must take the hardware and software available in the LAN and turn it into a means of information interchange for the subscribers. Based on this charge, the LAN Manager must identify the subscribers to the LAN and ensure that they are using no more than is required.

To determine if LAN usage is under, at, or over what is required by a subscriber or group of subscribers is simple in description but complex in application. A subscriber with a dumb terminal who accesses an application on a remote computer needs throughput of approximately 9600 Bps. A draftsman who retrieves a drawing from a library of such drawings, modifies it at a local intelligent workstation, and returns it to the library needs throughput in the 1.5–2 Mbps range. So far so good. Now, how often do these people perform these actions? The user with the dumb terminal opens the connection and keeps it open all day. The draftsman retrieves and returns a drawing perhaps once every two or three hours. Add to this load the secretary who, after typing a memo, transmits it to many users through the electronic mail facility. This memo is probably in the 2–3 Kbps range.

Whereas it may appear that consumption of bandwidth is additive, in all reality it is not. Consumption is random, with peaks usually occurring between 9:30 to 11:30 AM and 1:30 to 4:00 PM in most one-shift organizations. The LAN Manager must ensure that there is enough bandwidth that users will not be exposed to response times that exceed 5 to 7 seconds during peaks of usage. The key point to remember is that LAN usage must be allocated in a cost-effective manner.

Unused Equipment: Another method of cost savings that results from configuration management is that of canceling leases or rentals of equipment that is no longer needed. If a remote element of the organization requires a temporary connection to the LAN, the equipment can be leased rather than purchased. When the temporary demand is over, such as seasonal fluctuations, there is no need to retain the equipment with its concomitant expenses. By making the LAN Manager responsible for procurement and return of the hardware, the organization ensures that rental or lease expenses are kept to a minimum. The LAN Manager may also be charged with the responsibility of selling used or out-of-date LAN hardware. This is a way to recoup costs for equipment that has either been fully amortized or is no longer compatible with current LAN configuration.

Site Licenses: In a large LAN, it is advisable to have commonality in software as well as in hardware. To ensure that no pirated copies of this software exist, the LAN Manager should be responsible for procurement of LAN software on a site license basis wherever possible. Not only is site license software cheaper than individual copies, the upgrades or fixes to defective applications are easier to obtain and apply. By relying solely on one vendor for software, the LAN Manager has much more leverage when negotiating for additional site licenses and new applications. Interoperability between locations is guaranteed.

Many people wink at the dissemination of illegal copies of software. When the original buyer of an application brings a copy of it into the workplace for his own use, this is skirting the limits of legality. When coworkers duplicate the second copy, it is theft. This theft has taken place in the worker's place of employment. Courts could regard this action as being condoned by the employer, making the employer an accessory to theft. This makes the employer liable to both criminal and civil penalties. Although LAN Managers cannot be held responsible for nontelecommunications software piracy, they may be held liable for internal and unauthorized duplication of telecommunications software. Each organization must evaluate these responsibilities on a case-by-case basis.

Manpower Savings

The imposition of formal configuration management can, in some circumstances, eliminate some manpower expenses. When more of the equipment in the LAN becomes common, fewer people with equipment-specific skills are needed. As LAN equipment matures, the need for low-level skills such as parameter loading become unnecessary due to the automation or centralization of the process. This same maturation also eliminates the need for some highly paid engineers. Many tasks that now require an engineer are automated within newer equipment. For example, port speed levels are now automatically sensed and adjusted, or are made simple enough for a technician or analyst, not an engineer, to set or modify. Because so much of this automation is being done in software, technicians and analysts will have to become more software literate to accomplish their assigned tasks.

Restoration of the LAN

Sooner or later, equipment that makes up the LAN fails. The failure can be so minor that only one subscriber is out of communications, or so major that the entire LAN is nonfunctional. In either case, the goal of the restoration process is a recovery that is as rapid as good safety practices will allow. Configuration management gives those charged with restoration tasks a complete knowledge of each item in the LAN that could be defective.

When high degrees of commonality exist, another benefit is gained. Technicians soon learn that a such-and-such type of file server will exhibit certain symptoms only under thus-and-so conditions. This type of knowledge shortens the amount of time spent in eliminating conditions that could also have caused the symptom noted. The requirements for speed in the restoration activity should be obvious. However, they are the subject of Chapter 5, "Fault Management".

Repair Parts/TMDE

Parts of electronic equipment that make up the LAN fail with some regularity. Restoration of communications can be expedited if these repair parts are kept on hand. Technicians can usually replace what is known as LRUs, or line replaceable units. These are normally whole items such as modems, or printed circuit boards in larger assemblies. How many of which types of items to keep on hand is difficult to determine without some historical record of failure rates. These failure rates should be derived from records kept of failures that have been experienced in the past.

As a rule of thumb, an organization should have enough LRUs for a two-week period of operation. Let us assume that the organization uses a token ring LAN. Each personal computer attached to the LAN uses vendor A's interface board. It is known that one of these boards fails every six months. There are 12 of these PCs on the network. Therefore, the LAN Manager can expect one of these interface boards to fail every two months.

Based on this computation, the correct stockage level of interface boards is one. Note that the failure level of the interface board is one every two months, and the suggested period of two weeks is much less than two months. If the two-week period were an inflexible standard, the authorized stockage level would be one-quarter of an interface board. The attempt to stock one-quarter of a LRU is always bound to fail. When computing the stockage level, always round up. Additionally, there is always some subscriber who must be connected to the network immediately. The LAN Manager who can support this type of "short fuse" requirement is always appreciated by upper management.

TMDE is like insurance. No one likes to pay for insurance, but there is no substitute when it becomes necessary. Configuration management ensures that the costs for purchase and upkeep of TMDE are held to a minimum. A word of caution is required at this point. As the perversity of the universe tends to a maximum, the LAN Manager can rest assured that a piece of TMDE will be required when it is either in use in another location or unavailable for other reasons. Too much TMDE is better than not enough.

Review

This section addressed the positive aspects of configuration management. Basically there are two positive aspects: reduced operating expenses and increased ease of operation and maintenance of the LAN. This is not to say that configuration management by itself is easy or cheap. Configuration management requires attention to detail and very precise recordkeeping.

Negative Aspects of Configuration Management

Two negative aspects of configuration management must be addressed: the "frozen" development of hardware and software and various forms of dissension within the organization. The first is purely technical; the second is managerial.

Development Is Frozen

The previous section stated that commonality of equipment was a goal worth pursuing. Such a goal is not without its drawbacks. The major drawback is that if only Vendor A's modems are purchased, the LAN Manager may not be able to introduce Vendor B's modems if such modems are technically superior and cost about the same. Modern modems are not always interoperable. This is particularly true when using higher speed modems, that is, those in the 9600-bps range and above. Vendors of these high-speed modems use different internal algorithms to encode data at one location and decode it at the other location.

Multiplexers are another type of hardware that may not be

interoperable if they are from different vendors. There are no standards to which all vendors can be held in producing their telecommunications equipment, as there are in mechanical devices such as screw sizes or thread pitch. This is not to say that in the future, such standards will not be available. (Also see Chapter 9, which addresses telecommunications standards.)

Software is not quite so frozen in development as is hardware. Assume that one central computer is servicing multiple dumb terminals as well as PCs that can emulate dumb terminals. These PCs require software to permit this dumb terminal emulation. Several different vendors' software can be used for this purpose without affecting the central computer. The other side of this coin is that telecommunications software, no matter how well designed and debugged it is before it is released, will be updated much more often than telecommunications hardware. These updates cost money. Perhaps it does not cost a lot, but such updates are an expense that may be eliminated. Such expenses can be reduced by site licenses or bulk purchases of such software. Of course, if the vendor has stopped supporting this particular version of software or has gone out of business, the expense of replacing every copy of telecommunications software becomes exorbitant.

Another negative aspect of configuration management is that of restricting growth by reliance on out-of-date technologies. Consider the following example. For many years only two types of multiplexing were available, frequency division and time division. Both of these were somewhat wasteful of bandwidth. With the advent of statistical time-division multiplexing, LAN Managers could make much better use of available bandwidth. However, if these new multiplexers were not purchased or could not interoperate with existing equipment, the LAN Manager could not take advantage of the more intelligent use of bandwidth and was forced to purchase more bandwidth as the demand grew.

The LAN provides one thing, information interchange. It is the LAN Manager's task to use LAN hardware and software in the most cost-effective manner. The LAN Manager must also conserve the organization's financial resources in pursuit of this goal.

When a new technology creates a tension between subscriber

satisfaction and the organizations's financial resources, the LAN Manager must decide which has priority in light of other corporate goals and missions.

The CSMA/CD Ethernet type LAN offers a throughput in the 10-Mbps range. When subscribers have outgrown this bandwidth, what should be done to ensure that these same subscribers have sufficient throughput, yet stay within the commonality of equipment goal, which was addressed earlier? Should the LAN Manager install another CSMA/CD LAN in parallel with the existing one, or should the network topology be changed to entirely different transmission media? Does a third option exist? These questions are brought forward to identify a very important point: LANs are not static; LANs change as subscribers' needs and organizational goals change.

If, during the design phase of a LAN, there is a question as to whether or not the transmission media has enough bandwidth, you can put in a parallel run of transmission media when the initial run is constructed. The cost of installing additional transmission media is a very small percentage of the total cost during an initial installation. The cost of installing transmission media on demand is quite high. Such installations are labor intensive. Labor costs can be as much as one-half of the total cost of LAN installations.

Dissension Within the Organization

There are three general groups within an organization that may oppose configuration management. The LAN Manager is responsible for creating, within these three groups, a consensus that supports configuration management.

Subscribers: The first, and perhaps most vocal, of these groups includes the subscribers that the LAN supports. As more and more subscribers become computer literate, they develop attachments to their favorite brand of computer or type of software. As a rule of thumb, the LAN Manager should allow this hardware and software on the LAN only if it interoperates with the existing LAN equipment. The burden of proof of interoperability rests with the subscribers. However, the LAN Manager should not turn a deaf ear to these people either. Newcomers or "gurus" can bring good, as well as bad, ideas to the organization. These ideas should be evaluated on their own merits, not discarded just because they are different. Remember to be fairly skeptical of any box or diskette of telecommunications software with "V1.0" or "Release One" printed on it.

Individualists: The second group that may create dissension when configuration management is begun includes those who feel that they have a right to design and install their own LAN. These people assume that, as the subscribers, they know what support they need to complete their assigned duties. This is not a fallacious position. Many of these people may have experience in this area, and they are somewhat knowledgeable of the subject of LANs. What they do not have is the "big picture" of how the LAN supports the organization, and how their arbitrary decision will impact the future growth of the entire LAN.

The LAN Manager will do well to tap the resources present in such a group. An old adage states, "If you can't lick 'em, join 'em!" However, the LAN Manager's position makes joining this group impossible. Instead, the group that wants to go their own way must be persuaded to join the LAN Manager. The easiest way to accomplish this is to develop a consensus between all involved.

For example, if the engineering department needs to pass data from several sources at different times and finds that such-and-such a LAN serves their purpose the best, they will attempt to install such a LAN through the entire organization. The LAN Manager should solicit these peoples' help in the early design phases. Make the department that wants to be different justify its requests. After all, they are engineers, are they not? They can conduct research on technical subjects such as throughput, response times, and reliability computations including Mean Time Between Failures (MTBF) and Mean Time To Repair (MTTR). Of course, if they find that this is taking up too much of their own time, they may just pass the whole thing back for the LAN Manager to decide—which is something the LAN Manager wanted to do in the first place.

When the LAN Manager has responsibility for all LAN functions, the purchasing department must obtain the LAN Manager's approval for anything that is connected to the LAN. This is another layer of bureaucracy in the organization, with all the drawbacks inherent in such a layer. A method for getting around such authorization for each purchase is reasonably straightforward. A list is made of LAN hardware and software that may be purchased without the LAN Manager's approval. The purchasing department checks each purchase request against this list. If the product(s) are not on the list, the LAN Manager must then approve the purchase.

Physical Plant Support Staff: The third general group that is involved with the LAN on a nonsubscriber basis is the group that is responsible for the organization's physical plant.

Assume that another building in the industrial park is purchased for expansion purposes. The LAN Manager must be invited into the planning stages as soon as possible. Some types of LANs are limited by distance. Other types require long lead times for VAN and WAN circuits. If microwave transmission media is used, lead times can range from 12 to 18 months in some areas. The LAN Manager must survey the new building for connections, taps, and drop cable locations.

Routine maintenance on the physical plant requires the LAN Manager's approval in some instances. The transmission media that carries the LAN traffic is routed throughout the building(s). Any modification to these buildings may have a negative impact on such transmission media. If a tradesman is running electrical conduit through a wall and cuts the "backbone" transmission media in a token ring network, the entire network is down until the break is found and spliced. Some types of transmission media are subject to interference generated by fluorescent lights, arc welders, or electric motors. The relocation of a production line that does not use the LAN can induce electrical noise in the LAN. This noise acts to corrupt the data flowing through the transmission media, causing retransmissions and increased throughput.

Prevention of Dissension

The easiest way to eliminate the dissension caused by configuration management is prevention. Prevention is as simple as building consensus among all involved when an action or activity can have an effect on the LAN. Everyone should be brought into the planning stages at the earliest possible opportunity and be given a chance to explore how this change impacts the way they now accomplish their assigned tasks. Although consensus does not always mean approval, it does mean agreement. There is a distinct difference between approval and agreement.

Review

This section has shown some of the negative impacts inherent in a configuration management program. In some circumstances, configuration management may not be appropriate, but these are few and far between. If an organization is large enough to require a LAN Manager, the LAN is large enough to require configuration management.

Implementing Configuration Management

If you do not know where you are and you do not know where you are going, one direction of travel is just as good as another. Configuration management has a goal of supporting the organization's data communications needs. How these needs are ascertained, and then supported, is the subject of this section.

Organizational Goals

As a member of the management of the organization, the LAN Manager must have an in-depth knowledge of not only what services the LAN subscribers need, but also of how these services help the organization achieve its goals. Is the organization's goal better products, better services, or faster delivery? This is a three step process:

1 Understand the organization's goals;
2 Examine the LAN;
3 Standardize hardware and software.

Step 1–Understand the Organization's Goals: Having determined the goal(s) of the corporation, the LAN Manager must analyze the LAN capabilities that support the subscribers' attempts to achieve the goal. If one goal is better quality products, how can the LAN support the quality control effort? What information interchange is required to eliminate, or help eliminate, defective products during the manufacturing process? Some say that an automated assembly process reduces production mistakes. Can the LAN support such an automated (robotic) assembly line?

Service industries can also benefit from LANs. Banking is such a service industry. One of the more familiar automation efforts is that of the automated check handling. By automating check handling procedures, manpower requirements have been reduced. And, as labor is the single most expensive component in a service industry, LANs that replace labor not only support the corporate goal of service, but also save money by eliminating some salaries.

In most organizations, data processing began in support of the finance and accounting function. Soon the computers in this area were networked to outlying locations (through WANs or VANs) for ease of information interchange. Sometime thereafter the LAN was connected, making remote entry and file transfers available to all workers. Other elements of the organization copied this capability. Now, the challenge for the LAN Manager is to draw order from this amalgamation of networks in order to meet the following requirements:

- Provide support to the organization.
- Be cost effective; no more or no less than needed to accomplish the assigned tasks.
- Have a technically elegant design.
- Be easy to modify as conditions change.

Step 2–Examine the LAN: Once the LAN Manager knows how the LAN can be used to support the attempts to achieve established organizational goals, the next step is to examine the LAN contents. This examination results in two categories of hardware and software: those that support the attempt, and those that do not. Those items of hardware and software, or circuits, that fall into the latter category should be eliminated or sold for salvage value in a manner consonant with corporate policies and good management practices.

To this point, two actions have been accomplished. The first action is to identify methods in which the LAN supports organizational goals. The second action is to eliminate hardware and software within the LAN that contributes nothing in support of these organizational goals. In some cases, this type of hardware and software inhibits achievement of assigned goals.

Step 3–Standardize Hardware and Software: The act of standardization has been discussed previously in the area of commonality of equipment. However, the LAN Manager may not want to take on this decision. Although LAN Managers are probably the ones most knowledgeable of appropriate hardware and software, they may not be the most knowledgeable of the way in which the subscribers accomplish their assigned tasks.

As soon as possible, division, department, and section managers, or their assigned representatives, should be polled for their opinions on what type of services the LAN should provide. Note that these people should not specify which type or brand of hardware and software should be purchased; rather, they should specify functionality.

Their specifications could include things such as memory capacity or speed of transmission in hardware. Software specifications should include things such as the maximum size of the spreadsheet, how large a database to use, or what features should be included in a word processing package. If these procedures are not followed, the result will be a "want list" of brand X computers, brand Y spreadsheets, and brand Z word processing applications. The only problem is that recommendations for brands X, Y, and Z will differ from department to department. The LAN Manager must stress that functionality, not brand name, is the most important decision-making factor.

To avoid appearing to be an autocrat, the LAN Manager must review the recommendations from various users, eliminate those that will not work well in a LAN environment, and return the remaining recommendations to the subscribers explaining why their choices were not selected. Then the subscribers decide, within a given time period, which hardware and software will be installed in the LAN. If the subscribers do not make recommendations by the allotted deadline, the LAN Manager can truthfully point out the subscribers' obvious lack of interest.

In Counterpoint: The other side of this problem should also be discussed. If certain hardware and software are installed in the LAN, this process is not required. However, if a new product is being considered for inclusion in the LAN, the LAN Manager may want to circulate descriptions of the product through the organization, particularly to those who are either technically sophisticated, or who are thought of as opinion leaders, for their comments. These comments can help buttress the LAN Manager's recommendation for or against the proposed new product.

The result of obtaining input from present or future subscribers of LAN hardware and software will be a suite of products that first and foremost support the organizational goals, but also have the approval of as many of the subscribers as possible. Essentially the activity is building consensus, while simultaneously offering subscribers the chance to feel as if they belong to the organization.

Once the hardware and software have been standardized, the LAN Manager must complete a formal inventory of what is on hand. (This was mentioned very briefly at the beginning of this chapter.) The required information for this inventory can be very large. Some of the more important items for recording are listed here.

Serial number	Make/Model	Date purchased
Maintenance cost	Location	Revision number
Channel capacity	Bandwidth	Bit rate
Initial cost	Residual value	Status—hot/cold
Port capacity	Standards	Length (cable)
Operating system	RAM capacity	Address (LAN)
Drop locations	Connections	

Note that this inventory should not include WAN or VAN circuits. These should be inventoried separately. (The reason for this is discussed later.) Note also that unauthorized persons who gain access to this data could wreak havoc with the LAN. The LAN Manager must treat this inventory with care. The inventory is corporate proprietary data.

Once completed, the inventory must be stored such that two objectives are reached, even though these objectives may seem to be mutually contradictory. The first objective is to secure the data from unauthorized viewing. Aside from the fact that such data is corporate proprietary information, as was mentioned earlier, unauthorized dissemination of this information may alienate subscribers. Questions such as "Why does so-and-so have more ports than I do?" can be answered, but never really satisfied. The second objective is to make the inventory information available at a moment's notice for the LAN Manager's daily chores. Examples of this inventory information include:

- Where empty ports are located
- What sections of the LAN transmission media are not fully used
- What applications are available
- Where such applications are located

This information is required for continued subscriber support as well as for LAN redesign or growth.

Once the dichotomy between protection and availability is resolved, the means of storing the inventory information must be determined. The term "storage" in this instance has two meanings. One meaning is the entering of the actual data on some type of records; the other is the storing of the completed records themselves.

The data can be stored in manners as archaic as 5x8 cards and as up-to-date as optical disks. The storage media is determined by, among other things, the amount of data to be stored and the rapidity of access. Can the LAN Manager afford to spend a half hour trying to find the termination point of port 4 of the multiplexer located in the third floor of building 18? If so, 5x8 cards may be the answer. If not, magnetic media and a flexible database are required. There is no rule of thumb to guide the LAN Manager. Each choice of storage media must be made on a case-by-case basis. The only recommendation is to leave as much room for growth as possible since this data will grow as the LAN grows.

The complete records must be stored in at least three locations. All records pertinent to the LAN inventory must be in triplicate. The LAN Manager must have one complete set available for daily reference. Another set should be available, probably within the same building, in case the first set is corrupted or destroyed. A third set should be maintained outside of the organization's physical plant. All three sets of records should be updated no less frequently than weekly, and if the LAN is large enough, the updates should be done daily. Once again, the question of how often to update depends on the LAN's size and the LAN Manager's judgment.

Circuit Inventory

In addition to inventories of material in the LAN itself, a separate inventory should be made of the WAN and VAN circuits that connect to the LAN. There are two types of these circuits: leased (which include private packet networks) and dial-up circuits.

Inventories for leased circuits must list, at a minimum:

- End points of the circuits
- Contractual costs of the circuits
- Guaranteed availability (percentage)
- Guaranteed throughput (bits per second)
- Circuit start and stop dates
- Carrier's circuit identification
- Identity of the equipment that is connected to the circuit's end points, and where such equipment connects to the LAN
- A schematic or sketch of the circuit routing from the carrier's point of presence or demarcation to the connection to the LAN

Inventories for dial-up circuits, either analog or digital, must contain, at a minimum:

- Bandwidth of the circuit (bits per second)
- Carrier's circuit identification
- Where the modem connects to the LAN
- Data on the modem itself
- Telephone number assigned
- PBX data as required

From this information, the LAN Manager can ascertain certain management information regarding leased circuits. Such information is required to ensure that the organization is not paying for circuits that are not being used, for duplication of circuits, for leased equipment (for circuit termination requirements), for bandwidth consumption, and for WAN/VAN communications costs. Note that, if four leased circuits of a certain bandwidth, 1200 bps for instance, are in use, it is usually less expensive to have one circuit of 4800 bps under the control of a multiplexer.

The same type of information is not available on dial-up circuits. When a dial-up circuit is used, the actual path the signal travels depends solely on the common carrier's routing algorithms. The charge is based on time and distance. The distances

LAN Operations

are specified by V and H (vertical and horizontal) coordinates. These coordinates measure the geographical distances between end points of the circuit in use. The organization is billed on a routine basis. The LAN Manager must review the billing to ascertain what costs can be attributed to LAN subscribers. A careful record of this type of usage must be kept.

If these records show a large number of routine calls to a given series of locations, the LAN Manager may wish to investigate the possibility of replacing the dial-up circuits with leased circuits. There is no rule of thumb on this decision. Each common carrier has different cost schedules that must be evaluated in the light of calling patterns. If the organization has a private PBX, this same type of information may be available through the SMDR port on the PBX.

Configuration Management Results

The purpose of this final section is to define some of the steps required to begin a configuration management process for the LAN. Such actions are not taken in a vacuum. The LAN Manager, and eventually the organization, will benefit from configuration management in several ways, especially costs and forecasting.

Organization Goals and Costs: The first, and perhaps most important way in which benefits are shown is in the support of the organization's goals in the most simple and cost-effective manner possible. Nothing is purchased or installed that does not directly support these goals. Information required for network redesign is immediately available. The second way in which benefits derive from configuration management is in identifying cost data. Such data answers such questions as: How much are we spending now? What are we paying for but not using? Or, as sometimes happens, what are we using and not paying for?

Forecasting: Configuration management also supports the requirement of budgets. The inventories of hardware, software, and circuits will show how much has been spent last year, and in the preceding years. The LAN Manager can, from historical data, forecast future budgets with some degree of confidence. If large growth is foreseen, this same data can be used to extrapolate additional charges resulting from such growth.

Technical data is available to ascertain the performance of the LAN under loading. If measurements show that with 30 subscribers the response time for a software application is about 3 seconds and that with 40 subscribers the response time goes up to 18 seconds, the LAN Manager should be thinking about LAN redesign. Response time is not the only parameter to be included in such preparation. The total performance of the LAN must be measured—but that is the subject of Chapter 6.

Summary

This chapter covered some of the more important aspects of configuration management. It has discussed:

- What configuration management is, including,
  — A basic knowledge of the LAN
  — Control over LAN assets

- The positive aspects of configuration management, including
  — Records and history
  — Commonality of equipment
  — Elimination of unnecessary expenses
  — The impact on restoration of the LAN
  — Stockage of repair parts and TMDE

- The negative aspects of configuration management, including
  — How development of the LAN is frozen
  — How dissension is created and controlled

- Implementation of configuration management, including
  — The support for organizational goals
  — The development of LAN inventories
  — The results of these efforts

Similar to Chapter 3, Chapter 4 is not all inclusive, nor was it meant to be. LAN Managers must adapt configuration management to support their organization, not the author's. This requires a study of the organization, its goals and mission, and the subscribers who act in the attempt to reach these goals.

Case Study

Section 1: Factual Data

The firm under discussion is a medium-sized manufacturing firm with several plants located in one state. Each location has its own LAN, and the LANs are connected through dedicated leased lines to each other. F. Wisnowski, the previous LAN Manager had retired recently after many years of faithful service. He declined to be retained on a consultant basis as he and his wife planned to retire to the Southwest. The firm searched for three months before it found a replacement. The new LAN Manager, M. Jones, got her first major project three weeks after she walked in.

Section 2: What Happened

Numerous subscribers were complaining about the slow speed of data transfer through the dedicated leased lines. Jones thought the best thing to do would be to add more leased lines, but senior management decided that the increased cost would not be acceptable. Jones was told to find another way. After several months of fruitless research, with complaints still coming in, Jones contacted the vendors of the hardware (gateways) being used to interconnect the firm's LANs. She hoped that perhaps new software or firmware had been released for the gateways to increase their throughput. Much to her surprise, she found that the gateways that her firm had in use had variable speeds, adjustable to match the media used on the leased line side. She contacted the various common carrier vendors and found that all the dedicated circuits being used to interconnect the LANs were rated at 9600 bps. By upgrading the leased lines and fine-tuning the equipment parameters, she was able to eliminate the subscriber complaints that were based on slow response time.

Section 3: Losses

Subscriber satisfaction was lost during the almost seven months it took to identify and correct this problem. Part of this can be attributed to management's slowness in finding a replacement for someone who, in all likelihood, management knew was going to retire. Someone should have been training Wisnowski's replacement over a year ago. Management had also been depending on institutional memory. Equipment parameters and capabilities should have been noted in some type of organized fashion, not in someone's memory.

Section 4: Lessons Learned

Failure to maintain accurate records, lists, inventories, and descriptions of LAN hardware, firmware, and software lead to, among other things, loss of subscriber satisfaction. The LAN Manager must keep in mind that his part of the organization was created solely to support those people who are charged with increasing the firm's revenues. Anything that interferes with this effort cannot be allowed to be traced to the LAN Manager or his staff. The LAN Manager and his staff must know what they have to work with to accomplish this goal.

5 *Fault Management*

"Leave 'em alone and they'll come home, waggin' their tales behind 'em."

—Nursery Rhyme

This chapter introduces the concepts of fault management within the LAN, including the following areas:

- Fault management as the prevention and correction of defective conditions.
- The positive aspects of fault management.
- The negative aspects of fault management.
- The methods used to implement fault management techniques.
- Fault management and organizational growth.
- Expert systems and their relationship to fault management.

Preventing and Correcting Defective LAN Conditions

Fault management takes place in two modes, proactive and reactive. Although proactive is the better approach, no amount of proactive fault management can totally eliminate reactive fault management.

Proactive Fault Management

The first step in proactive fault management is to evaluate network performance. (The discussion of performance evaluation of the LAN is covered in Chapters 3 and 4, which cover accounting management and configuration management, respectively.) Why is such emphasis on performance evaluation required? The LAN is like any other support device. The LAN enables those who are charged with producing the good or service to finish their assigned tasks quicker, better, or cheaper. Anything that interferes with this completion, either slows production down or helps to create errors. Either condition, in the short and long run, lowers profits or market share.

Quality of Service

In previous chapters, the evaluation of LAN performance was more concerned with how much the LAN was being used (accounting) or how much capability was there (configuration). The LAN evaluation within fault management is more concerned with how well is the LAN functioning. Such evaluation begins by identifying two specific criteria: the points of stress within the LAN and the single point(s) of failure.

Stress Points

Points of stress within the LAN are not those of mechanical stress, but those of traffic loading. One of the rating factors in evaluating any LAN is throughput. If the organization supported by the LAN has only one topology and no identified subLANs, there should not be a single point of stress in the LAN. Rather, all parts of the LAN are stressed equally. But when subLANs are created, different points of stress are created. These points of stress vary from time to time, particularly if the product or service is seasonal.

A department store uses point-of-sale terminals to track inventory of products on the shelf. During the Christmas rush, the subLAN supporting these terminals may be working at peak performance. Any error conditions that may arise are magnified by the extra heavy load. All LANs show definite peaks and valleys of usage. Peaks are noticeable between 9:00 AM and 11:30 AM and between 1:30 PM to 4:30 PM during the normal business day. Once again, actions having even a slightly negative effect on the LAN's performance are magnified well out of proportion to its size when the LAN is heavily loaded.

Single Point of Failure

The other operational characteristic of LANs that must be identified for proactive fault management is that of the single point of failure. A small LAN with one large file server and several printers has, as a minimum, two single points of failure. These are the file server itself and the media that connect subscribers to the file server. In a token ring topology, any break in the "backbone" transmission media disables the LAN. No one can communicate with anyone else. A LAN with a bus topology and the same break in the transmission media will prevent those subscribers who are "downstream" of the break from accessing the file server. In most LANs, duplicate transmission media is the exception, not the rule. Therefore, almost all LANs have a single point of failure.

Alternative Routing

Once the stress conditions and single point of failure have been identified within the LAN, the LAN manager has the task of creating alternative routes for traffic. The term "alt routing" will be used in this text to identify all alternative routes and the action taken to use these routes.

Alt routing is the manual or automatic switching of traffic to different transmission media or LAN hardware. Switching to hardware is normally conducted through either a matrix switch, sometimes called an XY switch, or through a patch panel using specially designed plugs, receptacles, and patch cords. The patch panel approach is less expensive to install, but it has the drawback that reconnection is slow and remote telecommunication sessions can "time out." This time out could cause subscribers to lose data that have been entered, or it could corrupt open files. The matrix switch is much faster, but also more expensive. There is no rule of thumb as to which approach is better. Speed prevents a loss of data. A slower approach is cheaper.

Alt routing of transmission media is a rule that is honored more in the breach than in the observance. Transmission media, particularly coaxial cable, are somewhat expensive to purchase and much more expensive to install. The chances of coaxial cable being damaged are slight, particularly if the cable is run in raceways, plenums, or ducts. However, when such media are damaged in these areas, the damage is almost impossible to detect without resorting to specialized TMDE. Very few organizations are willing to expend the funds necessary to duplicate the transmission media on the chance that they may fail.

One major problem with duplicating transmission media is

the physical layout of both the primary and alternative routings. There is usually only one truly convenient and acceptable path for transmission media to follow. We have seen both primary and backup transmission media following the exact same physical path. This is not the recommended approach. Any agency that damages the primary transmission media will most likely damage the backup transmission media in the same incident.

When, and if possible, the backup transmission media should be of a different type and run at physical right angles to the primary transmission media. For example:

If the primary transmission medium between two buildings on a campus is thick ETHERNET cable, buried in underground raceways, the backup transmission medium should be line-of-sight radio or free-space light. If the primary transmission medium is a wide bandwidth, WAN/VAN circuit, the backup should be an equally wide band circuit through an alternative WAN/VAN vendor, or a point-to-point satellite communications link. The serious student of alt routing is advised to study, in some depth, the approaches taken by those who provide life-sustaining telecommunications, or the redundancy present in military telecommunications.

Monitoring

Once the LAN has been evaluated, stress conditions and single points of failure identified, and alt routing selected, the LAN Manager has one more step to take in proactive fault management. The LAN must be continually monitored.

In previous decades, network monitoring was performed by humans who were alerted to failing conditions by primitive, but highly functional, alarm devices. With the high speeds present in data communications, this approach simply does not work. The human observer cannot notice transient conditions lasting less than 0.001 seconds, one microsecond, but they will disrupt data transmission on the LAN. This transient disruption causes an increase in the number of required retransmissions, which in turn causes an extra load on the LAN. If the LAN is operating at or near peak, this extra, but transient load, may be just enough to bring the LAN to its figurative knees.

As the cause of such transient conditions may be unknown and are quite rapid in nature, human perceptions are not enough to capture actions prior to and immediately after such incidents. There must be some mechanism or agency that constantly monitors the condition of the LAN for interruptions. (Chapter 6 discusses the concept of performance management within the LAN.) Some of the techniques used with performance management can be used to capture transient conditions. But, such capture requires continuous monitoring of the LAN.

The hardware and software required to continually monitor any type of LAN varies with the size, topography, and topology of the LAN in use. Certain types of TMDE, protocol analyzers, and network management hardware to name two, are used for this monitoring. Yes, these devices are not cheap.

The result of continuous monitoring of the LAN is an intellectual and "gut level" understanding of exactly how the LAN performs under varying loads. This understanding is important. What is more important is the fact that the LAN Manager can identify problems that cause subscribers to complain before the subscribers see them themselves. Proper application of the results of constant monitoring of the LAN allows alt routing to take place before, or at least immediately after, the traffic load becomes so heavy that LAN performance is degraded.

Reactive Fault Management

Reactive fault management cannot be eliminated no matter how much proactive fault management is practiced. Proactive fault management does not prevent equipment from failing through internal component failure, accidents, or acts of nature. Transmission media that are exposed to the elements—rain, dust, fog, ice, snow, and lightning—long enough will fail.

Rapidity in Restoration

The most important factor in reactive fault management is speed. Subscribers need and use the connectivity provided by the LAN. When this connectivity is missing, production slows or stops, and management is made aware of that fact. There are many ways to ensure that a defective condition is set right. The most common method is that of spare equipment.

There are two types of spares, hot and cold. A hot spare is one that is connected to either a matrix switch or a patch panel, turned on, and where necessary programmed and ready to run.

A cold spare is one that is mechanically ready to go, but sits on a shelf or in a closet and must be brought to the place of the defective device, installed, turned on, and where necessary programmed.

The hot spare can only be used where it is connected to the LAN through the matrix switch or patch panel. For instance, if a 12-channel multiplexer is in a hot standby status and a like multiplexer has become defective at a remote location, it is difficult to remove the hot spare in preparation for transport and installation. Yet, if the same multiplexer is on the shelf, it is ready to go as soon as it is put in the box. However, if a multiplexer is just sitting on the shelf, it is a wasted resource. Further, the time spent in moving it to the defective location, installing, preparing, and integrating it into the network translates into lost traffic and disgruntled subscribers.

When deciding whether it is advisable to have hot or cold spares, look to the procedures used by the various telecommunications vendors. When was the last time one of your voice connections just "died" in the middle of a word? The decision to go with hot and cold spares is not intuitive. The LAN Manager should perform a cost-benefits tradeoff study before reaching a decision.

Hot Sites

Routine failure calls for routine restoration. What would happen if a fire destroyed the transmission media, file servers, and some of the terminals attached to the LAN? The LAN Manager may wish to consider the possibility of a "hot site." The concept of hot site is a natural extension of the hot spare approach to LAN restoration. Within the hot site, all hardware, software, and services that the subscriber normally has access to is duplicated. Data stored in the file servers are updated continuously. The latest revision to the operating systems and applications are also available at the hot site.

What is the cost of the hot site? This question can be answered in one word: plenty! Is a hot site worth the cost? That question cannot be answered without much hard study and long soul searching. If the LAN supports several clerks, an accountant or two, three secretaries, and a draftsman, the answer is probably not. But, if this same LAN supports the entire accounting department, the legal department, and marketing, perhaps the answer is yes. If the LAN *is* the organization, such as the LAN that provides interconnectivity for check clearing in a bank, the answer is an unqualified yes, the expense is worth it. An unbiased source of guidance in such questions may be found in the firm that provides business insurance for the organization supported by the LAN. Find out from them if a previously prepared hot site will have a positive impact on the annual business insurance fees.

Contingency Planning

Reactive fault management requires all the preceding procedures, plus one more. Contingency planning is the sine qua non of LAN management. Without contingency planning, restoration is extremely difficult to accomplish. What is contingency planning, and how is it employed within a LAN?

In a nutshell, contingency planning is planning for the worst possible combination of circumstances. What is "worst possible?" Recent philosophers have codified it in Murphy's Law; "That which can go wrong will go wrong." Consider a violent thunderstorm, perhaps associated with a tornado. First, the local power goes out. This should be no problem because we have standby generators. Fine, but in the few seconds between the loss of commercial power and the start of the generators, one of the multiplexers lost its programming. No one had checked to see if the battery-backed RAM's battery was up to capacity. The only engineer who can reprogram the multiplexer is either on vacation or stranded due to storm-damaged bridges and roads. The manufacturer no longer supports that model, and the manual of reprogramming instructions cannot be located. The new technician who was scheduled to be available during the period has never seen that device, and the engineer was scheduled to start training him next week. Now what is to be done?

Consider another scenario. A subscriber complains because she cannot open a connection to a file server, which happens to be physically located in another city. The multiplexer used to consolidate traffic over the trunk to that city seems to be working, so the technician contacts the common carrier vendor. The vendor,

"Fly-by-Night Telephone Company and Yacht Sales," has no technical personnel on duty. What are the next steps to take?

Prioritizing Efforts

The benefit of daydreaming (day nightmares?) about these types of scenarios is reasonably obvious. Scenario building is a way of identifying possible error conditions and preparing now, so that they will not happen in the future. Perhaps one of the simplest means of preparation is to prioritize effort. Assume two trunks are found to be defective simultaneously. Only one engineer or technician is available to work on the problems. Which trunk is to be fixed first? How is such a decision made on the spur of the moment? No matter what happens, this will be a BAD decision, that is, a decision based on the Best Available Data. The key word here is "available."

Another question should be posed: When two or more subscribers complain, which one is serviced first? If one of the subscribers is the executive secretary to the vice president of operations, and the other subscriber is a clerk in the shipping department, the answer is reasonably obvious—or is it?

By prioritizing the restoration actions before a defective condition is noted, the LAN Manager can be absolved of a lot of blame for what appear to be hasty decisions. During routine LAN operations, the LAN Manager can identify those pieces of equipment or transmission media that may require the first priority of effort in restoration. Whether the LAN Manager feels that these decisions need approval from the executive suite is a matter best left to that person's own discretion and understanding of the organization's policies and procedures.

Besides identifying weak areas in hardware and software, the LAN Manager should also identify those persons who need additional training in the procedures of installation, operation, and maintenance of the hardware and software that constitute the LAN. If only one technician is able to repair or reprogram one or more devices within the LAN, the LAN Manager can be at that person's mercy. Further, there is no way the LAN Manager can, in good conscience, allow this person time off. What happens if the router in one of the subLANs breaks down and the only person who can repair it is vacationing in the wilds of Alaska? Cross training and retraining of all technical personnel within the

LAN Manager's organization should be going on now, not sometime in the future.

In sum, contingency planning is preparation for whatever combination of circumstances could come together to shut down the LAN. Consider the following set of circumstances. When an older piece of equipment is turned on, a weak component causes the fuse to blow. There is no replacement fuse in stock. Part of the LAN no longer functions. Management wants to know why a fuse, which costs less than $0.50 in small quantities, is not available for replacement. A resignation from the LAN Manager may not be called for, but the LAN Manager's raise that year may be less than what was expected.

Positive Aspects of Fault Management

Fault management cannot, under any circumstance, prevent faults from occurring in LAN management. What fault management can do is minimize the impact of such faults and speed up the restoration of communications to the subscribers. This section addresses some of the positive aspects of fault management and defines the difference between fault and event.

Positive Aspects

There are two positive aspects: decreased restoration time and increased productivity.

Decreased Restoration Time: The first benefit that the subscribers will note is decreased restoration time. Senior management's first question should be something like: Why should the organization pay thousands of dollars so some clerk in accounting won't have to wait an additional three minutes to get back on line? It is a reasonable question, and the LAN Manager should have a reasonable response. Unfortunately the answer is not intuitively obvious.

More than just "one clerk in accounting" is the unit of measure here. In all likelihood, if just one clerk is out of communications, minor equipment replacement or repair is probably required. Such replacement requires skilled troubleshooting, and that takes expensive technician and engineer time. The sooner these people can move on to the next problem, the fewer engineers and technicians are required. The trouble call from the accounting department may also be only the first of many calls caused by a larger common problem.

Continuing with this same clerk, what if the clerk was preparing data that was to be included in a proposal or sales/marketing effort, and the deadline for the clerk's input was ten minutes before the problem was found? Every minute spent in restoring telecommunications is one minute closer to meeting the previously imposed schedule.

Although corporate espionage is outside of the normal realm of possibility, a subscriber's complaint can be evidence of tampering with the LAN's structure. Sometimes covert taps put on transmission media by sloppy espionage agents interferes with normal telecommunications. Additionally, a defective piece of equipment may counter all of the security measures previously put in place. A defective LAN is an opening others can exploit.

Decreased restoration time has another, not quite so obvious benefit. Increased subscriber satisfaction is a real goal for the LAN Manager to try to attain. Some may say that the subscriber has no option but to use the LAN for information interchange. The answer to this argument, in a word, is: Wrong! Information can be manipulated into many formats and then physically carried from point to point. When it reaches the destination, it is then changed to an electrical format, never having reached the LAN. Consider the following example.

One of the sales staff has completed his monthly summary of sales. He must get this summary to the regional office. He is unsatisfied with the quality and quantity of service the LAN provides. When he completes the report, he copies it to a floppy disk or tape cassette. The disk or cassette is put in an overnight envelope and is in the regional office the next day. The data is read from the magnetic media and folded into the finished report.

Why was this method chosen over the LAN? The causes are simple to state and difficult to correct. The salesman was unsatisfied with the quality and quantity of service provided by the LAN. Personal experience has shown that people, either through ignorance or design, will go out of their way to find alternative methods of information interchange if the corporate method is too difficult or untrustworthy.

Proactive fault management helps convince the subscriber

that the LAN is a quality means of information interchange, one that can be depended on to deliver accurate information in a timely and cost-effective manner. Training, or propaganda (depending on the reader's point of view), may be necessary to convince subscribers that they have a quality resource available. This is not to say that the subscribers cannot be forced to use the LAN. However, if they are forced to use the LAN, they will use it to the minimum. Most modern LANs are so rich in features that the subscriber who is forced to use it will never discover all of its functionality.

Increased Productivity Through Shared Resources: One of the most commonly cited reasons for installing a LAN is to share resources and by doing so increase productivity. The claim of increasing productivity does not bear close scrutiny under certain conditions. If one person is charged with producing a product alone and shares nothing but the finished product, a LAN is not necessary. Only when the information in the finished product needs to be shared with others, such as a memo in an E-mail system, does the LAN increase productivity. Proactive fault management ensures that the finished product is shared as quickly and accurately as possible.

The shared resources claim does bear up under close scrutiny under certain conditions. Printers that produce executive quality correspondence are expensive. If "mahogany row" can share expensive printers, cost savings result. Proactive fault management ensures that these shared resources are available to all users as much as is technically and humanly possible.

Fault Versus Event

Many people are either unaware or confused about the difference between a fault and an event. A fault is an unforeseen interruption in service; an event is a planned disruption in service. Faults occur when hardware or software malfunction. Events occur when hardware or software is taken out of service for repair or reloading. A fault is an uncontrolled outage; an event is a controlled outage. A fault decreases LAN availability; an event may interrupt service, but is not computed as a diminution of availability.

Negative Aspects of Fault Management

Fault management, whether proactive or reactive, has a requirement for additional resources. These resources are not without cost. This section addresses some of the costs associated with the negative aspects of fault management.

Personnel

The single greatest cost involved is manpower. The single alternative to accepting this increased cost for internal manpower is to contract out the maintenance for the LAN. Yet, contract maintenance for the LAN does not provide the speed of restoration that an in-house maintenance staff can provide. We cannot sufficiently stress that speed of restoration is the primary goal of either proactive or reactive fault management.

Fault management involves four types of maintenance "jobs":

- Clerical
- Analyst
- Technician
- Engineer

The lowest-level job involved in fault management is *clerical*. This job is concerned with data gathering and initial contact with current or future subscribers to the services provided by the LAN. Although the details of this clerical job vary from organization to organization, some elements are common to all cases.

Data gathering is the technical aspect of the job. This person monitors read-outs, takes meter readings, and notes abnormal conditions or alarm indications for more technically oriented persons to evaluate. The more important aspect of this job is the daily interaction with subscribers. The clerical job includes answering nontechnical questions, taking reports on error conditions, and translating "technical-ese" into terms a layman can understand.

The next level of job classification is that of *analyst*. This type of job requires an in-depth understanding of the technical terminology and operating characteristics of the hardware and software that make up the LAN. This person should be able to identify abnormal conditions that derive from improper operating procedures. The job also requires the ability to use, at a low level, certain types of internal or external fault-locating devices. This includes diagnostic lights, meters, or other built-in devices.

The third level is that of *technician*. This individual can install, initially set up, take down, and remove any type of equipment that makes up the LAN. The technician should know how to use all the test, measurement, and diagnostic equipment on hand. The technician should be able to perform board level or LRU (line replaceable unit) level troubleshooting. To complete these tasks, the technician should also be familiar with the use of hand tools and safety requirements.

The fourth level of technical skill is that of the *engineer*. This person should have all the skills and abilities of the technician, plus others. These other skills include system design, evaluation of the impact of new equipment and procedures. The engineer should also be able to create low-level software, particularly small programs using the C language or other telecommunications-specific language(s). The engineer should have a working knowledge of the various telecommunications protocols that may now, or in the future, impact the LAN's operation. Either the engineer or the technician should have sufficient skills and knowledge to be able to train subscribers or others to use the LAN and its resources.

Test, Measurement, and Diagnostic Equipment

Test, Measurement, and Diagnostic Equipment (TMDE) is sometimes thought to be a negative aspect of fault management. The newer hardware and software that is used on and in LANs does contain a plethora of self-diagnostic capabilities. Yet many older items do not, and there are occasions when such internal test procedures are not sufficient. The internal test procedures cannot find every deficiency, or they may not be accurate enough.

Several different types of TMDE are required. Chapter 8 discusses them and their applications in detail. For now, it is sufficient to state that TMDE fills in the gaps where internal troubleshooting capabilities are missing and extends the senses of the technician or engineer.

Spares

The cost of hot and cold running spares has always been a bone of contention for any LAN Manager. The LAN Manager must work within a certain budget. The LAN Manager who asks for more money for equipment that is not being used to carry traffic may have to do some fast explaining. Perhaps the best argument is the potential cost of doing without backup equipment. The LAN Manager must show others the impact of delayed restoration of active circuits by posing such questions as: What would happen if the such-and-such department lost all connectivity to the WAN/VAN circuits that tie them to a distant resource? What would happen if all field agents were prohibited from calling in orders or reports?

Assuming, for the sake of discussion, the LAN Manager has been given money to purchase some spare equipment, the next problem is where to install the equipment. Having achieved an intellectual and practical understanding of the LAN and its weak points, the LAN Manager may be able to position the spare equipment to the organizations's best advantage. This is a learning process. Such knowledge does not spring full blown to mind. Only experience will show what equipment is most likely to fail or which parts of the LAN are under the most stress through heavy traffic load.

Implementation of Fault Management

Proactive fault management requires more than just a "can-do" attitude. Effort must be put forth in several areas. This section addresses the methods involved and some of the decisions required in fault management.

Technical Control

Large LANs require a formal technical control center. The degree of formality in a technical control center depends almost solely on the organization the LAN supports and the size of the LAN itself. If the LAN consists of several file servers, two or three printers, and a single integrated LAN (no subLANs), the technical control activities will probably be a subset of the LAN Manager's job description. A larger LAN should have one or more persons with a technical controller's job description. Those persons charged with technical control have certain functions and authority.

Functions: The single most important function of technical control is that of LAN restoration. Regardless of how much planning has been done, equipment will fail. The technical control personnel must perform or direct the restoration of failed hardware, software, or transmission media. The restoration activity can be stressful. The person doing this is under pressure from the subscriber, the subscriber's immediate supervisor, and the LAN Manager. The best approach is to leave this person alone to work out the problems as soon as possible. Constantly querying "When will it be done?" serves no purpose other than breaking the worker's train of thought. Besides, the worker is likely to answer "When it gets done," or "When I get around to it," or words to that effect. Technicians have been known to put their tools down and take a coffee break in the middle of a major outage because senior management personnel were constantly asking for updates when a few moments thought would have shown them that the effort was stalled for lack of information or equipment.

Authority: As long as the technical control personnel are responsible for maintaining the LAN, they must be the final authority in regards to such maintenance. If people performing the restoration function need to shut down a circuit for testing during restoration, they must have that authority. Clearly other subscribers who may be affected should be forewarned, but the restoration activity does not wait for one subscriber when more than one subscriber is without communications. (Recall our previous references to prioritizing circuits and trunks.) Although the technical control person's opinion is not final, anyone who challenges that opinion should have some objective evidence to back up the claim. If the engineer or technician says that the circuit or equipment is operable, a subscriber who disagrees should be able to disprove operability through tests.

Recordkeeping: The technical control center also has the responsibility for keeping all the records that pertain to the LAN. What these records are and the frequency of updates is a matter of professional knowledge and the LAN Manager's personal management philosophy. Chapter 11 discusses in some depth the reports the LAN Manager needs to evaluate proper operation of the LAN. Data gathering and recordkeeping are required to prepare these reports. Who better to gather this required data and prepare the reports than those persons who are most intimately involved with the functions of the LAN? The technical control function must continuously keep its collective finger on the pulse of the LAN.

Security: The technical control center is a weak point in the security of the LAN and of the devices attached to the LAN. The technicians and engineers who work in technical control must be able to evaluate the functional capabilities of all LAN equipment. This includes encryption devices and password protected files. Does this mean that a technician, in the process of troubleshooting a file server, has access to accounts payable data? The answer is no. But, this same technician must be able to test the file server for functionality, which means being able to open the database that holds that information.

Someone must bear the responsibility for the technician's conduct. This is usually the LAN Manager. It should not be beyond the realm of consideration to look into the possibility of bonding or insuring one or more of the engineers and technicians to protect the organization in case of accidental or deliberate sabotage by people who perform the technical control function.

Help Desk: In addition to the technical control function, many organizations have a help desk associated with the LAN Manager or technical control. The help desk is very close to what its name implies. The help desk is manned by one or more persons who are knowledgeable of the LAN and its functions. The help desk provides assistance to untrained subscribers in some of the more routine problems.

The help desk may well be staffed by one of the technical control personnel who is not involved in other duties at that time. One problem arises here. The help desk person must be technically astute concerning the hardware and software that is part of the LAN. This same astuteness ensures that the knowledgeable person is going to be one of the first sent out for restoration activities, leaving the help desk staffed with someone not quite so well qualified.

The help desk has limited functionality. The people working there cannot go out to a subscriber's location to do troubleshooting. The help desk staff cannot take down part of the LAN for troubleshooting. The help desk staff can give help over the telephone or locate the right person to contact for more technical questions. The help desk staff may be able to provide information from manuals the subscriber normally does not have immediately available.

However, none of these activities addresses the most important function of the help desk, which is to represent the LAN Manager to the subscriber community. Those persons who work the help desk are the "LAN Manager" in the eyes of the subscriber. They must be helpful, calm, and professionally poised to deal with irate or frustrated subscribers. Yet the persons who normally are assigned to the help desk are those who are of little help elsewhere in the technical control function. When these people become technically qualified, they move from the help desk to the technical control center and/or the restoration function.

Contract Maintenance

In the implementation of fault management, the LAN Manager must at one time or another evaluate the cost tradeoffs between maintenance provided by internal versus external organizations. When making this decision, keep in mind at least these four criteria:

- Cost
- Response time
- Competence
- Security

The first, and perhaps the most important criterion, is that of costs. Of all the costs associated with any enterprise, manpower costs are the hardest to control. You may think that eliminating manpower would decrease LAN fault management costs. Contracted maintenance of the LAN may look attractive. Looks can be deceiving. Organizations that provide contract maintenance have the same manpower costs as the organization that owns the LAN. True, contract maintenance organizations may be able to practice economies of scale, but they cannot escape the continuous upward spiral of wages and benefits. Who is charged for such increases in manpower costs? It is hard to believe that the vendor would absorb such increases in the name of goodwill. The only true benefit derived from contact maintenance is the knowledge that manpower costs will not rise during the period of the contract. The same effect can be achieved by employing job shop personnel for the same period of contract time. Further, if contract maintenance organizations are required to provide repair parts, most LAN Managers know that a profit will be made on these repair parts. In sum, contract maintenance does not ensure less expensive LAN maintenance. We should also state that this rule does not apply to small LANs where the only "technically" qualified person is the LAN Manager.

The second consideration is response time. As the response time grows smaller, the cost of the maintenance fees grows larger. In some cases, exponentially! A little comparison shopping among the various firms offering contract maintenance may prove this to the most doubting LAN manager. Remembering that speed in restoration is the single most important component of fault management (except personal safety), the LAN Manager soon realizes that contract maintenance may not be the best way to go.

The third point to consider is the competence of the contract maintenance personnel. If the LAN is composed of only one vendor's equipment, this point is not as important. But, if the LAN under consideration is similar to most, such competence is much more important. Assume for the sake of discussion that you have Vendor A's file servers, Vendor B's bus interface units, Vendor C's terminal servers, Vendor D's terminals, and Vendor E's telecommunications software. Additionally, the local regional private operating agency provides inter-LATA WAN circuits and a national telecommunications company provides intra-LATA connections. What maintenance contractor can provide enough knowledgeable personnel to provide rapid and efficient maintenance on all of these various vendors' equipment and connectivity? The situation can be exacerbated if some of the equipment is still under warranty and the maintenance contractor refuses to perform repairs to that equipment for fear of legal liability.

The final, and in some circumstances most telling, argument against contract maintenance is that of security. Who wants to give a complete stranger the potential of accessing the organization's most sensitive data? True, the contractor may boast of being insured or bonded, but is the amount of insurance or the size of the bond sufficient to cover any or all potential losses? If, in counterpoint, the argument of suing for breach of confidentiality is raised, experience has shown that a court's judgment against a contractor is, in the end, nothing more than a hunting license. If the contract maintenance firm is something like "Start-Up Maintenance Services and Software Development Inc.," the winner of the judgment may not have a lot to go after.

In the end, the cost of contract maintenance normally exceeds the gains for any organization except those supported by either the smallest LAN or the largest LAN—the smallest because of its limited maintenance requirments and the largest because of the bargaining leverage held by national or international firms. Yet consider that the largest and most powerful of the long-distance telecommunications vendors do not contract out all their telecommunications maintenance.

Disaster Recovery

The final stage of implementing proactive fault management is that of planning for disaster recovery. The concept of hot spare equipment is somewhat self-explanatory. The concept of a hot site is a logical extension of hot spare equipment. This is one type of disaster recovery planning. What other types exist? That question can only be definitively answered when every potential disaster can be identified. What then are some of the more common disasters that can be planned for, and what planning is required to overcome the effects of these disasters?

Power problems are perhaps the most common type of disasters that can strike the LAN. This can be through a malfunction in the commercial power distribution grid, through an industrial accident, through sabotage, or by natural causes. These types of disasters are prevented by using voltage regulators for surges or standby power supplies and/or generators for voltage losses.

Another type of disaster the LAN Manager must plan for is that of water. Water can come from floods, holes in walls or the roof, burst pipes, or water used to put out fires. Enclosing wire and cable in sealed conduits prevents moisture from finding an opening. Placing equipment up off the floor reduces the chances that flooding will damage electrical circuits. Do not place equipment where a technician or engineer might place a coffee cup on it. An alternative is to rack mount the various hardware. Put spare equipment in closed and reasonably tight cabinets or enclosures.

Other damage can result in the simple failure to foresee the thoughtless acts of others. Many times, sensitive electronics equipment is placed in broom and mop closets. Custodial staff members can throw a mop in the closet at the end of their shift. The fibers of the mop block the air intake ports on the electronic equipment. The equipment overheats and fails. With some good luck, the equipment does not catch fire and burn. All unattended electronics equipment must be fused with the appropriate value of fuse or circuit breaker.

In sum, the LAN Manager must evaluate any potential combination of circumstances and protect the LAN equipment from those circumstances. There is no one disaster recovery plan that can be applied to any organization. Disaster recovery planning must be done on a case-by-case basis. If protection is impossible, the LAN Manager must be prepared to restore the defective equipment and circuits as soon as possible within the constraints of safety and good engineering practices.

Growth of the Organization Supported by the LAN

Any organization changes as time goes by. If the organization shrinks in size, the fault management function becomes easier because there is less equipment to maintain. However, the reverse is not true. Growth can come in two different forms, single network growth and multiple network growth, and each form of growth must be treated differently.

Single Network Growth

Growth in size requires more of everything—more engineers, more technicians, analysts, and clerical personnel. This growth in personnel forces the LAN Manager to decide whether to continue to function in the current manner or to delegate some operational control to subordinates? To a large degree, the answer to this question depends on whether the LAN Manager is even capable of delegating authority along with responsibility. The failure of senior management to delegate authority cripples anyone who has been charged with responsibility. The second consideration is whether the LAN Manager's management philosophy allows such delegation. A third consideration is how large the LAN Manager's span of control is. In the end, the LAN Manager's choice of action in this area must be defended to senior management.

Growth also requires the purchase and use of additional TMDE. If the LAN is merely growing in size, this may not be that large an outlay. After all, an oscilloscope is not in use 24 hours a day, seven days a week. How often is a time domain reflectometer used? What the LAN Manager must watch out for in this type of growth is conflicts between groups of users. If two separate groups of engineers and technicians need a piece of TMDE to restore a circuit, someone must decide who has priority. No matter what the LAN Manager decides, one of the two groups becomes alienated. This could turn into a lose-lose situation very easily.

Because LAN Managers are more involved in management rather than technical questions, they may become removed from the products and services rendered by WAN/VAN vendors and their involvement in circuit restoration. The LAN Manager must stay on good terms with these vendors. They are the ones who make the LAN Manager look good or bad, depending on the circumstances.

As the entire network grows, LANs can appear in remote locations. These remote locations can be either manned or unmanned, depending on various circumstances. Manned remote locations can be thought of, in medical terms, as potential sites of infection. Without leadership, people at these remote sites can lose track of the goals of the network, let things slide, and generally do as little as possible without attracting management's displeasure. The LAN Manager must "show the flag" at these remote locations on frequent, but unannounced and random, intervals. Those who work at these remote locations must be made to feel like one of the whole group, not just "that bunch out there."

Unmanned remote locations are another trouble spot. Routine preventive maintenance and close attention to equipment operational life spans are required at these remote locations. This requires constant travel with its attendant expenses. Automatic alt routing and equipment switching should be employed wherever possible when unmanned remote sites are part of the LAN. If the organization is blessed with technically qualified personnel at these unmanned remote sites, the LAN Manager must make every effort to ensure these people are trained in low-level maintenance and replacement of LAN equipment.

Multiple Network Growth

LAN growth that involves different types of LANs presents different problems for the LAN Manager. Different types of LANs require different types of skills to maintain them. If a token ring LAN and a bus LAN are at the same site, engineers and technicians with skills for both types of LANs may be required. An engineer or technician who is equally skilled in all types of LANs is a jewel beyond price and should be treated accordingly. If several types of LANs are in use, the LAN Manager must, at the earliest possible moment, begin cross training the support staff in the technology pertinent to both types of LANs.

When several types of LANs are in use, several different types of specialized TMDE are required. Network analyzers are designed for use with certain types of LANs. A network analyzer that is designed for a token ring LAN is worthless when used with a CSMA bus topology LAN. Common TMDE can be used on both. But there still is contention for common TMDE. Larger LANs of different topology require not only more, but different, TMDE.

WAN/VAN vendors become even more important when linking different topology LANs. If one group of subscribers is working with a token ring LAN and another group of subscribers is working with a bus LAN, it is difficult, if not impossible, to link these two types. Linkage may be made by using WAN/VAN circuits and gateways. When problems arise, the token ring group blames both the WAN/VAN vendor and the bus network group. The bus network group blames the WAN/VAN vendor and the token ring group. The WAN/VAN vendor shrugs his shoulders and says, "They're both wrong, there's nothing wrong with our circuits." The LAN Manager is left to sort things out.

Remote manned locations can generate problems with mixed topologies. Those who are responsible can say, with some impunity, that the problem belongs to someone else. Their equip-

LAN Operations

ment is working fine, even if that is not the case. Then, when the LAN Manager tries to find out what is wrong, the problem magically clears itself. The remote group has drawn attention to itself, without drawing blame for any failure.

Remote unmanned locations are not the problem that remote manned locations can be. No individual egos are involved. Equipment once working will continue working until something is done to change its condition. Simple troubleshooting is normally all that is necessary. Otherwise, the same comments made earlier concerning remote locations of the same type of LAN apply here, too.

Impact of Expert Systems on Fault Management

The current state of expert systems (artificial intelligence) is such that these systems are beginning to make inroads into fault management in LANs. They have progressed from a laboratory curiosity to the start of a useful tool.

Expert systems are built on a rule base. The system compares the LAN's current conditions to its previous conditions. It then evaluates the current conditions against a series of if-then-else rules and historical data to see if the current problem matches a problem that occurred in the past. If the current problem does match, the expert system presents the engineer or technician with one or more reasons why such a problem can exist. The engineer or technician then evaluates the possible problems by using hardware, software, or TMDE to eliminate the possibilities presented by the expert system.

One of the current problems with expert systems is the length of time it takes the expert system hardware to evaluate all the rules that apply to the situation at hand. This will change with the advent of more sophisticated programming techniques and faster computers. Eventually expert systems will replace many of the routine troubleshooting procedures currently in use in fault management.

Summary

This chapter introduced fault management, and discussed the following areas:

- The prevention and correction of defective conditions, including
  - Proactive and reactive management styles
  - The identification points of stress and single points of failure
  - Alt routing of traffic
  - The monitoring of LAN performance
  - The use of both hot and cold spares
  - Contingency planning for fault management

- The positive aspects of fault management, including
  - Decreased restoration time
  - Increased subscriber satisfaction
  - Increased LAN usage

- The negative aspects of fault management, including
  - Increased manpower costs
  - Increased population of hardware and software

- Implementation of fault management, including
  - The creation of a tech control
  - The creation of a help desk
  - The possibility of external maintenance
  - Disaster recovery operations and planning

- How growth affects fault management, including
  - The need for more of everything
  - The impact of remote locations
  - Management problems arising from growth

- The advent of expert systems in fault management

Case Study

Section 1: Factual Data

The organization involved is national in scope. It has regional offices located throughout the United States, including Alaska and Hawaii. The headquarters are located in a major city on the East Coast. The telecommunications division runs on a 24-hour-a-day basis, year round. The regional and local offices are responsibile for taking orders from customers, electronically transmitting the orders to the headquarters, and ensuring that the customer received what was ordered. Additional administrative and clerical information is also transmitted through the same network. Within the headquarters, several LANs were dedicated to certain internal functions; others were connected to leased circuits through gateways through leased circuits and then to the LANs in the regional offices.

Section 2: What Happened

One of the leased circuits from the headquarters to a regional office was rated at T-1 (1.544 Mbps). On the headquarters side, a statistical multiplexer was used to combine LAN traffic and other dumb terminal traffic on this T-1 circuit. The multiplexer developed problems late one afternoon. The regional office was not able to pass traffic to headquarters and vice versa. Early the next morning, one of the workers at the regional office tried to submit an order to headquarters several times, each time receiving what amounted to a busy signal. The marketing manager at the regional office was appraised of the problem. He in turn contacted the vice president of marketing at headquarters. It is now slightly before 2 o'clock in the afternoon. The vice president of marketing called the vice president of telecommunications to find out why customer orders were not being transmitted. The vice president for telecommunications was "in a meeting" and could not be disturbed. The vice president for telecommunications received a personal visit from the organization's chief of staff about 45 minutes later. No further description of that discussion is required.

Section 3: Losses

Essentially everyone lost in this case. The organization under discussion may have lost orders from dissatisfied customers. The organization lost the money it was spending for the T-1 circuit. The vice president for telecommunications lost all of her hard-won reputation within senior management. The vice president for telecommunications lost the faith she had in her staff. The engineers and technicians lost their reputation within the telecommunications division.

Section 4: Lessons Learned

The T-1 circuit that passed this traffic was vital to the well-being of the organization. Without it, gross revenue would be lessened.

Anything that affected this circuit and its traffic should have been protected against. Without such protection, losses were inevitable. This is the perfect example for the need for a hot spare multiplexer. Perhaps the worst result of this outage was that the vice president for telecommunications was not informed of the problem. Her technical staff thought the restoration would go quickly. Actually it took over three days to correct the problem. None of the circuits or trunks within this organization were prioritized. Restoration was on a catch-as-catch-can basis. Perhaps the very worst part of this case study is that, as far as we know, the same people are in the same parts of the organization and have not changed their way of doing business.

Performance Management

Sufficient superlatives do not exist to describe this person's abilities.
—*From an annual performance review*

This chapter addresses the question of how the LAN Manager evaluates the performance of the LAN. Areas for discussion include:

- The positive aspects of performance management.
- The negative aspects of performance management.
- How to implement performance management.
- The impact of growth on performance management.

The underlying idea of this chapter, if not of all management functions, is this: If you cannot measure something, you cannot manage it. Failure to realize and implement this concept severely handicaps the LAN Manager before the first task has begun.

Components of Performance Management

The LAN is an assemblage of hardware and software. These components respond in accordance with the laws of physics and mathematics. Functions in physics and mathematics are rigorously defined by objective data. This same adherence to objective measurements of the LAN must be the rule of performance management.

Objective Standards

When evaluating the functionality of the LAN, the LAN Manager must measure the following three objective standards:

- Throughput (bits per second)
- Response time (seconds or fractions thereof)
- Availability (hours, days, or weeks)

Throughput: Throughput, in bits or multiple bits per second, is a function of the topology of the selected LAN. Some CSMA-type LANs have design throughputs from as low as 1 Mbps to as high as 10 Mbps. However, mathematical analysis and field experience shows that when the LAN is lightly loaded, sometimes as low as 25 percent, the response time degrades to the point where subscribers note a loss of functionality. Some experts say that CSMA-type LANs are best for "bursty" traffic, where small transmissions, normally less than 10 kilobits, are the rule.

By measuring the LAN's throughput, the LAN Manager can identify the amount of traffic that flows through the LAN. Knowing that the peak traffic is roughly 30 percent of the available bandwidth, the LAN Manager may want to start querying subscribers for their perception of delay times. Even if the subscribers note no perceptible delays, the LAN Manager has objective proof that the LAN is approaching the point where redesign may be needed.

Objective Response Time: Objective measurements of response time can be performed with either a stop watch, or if more precision is required, with generalized TMDE, specifically an oscilloscope. Normally an oscilloscope measurement is required only in laboratory situations. Alternatively, some types of modern telecommunications software will provide the actual transmission speeds when certain types of file transfers take place. This software does not provide this type of information when terminal emulation is the normal mode of operation.

The LAN Manager should have a test file of sufficient size, 100 kilobits or so, as a standard. This 100-kilobit figure is an extremely rough estimate. The LAN Manager must refine the file size in light of the operational characteristics of the traffic that flows through the LAN. In the early stages of the LAN installation or during a nonpeak period of usage, the LAN Manager should transmit and retrieve this test file from one or more file servers (or hosts) on the network. The length of time required for transmission and also for reception should be noted. These same tests should then be conducted during periods of peak usage. Results should be recorded and analyzed. The same test should be conducted on a daily or weekly basis during both peak and nonpeak periods for as long as the LAN is in use. Analysis of times noted will show the response time and changes in that response time under varying conditions.

The results of this analysis provides the LAN Manager with two types of data:

- Objective data
- Historical data

Objective data is available to present to subscribers when they comment on subjective delays in transmitting or retrieving files from other locations. Historical data supports the requirements for network redesign, which will, in most circumstances, come only too soon.

Availability: The third and final objective standard with which the LAN Manager must be concerned is that of availability. Before defining the availability of the LAN, the LAN Manager must specify how such availability is computed. What follows is one of the several possible approaches to such computations. The approach must fit the LAN Manager's managerial style and the LAN under evaluation.

The first decision is one of time: Is the LAN in use for eight hours a day, ten hours a day, or more? Availability is a mathematical function that follows the general equation of:

$$A = \frac{U - D}{T} \qquad \text{Eq. 6.1}$$

where A is the answer in percentage, T is the total operational time available, U is the total amount of time subscribers have the option to connect to the LAN, and D is the amount of time the LAN is "down" for error and recovery.

If T is less than $U - D$, the LAN will have more than 100 percent availability. This condition is impossible by definition. In

Eq. 6.1, substitute the integer values $T = 45$, $U = 50$, and $D = 2$. The result is:

$$A = \frac{50 - 2}{45} = \frac{48}{45} = 106.67\%$$

If T is less than U, the LAN will never have 100 percent availability. In Eq. 6.1, substitute the integer values $T = 50$, $U = 50$, and $D = 1$. The result is

$$A = \frac{50 - 1}{50} = \frac{49}{50} = 0.98\%$$

Once the maximum available time T is defined, the LAN Manager must make another decision concerning how to compute availability.

If the transmission media is defective, we can say that availability for the entire LAN has dropped to zero. However, this may not be the case. Depending on the topology in use, other subscribers may have access to the LAN and the services it provides. What if only one subscriber is out of communications? For that subscriber, availability has dropped to zero, but other subscribers will not perceive the conditions to be the same. Here we have identified the end points of the spectrum of possible error conditions: one is a single subscriber disabled, the other is the entire LAN disabled.

Perhaps the simplest way out of this problem would be to say that availability is determined by the total possible available time multiplied by the number of components in the LAN less the sum of the times each component is out of service. For the sake of discussion, the following assumptions are made:

- The LAN is operational 10 hours a day
- The LAN consists of
  - 1 file server or host
  - 2 terminal servers
  - 3 printers
  - 5 modems
  - 10 personal computers
  - 15 dumb terminals

This LAN (illustrated in Figure 6.1) consists of 36 components, disregarding the transmission media. Multiplying the

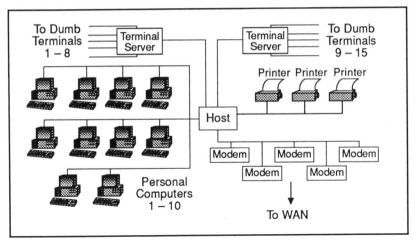

FIGURE 6.1

hours per day, 10, by 36 gives a maximum availability of 360 hours. One of the modems becomes unserviceable through a defective power supply. The time required to diagnose and repair the modem is 15 minutes. If no other defects occur during that day, the availability of the LAN (Equation 6.1) is 360 hours less the 15 minutes divided by 360 hours, or 359.75/360, giving an availability of 99.93 percent.

So far, the computations have been easy. For the next, slightly more complex, discussion, we will assume that 10 of the 15 terminals are attached to the two terminal servers, with 5 terminals on each server. One of the servers becomes defective. Whenever this happens, the other devices cannot communicate with the defective one. Therefore, all terminals attached to the server are not available. Repair of the defective server consumes two hours. Availability now is reduced by 2 hours times 5 devices, or 10. Availability equals (360 − 10)/360 or 350/360, giving an availability of 97.22 percent.

Regarding the two-hour period discussed earlier, let us assume that another modem became defective. Restoration time took 15 minutes. The nonavailability is cumulative. Because of the server, restoration availability was 97.22 percent. Our first example showed that a single-item, 15-minute outage reduced availability by 0.07 percent. Subtracting 0.07 from 97.22 gives a combined availability of 97.15 percent.

Performance Management 115

The next example concerns the three printers attached to the LAN. If one of them is defective, but the demand on the devices is so light that no one notices the defect, does this affect availability? The answer is yes. As long as a device is connected to the LAN, it must be involved in the availability computation.

The final example in this area is that of the file server or host attached to the LAN. The file server, like the transmission media, is a resource shared by all. So, if the file server is defective, the availability of the LAN is zero; correct? Well, that may not be the case. After all, the printers may be available, the PCs work, and communications are available through the modems. At this point, computations of availability require the skills found only through experience or predetermined policy.

Is there a rule of thumb that constitutes acceptable availability? Obviously 100 percent availability is the goal. Is it a realistic goal? The author's experience shows that when measured over a 12-month period, 100 percent availability is completely unattainable.

Two guidelines are available when computing availability goals. Commercial long-distance vendors offer communications availabilities of 99+ percent. Mission critical military communications have at least 50 percent redundancy. But, even with 100 percent redundancy, these communications facilities still are not 100 percent available. The time required to switch from one piece of equipment to another incurs an outage. Stated differently, even with 100 percent redundancy, availability may not exceed 99.9995 percent. To achieve 100 percent availability, every component in the LAN must be duplicated and traffic must flow through both sets of components simultaneously. Such engineering is not only expensive, it creates multiple problems in, for example, file and print servers. If printers are duplicated and on line, a print command will produce two copies of the same document. You should aim for 99 percent availability and accept 98+ percent. Total redundancy of mission critical hardware and software must be evaluated on a cost-effective basis.

Measurement by Subjective Standards

There is only one subjective standard worth measuring, and that is subscriber satisfaction. Remember that since the LAN provides a service to the subscriber, the measurement of quality of service is subscriber satisfaction.

Availability: One of the first things that a subscriber is concerned with is the LAN's availability. The subscriber does not care that the LAN has a history of 98+ percent availability. If it is not available when it is needed, it is viewed as being not available—period!

Another aspect of availability is that of subscriber-required hardware and software. Every LAN has a finite amount of hardware and software. If the subscriber needs to use a modem to transfer a file to a remote location and all modems are in use, the subscriber views the LAN as unavailable, even if it is running at 100 percent efficiency. Software can also restrict the availability of a LAN.

When an individual purchases software, both the seller and the buyer have an unspoken understanding that only the buyer will use the software. This same understanding is present when a firm buys a piece of software. Yet a firm consists of many persons, each needing that piece of software. If only one copy exists, users will vie for it, causing contention between employees in both the personal and electronic senses of the term. With the advent of site licenses for software, this contention is negated, or at least diminished. Ensuring sufficient copies of popular software applications may not be the LAN Manager's job, but subscriber satisfaction will be less than optimum if insufficient copies exist. And, if that is the case, the LAN Manager will be the one who is informed of subscriber dissatisfaction in a most direct manner.

Response Time: The second area of subjective subscriber satisfaction is response time. Response time can be divided into two areas: network throughput and file server or host response. These two areas are lumped together in the subscriber's perception. The subscriber cannot say that slow LAN response time was caused by heavy loading on the transmission media or by heavy demand on the host. All the subscriber knows is that he must stare at a blank screen for an unacceptable length of time. By knowing the actual design throughput of the LAN's transmission media, the LAN Manager can identify one of the two causes of this slower response time, which are host-induced delays or the use of transmission media beyond design criteria. Both of these problems have solutions, which are discussed later in this chapter.

Ease of Use: The third major subjective component of customer satisfaction is ease of use. A pencil is much easier to use than a typewriter. Yet how many important business proposals are written in smudged pencil? Certain software applications written for personal computers are so esoteric that no one will take the time to learn them. Others are so obvious that the instruction manual is never opened. If the subscriber is forced to learn (or memorize) many strange and seemingly unconnected commands in order to use the LAN, the LAN will experience minimum usage.

The LAN Manager's responsibility is to ensure that the LAN has a certain amount of ease of use. However, if the LAN is too easy, certain functionality may not be present. A wrench that only fits one size of bolt is easy to use. But, if more than one size of bolt is available, the wrench's functionality is limited. The LAN Manager can make the LAN easier to use by customizing the LAN to the subscribers' needs. However, to make use of all features of the LAN is only good sense. To make sure that subscribers can use the LAN to its fullest capacity requires that they be trained on the features available. It is also part of the LAN Manager's responsibility to validate training given to new subscribers and to do follow-up checks on the subscribers' abilities.

Evaluation: Evaluating the objective standards that can be applied to LANs is easy, but evaluating objective standards does not give the LAN Manager a grasp of how the subscribers view the functionality that the LAN provides. To obtain this type of information, the LAN Manager must be aware of problems subscribers encounter in the day-to-day completion of their tasks. The reactive LAN Manager waits for subscribers to submit their complaints; a proactive LAN Manager samples subscriber satisfaction on a regular basis.

This sampling can be as simple as selecting a handful of subscribers on a random basis and asking for their opinions on an informal basis. Alternatively, the LAN Manager can create and chair a LAN Users Group, obtaining formal recommendations for ways to improve LAN performance or ease of use. An alternative proactive approach would be routine written surveys of user satisfaction, coupled with written responses to valid problems listing steps that will be taken to eliminate these problems.

Eliminating problems identified by the failure to meet either objective or subjective standards is a process that some experts call performance tuning. In this instance, tuning must be seen as separate from redesign. LAN redesign is addressed later in this chapter. Performance tuning consists of minor changes in operating characteristics. Without descending into the morass of technical details, LAN redesign concerns things such as buffer sizes, header information, header and trailer size, and disk access times.

Combining both objective and subjective standards in the process of measurement of the LAN, the LAN Manager accomplishes several goals. He is seen as not only technically qualified, but also concerned with the human aspect of technology. Management perceives the LAN Manager as someone who is attempting to employ corporate resources in the most cost-effective manner. Subscribers perceive the LAN Manager as being not only a technologist, but a person who is working with them in the accomplishment of their assigned tasks. The result of this measurement process is an attempt to tune the performance of the LAN in such a manner that both management and subscribers get the "biggest bang for their buck."

Positive Aspects of Performance Management

This section addresses the benefits gained by implementing a formal, continuous program of measurement of the performance characteristics of the LAN.

Resource Maximization

The first and perhaps most obvious benefit is that of maximizing current resources. If, for example, a LAN uses modems for information interchange outside of the organization's physical boundaries, the organization must pay common carrier vendors for circuits. Charges for these circuits, at least on a dial-up basis, are both time and distance sensitive. The billing for dial-up circuits is the same billing anyone experiences on their home telephone. Therefore, modem-based communications should be completed as soon as possible within the constraints of good business practices. Before using a dial-up circuit, answer the following question:

Does this data have to go through a common carrier network now or can it be done after 5:00 PM when rates are lower? Many types of computer software are available that will automate such after-hours transmissions and receptions.

In keeping with the concept of modem-based information interchange, circuit speed becomes a variable to consider. Many modems have multiple speed ranges, falling back to lower speeds as circuit quality degrades. Do the modems currently installed have this capability? Other modems require manual setting of data transfer speed. Are the modems currently installed operating at the highest possible speed consistent with circuit quality? Why does this make a difference? Consider the following example.

A LAN subscriber at one location wishes to transmit a 36,000-bit file to another location. The cost of the circuit between the two locations is $2.52 per minute. If the transmission takes place at 1200 bits per second, it will cost $1.26 (36000/1200=30(0.5 minutes) × $2.52 = $1.26). Doubling the transmission speed to 2400 bits per second halves the telecommunications costs (36000/2400 = 15(0.25 minutes) × $2.52 = $0.63). But, there is another less obvious gain by doubling transmission speed.

Assume a secretary is paid $12.50 per hour. It takes 30 seconds of his time to transmit a 36,000-bit file at 1200 bits per second—if everything goes right! Therefore, in addition to the $1.26 for transmission costs, we must add $0.34 of employee salary. If everything goes perfectly, the cost to transfer a 36,000-bit file is $1.60. If a 2400-bit-per-second modem is used, the total cost is $0.80.

A rule of thumb is that 16,000 bits of data are equivalent to one page of double-spaced text. Is the cost of mailing an 18-page document less than either $1.26, or $0.80? If the answer is yes, perhaps a file transfer process via a modem is not the most cost-effective means of information interchange. Also, even though it may be inexpensive to mail an 18-page document, if the information in the document must be converted back into an electronic form, the overall cost may be much greater.

The preceding dollar amounts are based on the assumption that transmission and reception of the information flows with 100 percent accuracy and completeness during the period in question. Random noise on the circuit may require retransmission of parts of the data. This, of course, increases the duration of the circuit

LAN Operations

use, thereby increasing the costs involved. The longer the circuit is in use, the greater the chance of random noise on the circuit. Keeping transmissions short saves money in many ways.

How does the preceding example affect maximization of present resources? By knowing the capabilities of the hardware and software that make up the LAN, the LAN Manager can ensure that all information interchange is accomplished in the most cost-effective manner.

Does this mean the LAN Manager must have a degree in engineering to maximize the resources available on the network? The answer is not necessarily. What the LAN Manager must have is the ability to understand the capabilities inherent in the hardware and software that make up the LAN. This can come from experience or from specialized training. Once the LAN Manager understands what the hardware and software can do, the process of maximizing these resources becomes a problem in forethought and planning.

Performance Constraints

The second positive aspect of performance management is that of predicting LAN performance degradation in the near future. Many things can constrain LAN performance—file server speed, memory capacity, and the software used for file transfer procedures, to name a few. Perhaps the most visible reason for performance degradation is transmission media. Measurement helps the LAN Manager identify which element of the LAN is degrading performance.

Note that such degradation is a gradual process. If LAN Managers do not pay constant attention to performance, they will not notice any remarkable changes. This "constant attention" is helped by taking and maintaining measurements of LAN performance criteria. One obvious criterion would be that of throughput. Another would be the delay time between logging in to an application on the server and actually using the application.

One of the most commonly blamed parts of the LAN is the transmission media. The transmission media cannot carry data any faster than the data can be injected into or received from the LAN. If the transmission media can carry data at 10 Mbps, but the terminal can receive no faster than 19.2 Kpbs, which is the slower device? If a personal computer user wants to download a

300Kb-file from the file server through a 10-Mbps transmission media, to a local disk, the file transfer should take 300Kb/10 Mbps, or 0.03 seconds. Yet this computation fails to take into consideration the time it takes to write the file to the disk. If the local disk write speed is less than the rated throughput of the transmission media, the file transfer takes longer than 0.03 seconds.

Earlier in this chapter, advice was given on using test files to measure the throughput of a LAN under different loading conditions. This historical data helps the LAN Manager identify the quality of the transmission media versus a slower device that has been connected to the LAN.

In addition to the transmission media, the LAN Manager must be constantly aware of the condition of the hardware and software that constitute the LAN. The LAN Manager must realize that just because a piece of software works, does not mean that the software is performing at its peak capacity. The only one who can speak to the capabilities of the software is its author or someone better qualified than even that person.

How does the LAN Manager evaluate the usefulness of LAN software? There are two metrics by which to measure such effectiveness: ease of use and throughput. The term "ease of use" is a subjective value, depending on the sophistication of the user in terms of software. Something that is easy for one user may be too simple for another. Too much simplicity may indicate a lack of available functions. Intuitiveness rather than capabilities may also be evaluated. Since throughput is an objective value, it is easy for anyone to identify. The LAN Manager should not be misled by raw numbers. The process of purchasing software is analogous to any other purchase. The "specs" can be evaluated on paper; functionality requires a "test drive." Using a common test file, as discussed earlier, measure the time a file transfer takes. Software that requires constant retransmissions, creates erroneous transmissions, or cannot handle multiple errors should be placed low on the list of candidates. Other objective values to consider in software may be things such as statistics offered, reports given, or name-to-address conversions.

The evaluation of LAN hardware follows the same basic principles as that of LAN software. However, with hardware, the major concern must be reliability. Both Mean Time Between Failure (MTBF) and Mean Time To Repair (MTTR) are statistics that the LAN Manager must evaluate with a large grain of salt. A vendor may give a MTBF of 20,000 hours. The LAN Manager should question how the vendor arrived at that conclusion. If the conclusion is based on historical data, the LAN Manager may be able to rely on it. Forecasted or mathematically derived estimates are just that—estimates. Reliance on those estimates may be thought of as playing "You Bet Your Job." Ease of use is of limited importance, because the person using LAN hardware is normally a trained engineer or technician. Hardware that requires constant retransmissions, creates erroneous transmissions, or cannot handle multiple errors should also be placed low on the list of candidates.

Complaint Prevention

The third and final positive aspect of performance management is the prevention of subscriber complaints. The LAN Manager is providing a means of information interchange to subscribers. By knowing the subjective and objective causes of the subscriber's unhappiness with the LAN's performance, the LAN Manager can concentrate on removing whatever creates dissatisfaction, simultaneously increasing the capabilities inherent in the LAN, all without purchasing additional LAN (telecommunication) hardware and software.

Negative Aspects of Performance Management

The single biggest negative aspect of performance management is that of consumption of corporate resources. Like every other task, performance management requires organizational resources that may be assigned to other functions. This section discusses three resources that are consumed in performance management: manpower, specialized TMDE, and computer equipment. Some of the results noted will also be discussed.

Manpower

Manpower is mandatory in data collection and analysis. Someone must "count the bits" as the traffic flows through the LAN. Someone must make connections to various points in the LAN to attach specialized equipment. One or more persons must interact with subscribers, perhaps even removing equipment from subscriber usage during test and data gathering functions. Someone must prepare the raw data for analysis by either human or electronic means. Once the performance data have been recorded and prepared for analysis, someone must do the required computations to show how well the LAN has performed. Fortunately, or unfortunately as the case may be, the LAN Manager is normally the only one qualified to evaluate the results of this collection and analysis function.

Specialized Equipment (TMDE)

The second corporate resource consumed is that of the specialized equipment used to collect the data that this performance management evaluation requires. Certain types of specialized TMDE (including software) are needed. Such TMDE may cost as much as one-half of the LAN Manager's annual salary—each! Several of these may be needed if the LAN is of sufficient size or complexity, or if it mixes topographies and topologies.

Any department of any organization has a budget. The manager of the department makes purchasing decisions based on that budget. As manager of the department, the LAN Manager must make the purchasing decision by asking, "Will specialized TMDE increase my ability to perform my assigned tasks, or not?" The assigned task under consideration at this point is that of evaluating the LAN's performance.

Data Processing Equipment

The third corporate resource consumed is data processing equipment. In a relatively small LAN, statistical analysis of traffic can be performed with a personal computer and less expensive software. Statistical analysis of a large LAN or of a LAN using common carrier vendor-supplied circuits may need a much larger computer with a much more sophisticated analytic software package. Since these larger computers have demands placed on them by other elements of the organization, the LAN Manager may experience a conflict of interest when attempting to use these more powerful computers and software packages.

Results

Besides consuming corporate resources, performance management shows no immediate gain from the effort expended. A thorough performance analysis can result in a one-line summary: "Circuit number 1234A56 is running at 37 percent of bandwidth at peak loading." A nontechnically sophisticated person would say, with a yawn, "So what!" The response from someone with a smattering of technical sophistication may respond, "What are you going to do about this condition?" The LAN Manager's answer must be something very akin to "We've got to plan for future expansion."

Note that the first sentence of the previous paragraph used the phrase "immediate gain." One of performance management's goals is to develop a body of data concerning the functioning of the LAN. As it is mathematically impossible to extrapolate from one point, it is almost impossible to evaluate the functioning of a LAN from one measurement. The LAN Manager must gather sufficient information to accomplish two tasks: to identify consumption trends and to fully understand the LAN.

Trends: The first of these tasks is to identify trends in consumption of LAN resources. These trends change with seasons when the organization has seasonal fluctuations, or with the marketplace if the organization is tied to market changes, or to the size of the organization if it is shrinking or growing.

Understanding the LAN: The second task is to obtain a gestalt of the LAN. The benefit of obtaining such an understanding is the ability to know how changes in technology, topography, or topology will affect how the LAN supports the organization in the future. The LAN Manager can never lose sight of the purpose of the LAN, namely, to support the goals and mission of the organization.

Changes

The final negative point of performance management is that the effort previously expended can be negated by a simple change in corporate structure. Organizations change from tall to flat, from centralized control to decentralized control, or in corporate culture. Much has been written concerning how the computer can eliminate many of the middle management positions and functions. Also much has been said about the functions of "knowledge workers." Is it a viable assumption to make that middle managers have merely changed their title from middle manager to "knowledge worker?"

A highly centralized organization, which in the past required many reports with text, graphics, and tabular information, placed a heavy load on a LAN. Raw data flowed from subordinate elements to the central control points. A decentralized organization may require the same amount of information interchange, but this takes place at a much lower level, and only the final report goes upwards.

Such modifications in information interchange activities will distort any extrapolations that have been made in the past, or that are to be made based on older historical data. The LAN Manager must be aware of how even the slightest change in organizational structure and culture can influence past measurements.

Implementation of Performance Management

This section addresses the way in which the LAN Manager can begin to implement performance management. There is a fine but distinguishable line between LAN performance management and the measurement of the LAN. Measurement of the LAN, which is discussed in detail in Chapter 8, is concerned with a fine-grained analysis of throughput of the LAN. Performance management builds on the results of measurement of the LAN. However, performance management requires some understanding of LAN throughput. Therefore, this section begins with a high-level discussion of throughput evaluation.

Throughput Evaluation

Previous chapters have alluded to the maximum rated throughput of the LAN and the actual number of bits per second that transit the LAN. For example, an early version of a major vendor's token ring topology LAN has a rated throughput of 4 Mbps. Yet, when the load offered to that type of network exceeds roughly 35 percent of rated throughput, the response time increases almost logarithmically. Why does this happen?

Most commercially available LANs use either token ring or CSMA access methods. Data that is finally injected into the transmission media is in a datagram or packet format. To ensure proper transmission and reception of the data in the packet, additional (protocol-required) information must be "wrapped around" the packet. Such information is commonly known as headers, trailers, frames, and/or checksums.

The following description is typical of how such protocol-required information affects packet size. Using the IEEE 802.3 (see CSMA in glossary) packet structure, the smallest packet that can be transmitted through the LAN consists of 60 bits. Of this 60 bits, 52 are protocol-required data. The largest packet can be 1514 bits, of which 52 bits are protocol-required data. If the software that is used to create the packet is limited to a 120-bit packet, the assumption may be that it would take 208.33 packets to transmit a 25,000-bit file. This is not so for two reasons. The LAN treats a partial packet as a defective packet, a partially filled packet is "padded" with null symbols. Therefore, under this assumption, 209 packets are required. This is an invalid assumption.

There is a second reason why more than 209 packets are needed. The 120 bits of file data minus the 52 bits of protocol data create a packet of 68 information data bits. Therefore, only 57 percent ($68/120 = 56.67\%$) of each packet contains user data. However, since protocol data is required, 298 packets are sent, creating a transmission of 35,750 bits for usable data of 25,000 bits. How is this derived? Since 57 percent of each packet contains usable data, 43 percent of each packet is protocol data. Then, 43 percent of 25,000 is 10,750. Adding the 10,750 to 25,000 gives a total of 35,750. When this total is divided by a packet size of 120 ($35,750/120$), the total number of packets equals 297.92. Remember, a partial packet must be padded. Therefore, the total number of packets for this transmission is 298.

What this mathematical explanation means is that the protocol-required data contributes to bandwidth consumption. How much extra bandwidth is used? With no protocol data attached, it would take 209 packets to transmit the 25,000-bit file. With the protocol data attached, the same transmission requires 298 packets. This has shown that approximately 43 percent of the total number of bits in this transmission is unusable by the subscriber. This unusable information is termed overhead.

Protocol-required data is not the only cause of less than perfect bandwidth utilization. When CSMA type LANs are in use, packets can electronically collide. When this happens, the packets cannot be understood, and all transmitting stations cease transmitting for a random time, and then try transmitting again. When token ring type LANs are in use, the token itself can become lost and must be regenerated. This regeneration procedure takes a small but measurable time as well. During the random wait for the CSMA LAN and the token regeneration in the token ring LAN, no traffic can flow through the LAN. This cuts throughput to 0 bps.

In packet-based networks, part of the packet is a checksum. The checksum is a numeric representation of the packet's contents. How this checksum is derived is good material for a Master's thesis when taking a post-graduate degree in mathematics. Suffice to say that each checksum is sufficiently unique so that the chances of checksum errors are vanishingly small. When a packet is transmitted, the checksum is calculated and "tacked on" to the packet. The checksum is recalculated when received. If the two checksums do not match, the receiving station requests packet retransmission.

Each time a packet is transmitted in error and a retransmission is required, additional bandwidth is consumed. If, for instance, 298 packets are required to transmit a 25,000-bit file, and the transmission time for that file is 8 seconds, a 10 percent retransmission request rate will, at a minimum, increase the transmission time to almost 9 seconds. This computation disregards such factors as the amount of time taken to create, transmit, and reply to each retransmission request.

Note that these computations have been made without the use of sophisticated mathematical models, expensive TMDE, software, or time-consuming statistical studies. The LAN Manager should, after exposure to the LAN, have an intellectual understanding of how the true throughput of that particular LAN is computed. By computing protocol-required data, retransmission requests, and zero availability times, the LAN Manager can truthfully say that the throughput of this particular LAN appears to be a given number of bits per second at a given instant.

File Transfer Time

Besides computing LAN throughput, the LAN Manager must also be able to measure two other important performance criteria, the file transfer time and the length of time it takes to invoke an application. For the purpose of this text, an application is a software package resident on a file server or host somewhere in the LAN.

File transfer is the length of time taken to transfer a given file from one location in the LAN to another. Under normal conditions, this would be from one computer to another or from a personal computer to a file server. This transfer time measurement has been alluded to in previous sections of this chapter. In these previous sections, 100,000 bits was the recommended file size as a starting point. The final test file may be larger or smaller, depending on the particular test procedure.

The process begins when the final keystroke is entered, and it ends when the subscriber is notified that the transfer is completed. This process is timed with a stopwatch or other accurate clock. Some of the more sophisticated file transfer software provides the actual time taken for the process.

Let us assume that the LAN under test is a token ring LAN with a throughput of 4 Mbps. Under ideal conditions, the transfer of a 100,000-bit file should take 0.025 seconds (100,000/4,000,000 = 0.025). Yet, a previous discussion stated that each packet contains overhead. If the packet size is limited, the packet information can increase transfer size by 50 percent or more, thereby increasing transmission time by a similar amount. If we assume a LAN with no other traffic, operating at 4 Mbps, with a 100,000-bit file, then a transfer time of 0.1 to 0.3 seconds may be more likely. If multiple users are passing traffic simultaneously, the transfer time could exceed three or more minutes. It is vitally important that the LAN Manager know how long such file transfers can take. The LAN Manager must be able to identify conditions that do not correspond to "normal" loading and take the necessary corrective action.

The second, and less important, measurement is that of the length of time it takes to evoke a response from a particular software application resident somewhere on the LAN. If response times increase dramatically, there is very little the LAN Manager can do for subscribers except notify the MIS department (if the host is under that department's control). File server or host response time for applications usually is not affected by LAN functionality. Yet subscribers will complain to the LAN Manager if they cannot access their favorite spreadsheet fast enough.

MTBF/MTTR

The third and final computation required when implementing performance management is that of MTBF (Mean Time Between Failure) and MTTR, (Mean Time To Repair). Of these two, MTBF is the more complicated computation.

MTTR: MTTR is computed or calculated very simply. Consider the following example. When Vendor A's modems fail, note how long the repair process takes. Take the average of these repair times and the MTTR is the answer. The MTTR can be computed on every failed part of the LAN, and if necessary, the LAN itself. The LAN Manager is required to know the MTTR of a class of items when deciding how many spares of what types of equipment are required.

MTBF: Deriving the MTBF is somewhat more complex. One idiosyncrasy should be mentioned before the explanation. MTBF is concerned with units of time: "The MTBF of this multiplexer is 9000 hours." How the LAN Manager derives the true MTBF for the LAN, or any part of the LAN, is based on experience and judgment.

Let us assume that a vendor of Bus Interface Units (BIUs) states that the MTBF for their model is 100,000 hours. This means that a single BIU should operate without failing for almost 11.5 years. The LAN Manager can assume that the BIUs can be installed and forgotten. This is not the case! If a LAN has 11 BIUs, can the LAN Manager assume that one will fail each year? This is not the case either.

Vendors' claims for MTBF ratings can be based on solid scientific and statistical analysis, or they can be sales gimmicks, with no more validity than a huckster's promise. For a vendor to be able to state truthfully that a given BIU has a MTBF of 100,000 hours, the BIU must have operated 100,000 hours without failure. Vendors' claims are based on statistical computations, which may be correct for a large universe of BIUs, but have no validity when applied to a specific BIU. The only way the LAN Manager can identify the MTBF for a specific device is to maintain maintenance records on that device. Even these cannot accurately forecast the next failure.

The second problem with computing MTBFs for a LAN is deciding what is a failure. If a multiplexer has 12 subscriber ports and only one port becomes defective, has the entire multiplexer failed? Are maintenance records kept on each port, or on the entire multiplexer? If records are kept at port level, is the failed component identified? Does anyone care if diode CR41 fails, or are they concerned with the port itself? There is no textbook answer to such questions. The only option the LAN Manager has is to solicit advice from users, consultants, logistics specialists, or statisticians. Having combined this advice with the goals and missions of the organization, the LAN Manager will be able to strive to provide the most reliable LAN possible.

At this point in the implementation of performance management, the LAN Manager knows, at least at an intellectual level, the LAN's functional capabilities—where the traffic is the heaviest, when peak loading of the LAN occurs, and approximately how often certain pieces of hardware fail.

Redesign

Combining the knowledge mentioned in the previous paragraphs with knowledge of the organization and its corporate culture, the LAN Manager may decide to redesign the LAN based on these performance measurement factors. The first step of such redesign may be to create what are known as subLANs.

A subLAN is a smaller LAN that serves only specific elements of the organization. One subLAN may be required for the entire Finance and Accounting Division or for only the Accounts Payable Section. What part of what element is included in the subLAN is decided by the amount of traffic flowing through the element. Alternatively a subLAN may incorporate a particular floor of a building. Note that if subLANs are installed, a device known as a router or bridge is required to connect them.

When subLANs are created, the address of each piece of equipment on the LAN must be installed in the router or bridge. As each packet flows through the LAN, the router or bridge reads the packet address and does not forward packets whose address is in the subLAN where the packet originated. Although this idea is simple to explain, the application is difficult and expensive. The router or bridge receives traffic from both of the subLANs to which it is connected. It must evaluate the address of each packet and decide whether the packet is to be sent on or dumped. This must be done at the speed at which packets arrive. Failure to do this incurs further delays on the entire LAN. This type of delay, reduced throughput, is one of the main reasons for redesigning the LAN.

Sometimes the reverse process must take place. LANs that are separated by large geographic distances must be interconnected. The following assumptions are made for the following discussion. An organization has three offices: Boston, Atlanta, and Detroit. If all three LANs are interconnected, traffic from one LAN can flow in all three LANs. If traffic in each LAN is roughly equal, each LAN now triples in traffic loading. This is prevented by using a router or bridge.

A bridge is similar to a router in that it evaluates each packet's address for the final destination. If packets that originate in Boston are destined for Detroit, but must flow through Atlanta, they are evaluated in Atlanta and then shipped to Detroit without entering the Atlanta LAN. Gateways are normally installed when LAN traffic is sent over WANs or VANs.

The previous discussion of routers and bridges has been simplified. This simplification has two purposes. First, further discussion of the what, how, and why of these devices serves no additional purpose in this chapter. Second, there are a great number of opinions by learned individuals as to the difference between a router and a bridge. Some pundits have coined a new term "brouter" for the device that they allege serves both purposes. The serious reader is recommended to evaluate the various definitions for these devices that have been given by some of the numerous standards bodies. This subject is also mentioned in Chapter 9. Note from this discussion that bridges and routers are required to eliminate the flow of traffic through the LAN to points where such packets are not addressed.

Financial Impact of Redesign

To redesign the LAN, the LAN Manager must evaluate more than technical criteria. At what point does redesign become financially worthwhile? If the San Diego office is closing in six months, is there really any reason to install subLANs there? How much does it cost if a draftsman must wait an additional minute for a file transfer? Can the same draftsman endure an additional three minutes? What about six minutes? If the draftsman is making $15.00 per hour, a one-minute nonproductive interval costs $0.25. If a router costs $2500.00, the draftsman would have to wait for 10,000 file transfers to make up the difference.

Other factors must be taken into consideration. If the San Diego LAN is sufficient now, what will happen if the organization hires two scientists, a half dozen engineers, eight technicians, several analysts, two managers, and four secretaries? In addition to this, two mainframe computers, eight personal computers, and six modems are attached to the LAN. Once the new equipment and personnel arrive, the subLAN may be required.

It seems as if everyone can tell the LAN Manager when network redesign is required. The subscribers are always clamoring for more bandwidth, faster response time, and more transparent service. The financial controller would probably be happy with number two pencils and yellow lined tablets. The technical types want to experiment with anything new, different, and expensive. Top management wants to shorten the return on investment because the stockholders want more profits. Oh, yes, the technicians are unhappy, too! Once the redesign phase is completed, the LAN Manager has another hurdle to overcome: How much redundancy is required to ensure how much availability for the LAN. (This was briefly mentioned earlier in this chapter when discussing the subject of availability.) Redundancy is a duplication of online LAN circuits or hardware.

Recurring Performance Failures

In implementing performance management, the LAN Manager soon identifies parts of the LAN or circuits from the WAN or VAN vendors that fail with depressing regularity. This knowledge comes from records of subscriber complaints or continuous online testing of circuits and equipment.

If a WAN vendor's circuit is continually failing, thereby cutting the Chicago office out of the network, the LAN Manager should identify different WAN vendors to provide circuit redundancy in the form of parallel transmission paths. Stated differently, if Vendor A's circuit gets particularly noisy every afternoon, try a parallel circuit from Vendor B. Then show Vendor A the results of your comparisons.

There will be two results from this test. The first result is the most favorable to the LAN Manager. Subscribers will be complaining less often, and throughput on the LAN, due to the increased reliability, will show up as shorter transmission times. The second benefit will come from the relationship with the WAN vendor. If the vendor sincerely wants to provide quality communications, he or she will jump at the opportunity to correct the problem. Otherwise, the LAN Manager will find out just how "sincere" the WAN vendor really is.

The requirement for redundancy is controlled by the priority of the traffic that flows through the LAN. If the organization does not establish priorities for LAN traffic, it is quite difficult for the LAN Manager to identify circuits or equipment that require redundancy. This question can only be solved by experience.

Organizational Growth and Performance Management

Organizations of any type change over time. The product or service line changes, the size changes, and the missions or goals change. These changes are based on society's demands and fluctuations in the marketplace. New management creates different philosophies, which guide lower management in new directions. Each of these changes influences the LAN's performance characteristics. This final section addresses how these changes influence performance management.

Subscriber Growth

As an organization grows, the number of subscribers grows along with it. The relationship need not be linear. Low- and mid-level managers may share secretaries. The addition of one new public relations artist would not affect LAN traffic to any great extent. However, the addition of four new engineers may increase LAN traffic by a large percentage.

Some types of LANs are limited to the number of subscribers or hosts that can be connected to them. Other types of LANs have physical limits to their size. When either of these limits is reached, a new LAN must be created and the two joined by a router or bridge. If the LANs are of different types, a gateway may be needed. (Routers, bridges, and gateways are discussed in Chapter 9 and in the Glossary.

New Hardware

Another growth factor, which the LAN Manager cannot control but must be aware of, is the capabilities inherent in hosts attached to the LAN. If a file server or host has a memory capacity of 150 Mbytes and there are enough users to consume this file capacity, the LAN Manager must either negotiate with the manager of that host to increase the file capacity or replace the file server with one of greater memory capacity.

If one print server had been sufficient for three secretaries and two more secretaries have been added to the payroll, another print server may be required. Where will it be located? How well does the new print server function with existing hardware and software? What training is required to make this device useful? These are some of the decisions the LAN Manager must face during periods of growth.

Shrinking Organizations

Organizations do not always require additional bandwidth and increased capability. If the number of personnel in the organization shrinks or the emphasis changes from products to services or vice versa, the loading of traffic on the LAN may diminish. Should the LAN Manager remove equipment or redesign the LAN in response to such changes? The answer is usually no. The cost of removing transmission media, hardware and software, or other LAN-required items often exceeds the salvage value of those items. This may not be the case if employees are being shifted from one location to another. Once again, LAN Managers must rely on their own intelligence, experience, and understanding of how the LAN supports the mission and goals of their organization.

Relocation

If the entire physical plant relocates, the LAN Manager is faced with a chance to become a hero or a bum in one blaze of glory. Assume for the sake of discussion that a small organization has the LAN working through twisted pair wiring in its present location. Business has been good, profits are up, and money exists for a new building with enough left over for a new LAN. At this point, the LAN Manager knows how well or poorly the present

LAN is performing. With the upcoming increase in traffic offered to the new LAN, will the same hardware and software be sufficient in the new location? If it is, institute no changes. If not, the LAN Manager must consider several major points.

Will the new LAN use the same topology as the old? What benefit is derived from using twisted pair wiring that cannot be improved on by using fiber optic cable? What additional services will be required on the new LAN that were not available on the old one? Is there need for more file servers, more printers, more WAN vendor provided circuits, or less of some of these? How will the new PBX, if there is one, integrate into the LAN? If a new topology is selected, how much time and money will be consumed training the subscribers on the new methods? Who will provide a technical "sanity check" for the design of the new LAN?

Unless the LAN Manager is very experienced in the area of creating new LANs, he should seriously consider some of the following sources for help and guidance in such planning.

Physical Plant Constraints: The physical plant constrains the transmission media under certain circumstances. What are the local fire codes for cables and wires that run in elevator shafts and air conditioning access ways? Do differences in ground potentials exist between buildings, or even between floors? If such potentials exist, a 60-Hertz hum may be present in parts of the LAN. This 60-Hertz hum can, under the wrong conditions, be strong enough to prevent the transmission of data through cables that connect buildings with different ground potentials. In the worst cases, the potential difference can be high enough to kill anyone who accidentally contacts it.

Where are the connections to the transmission media to be made? If the engineering department is on the second floor, in the northwest corner, how many subscribers will connect there? What if these people change offices between the time the plans are drawn and the time of the move? The LAN Manager must establish a point of contact within each element of the organization to act as a liaison during the planning stages, to be the "point man" for that element during the move, and to answer installer's questions after the move is completed and as the new LAN is installed.

Common Carrier Vendors: The LAN Manager must establish a close working relationship with the local and long-distance telephone companies that the firm will be using. Do these firms offer the same or better services than the ones used previously? Are their costs more than, equal to, or less than those of the previous firms? How much lead time is required for new installations of both regular and special services? The sooner the new WAN/VAN vendor knows what is required, the better the quality of the service that can be provided.

Commonality: How much of the hardware and software from the old LAN will work with the new LAN? If the change is from CSMA to token ring or vice versa, the answer is: Not much! Certain devices such as modems, file servers, print servers, and multiplexers are independent of topology. Bus Interface Units, communications software, terminal servers, transmission media, and certain types of specialized TMDE will be useless in the new LAN topology. The best action may be to sell it for whatever salvage value may exist.

Shipment Of Hardware: The equipment that can be used in the new LAN requires special attention when it is moved. Make sure that any original packaging is reused. Ensure that boxes are sturdy, cushioning material is used, vapor barrier protection is used on devices that could be damaged by moisture, and be particularly careful with the mover's inventory. Some LAN equipment and general TMDE bring good prices from dealers in stolen material. Precise inventories before and after the move are required to prevent loss and theft.

Subscriber Requirements: The LAN Manager should survey subscribers in the early planning stages of the move for their inputs on features that should be included in the new LAN. Would tape backups be better than the method used now? What additional features should new telecommunications software offer? Should subLANs be part of the new installation? Although very knowledgeable about the old LAN, the LAN Manager could learn a thing or two from the subscribers. If new hardware and software are required, these same subscribers should be able to identify the persons who are to be selected for the earliest training on the new LAN equipment and software. These trained people are responsible for helping those who are awaiting training or those who need more personal attention.

Review Plans: Finally, the LAN Manager must select someone to review the plans for the new LAN. If the organization has engineering talent available, so much the better. If not, now is the time to call in a consultant to provide a sanity check on all the elements of the new LAN. By doing this, the LAN Manager is not admitting to any incompetence. There just might be areas that have been overlooked, or areas where the LAN Manager's knowledge is less than complete. If senior management does not want to fund such experts, the LAN Manager may be forced to rely on guidance from the vendors of the new LAN equipment. Remember to have someone who is knowledgeable about the operational characteristics of the new LAN make sure that everything should work as planned. The LAN Manager really should not worry too much about such moves. Something will go wrong, at least according to Murphy: "The perversity of the universe tends toward the maximum."

Automation and the LAN

An increase in automation in a product-oriented organization may impose additional traffic loading on the LAN. Automation and robotics devices are controlled by microprocessors. The software necessary to run these microprocessors must be updated, changed, or debugged from time to time. Usually the connections from one or more central locations to the automatic equipment are permanently installed. These connections carry information required to monitor the performance of robotic machines, the flow of raw materials and completed goods, and locations of various incomplete assemblies.

Various standards bodies have created data communications protocols that are used solely for automation and robotics. If these protocols are incompatible with the LAN, another parallel network must be installed to support such protocols. If, however, the LAN Manager is made aware of impending automation, the networking requirements can be evaluated for inclusion in the new LAN.

There are physical aspects to installing a LAN in an automated environment that the LAN Manager should be taking into consideration. The actual equipment that performs the automated functions may be electrically "noisy." Such equipment can produce electrical pulses on the transmission media that cause interference with the traffic that flows through the LAN. The LAN Manager must evaluate how large transient voltages affect the packets that flow through the LAN if either it connects to such automated devices or the transmission media transits the factory floor.

Summary

This chapter discussed the five facets of performance management of the LAN, including the following topics:

- the two types of performance data required,
  — Objective
  — Subjective

- The positive aspects of performance management, including
  — A more cost-effective LAN
  — Maximized use of LAN resources
  — Performance data that can be used to predict future LAN performance
  — Prevention of subscriber complaints

- The negative aspects of performance management, including
  — Consumption of corporate resources that may have been more usefully employed
  — No immediate gains for efforts expended
  — The destruction of performance management efforts by changes in corporate culture

- Implementation considerations of performance management, including
  — Methods and results of measurement
  — MTTR/MTBF
  — Network redesign

- The impact of growth on performance management

Case Study

Section 1: Factual Data

The firm involved is a nationwide manufacturing firm with multiple locations in several states. Each location has its internal LAN, with connections to all other LANs through gateways and leased lines. A New England office of the firm was experiencing many subscriber complaints from slow response time when accessing data at the Chicago location. The slower response time did not affect the users' productivity, but it was a constant source of irritation. The situation was so bad that when subscribers logged in to the Chicago host, they normally had time for a rest break before beginning their work. No engineer or technician was assigned to the New England office, so the only person who could help was a subscriber, D. Wissle, who had a greater-than-average knowledge of personal computers.

Section 2: What Happened

Wissle spent some time observing the duration of the waiting period that subscribers experienced when trying to log in to the Chicago host. Apparently Wissle had some technical training because he was able to provide graphs of the delay periods. These graphs did not seem to quite follow the normal peaks and valleys associated with daily workloads. Waiting time would peak at about 10:30 AM and then again at about 2:30 PM. When comparing measurements taken during the same timeframe concerning connections to the New York office, subscribers had very short waiting periods for access to the information they required. Analysis showed that the delay was either the circuit between New England and Chicago or within the Chicago office itself. A few telephone calls to other subscribers outside of Chicago indicated the same pattern of slow response times. This pointed to a problem within the Chicago office. Eventually the problem was identified, but only after it had gone away. The same computer that remote subscribers were accessing was temporarily being used to do some rather intensive "number crunching" on an engineering project. Once the project moved out of the design phase, response times returned to normal.

Section 3: Losses

Luckily for all concerned, nothing of value was lost here. True, some worker productivity may have been eliminated, but this was temporary. This action did serve to point to some errors on the part of telecommunications management.

Section 4: Lessons Learned

When performance analysis is involved, it must be a continual effort. Just because last week or last month showed no increase in response time or traffic loading does not mean that such increases are not taking place. The LAN Manager must have detailed records of past performance on hand. These records not only help forecast future traffic patterns, they can help find reasons for current traffic problems.

Network Security

"Don't lock the barn after the horse has been stolen."
—*Traditional folk wisdom*

This chapter is concerned with security of the LAN itself and the devices that are either part of the LAN or connected to it. Security in a LAN is like insurance. You never think of security until it is too late, and you are never sure whether or not security works in your organization until your procedures fail. Security that has been proven 99.995 percent functional in other organizations may fail in yours. This chapter addresses the "why" of LAN security, some of the positive aspects of LAN security, some of the negative aspects of LAN security, and how to create and implement a security system for a LAN.

Why Institute LAN Security?

LAN security is management of access to the LAN and the devices that are part of the LAN and connected to it. LAN security should allow only those who are authorized to connect to the LAN, the resources that are part of the LAN, and those devices that are also connected to the LAN. LAN resources include such devices as file and print servers. Why prevent an unauthorized subscriber from using a print server? There are several reasons, not the least of which is corporate expense.

Preventing Loss of Corporate Resources

A print server consumes corporate resources. This includes paper, ink/toner/ribbon, bandwidth from the unauthorized subscriber to the print server, and the admittedly small amount of electricity required to run the print server. More important, as long as authorized subscribers are waiting for their outputs, some unauthorized subscriber is delaying official business. This delay is the least important aspect of LAN security.

Preventing Fraud and Theft

Various software applications are resident on the LAN or in devices attached to the LAN. These applications were paid for with private or corporate funds. With the file transfer capabilities inherent in modern LANs, an unscrupulous, unauthorized subscriber can break into the LAN, duplicate software applications, and sell them to persons outside of the organization. This is a fraud upon the organization.

If an organization purchases a given number of software applications for employees' use, only that number of applications can be used at one time. If employees duplicate the application for their own use at work, the organization has defrauded the vendor of the software application and is subject for both civil and criminal penalties. If this duplicated copy of the application is sold outside of the firm, the employees are committing theft, and the organization may well be liable as an accomplice. An attorney who practices in the jurisdiction involved can identify the legal liabilities of all parties to such frauds and deceptions.

Preventing Unauthorized Release of Information

The third area to be protected is that of organizational data. Data concerning costs of raw materials, subassemblies, finished goods, wages and salaries, or R&D work are always targets for industrial espionage. Personnel data are also targets of opportunity to those who can gain unauthorized access to the LAN. Consider the impact of every employee finding out what every other employee's salary is now and how much of a raise they got last year.

Think what would happen if a hacker got into the organization's financial data and wiped out all of the accounts receivable records.

Methods of Denying Access

Access to unauthorized LAN subscribers can be denied in five generic ways.

- Passwords
- Random number devices
- Encryption
- Biological metrics
- Dial back

Passwords: Passwords are used in a question and answer method. When attempting to access the LAN, the subscriber is prompted to enter a password—somewhat like the process used with a personal identification number on a bank's 24-hour teller card. If the subscriber is authorized to access the LAN, a connection opens for the subscriber to use. If not, access is prohibited. An alarm should sound if more than three unsuccessful attempts are made.

Passwords should be no more than eight, and no fewer than six, characters in a combination of letters and numbers. The usage of proper names, telephone numbers, or birthdays should be strongly prohibited. Passwords should not be written down and left in a drawer or on an appointment calendar. Project or product names should not be used for passwords. Passwords written on a piece of paper and taped to the user's terminal hardly constitute correct LAN security procedure!

When politics in a certain New England state was a little bit more freewheeling, an old-time politician was quoted as saying, "Vote early and often." The same principle must be applied to passwords—they must be changed often. A password should be changed no less frequently than every three months. If there is the vaguest possibility that a password has been compromised, change it. It is cheaper and easier to change a password than to correct the result of an unauthorized access to the LAN.

Passwords should not be recycled. A subscriber should not use the password "ABC123" for the first three-month period, change to "123ABC" the second three-month period, and then return back to "ABC123" for the third three-month period.

Passwords can be layered. The subscriber needs one password to access to the LAN and its resources such as print servers. Another password is required to get to each file server in the LAN. Still another password is required to access the hosts connected to the LAN. One more password is required to access each application or file within the host. Yet another password is required to perform maintenance on network equipment. Where does it end?

Passwords should conform to a set of rules established by those charged with security of the LAN and the attached devices. This does not mean that the password's content should also be set. The suggested approach is that subscribers select their own password within the constraints established. The passwords currently in use must also be on file in some secure location in case the employee dies suddenly or becomes disabled. If no one knows this person's password, it may be difficult if not impossible to retrieve data in that person's files and records.

If an employee terminates employment suddenly or involuntarily, all the files and applications to which the employee had access are now locked. No one can find out what this person knew or was working on. On the other hand, the passwords of an employee who was fired should be changed as soon as possible. This prevents the fired employee from performing any types of damage to corporate resources. As each password is changed, the old one should be thrown out and the new one put in its place.

A password should be treated as if the item was the combination to a safe or a key to one's home. Only the authorized subscriber and the security department should know what passwords are in effect for what devices and when the passwords were changed.

Before leaving the subject of passwords, the function of address should be discussed. An address is the electronic designation of a device on the network or attached to the network. The address, as an address, should never be available to the subscribers. Rather, a name-to-address conversion table should be created. Based on this, an authorized subscriber opens a connection to a named device. If there is ever a suspicion that a device's address has been compromised, the address can be changed and the name to address conversion tables modified to reflect this change.

Random Number Generators: Random number generators can work in several ways. Perhaps the most common approach is as follows. Within the LAN, or the devices connected to the LAN, is a special piece of hardware. This device generates a random number of up to eight digits. The user has a corresponding device that can range in size from a credit card to a small pocket calculator. These two devices are under the control of software.

When the user of the device first tries to access the LAN, she is greeted with a challenge in somewhat the same manner as with a password. First, she is asked to log in using her name or other unique identifier. Once this entry is made, she is presented with a four-digit number. She then enters the last four digits from the number shown on the device she was given. This eight-digit number is compared to the number stored within the device attached to the LAN. If the numbers match, the holder of the smaller device is assumed to be an authorized subscriber.

At first glance, this seems to be a somewhat foolproof approach. Analysis will prove otherwise. A loss of one of the devices carried by an authorized subscriber means a replacement and reprogramming of all devices carried by all authorized subscribers. If the subscriber is fired, and refuses to return the device immediately, the same actions must be taken. Also, the device the subscriber carries is battery powered. In keeping with Murphy's Law, the battery will fail just when it is needed most.

Such random number devices require both hardware and software maintenance. As they are electronic, they are subject to unforeseen failure. Another item to consider is the cost of such devices. They are not inexpensive, however, they are the cheapest hardware solution to LAN security.

Encryption: Encryption of LAN traffic does not necessarily prohibit an unauthorized subscriber from accessing the network. Encryption prevents the unauthorized subscriber from either gaining any benefit from the access or doing any damage to corporate resources. A caveat is required here. An unauthorized subscriber who gains access to encrypted LAN traffic can do two types of damage to the business: flood the LAN with gobbledegook characters and under certain circumstances do a rudimentary traffic flow analysis.

An encryption device takes a transmitted string or block of bits and scrambles the meaning of each bit within the string or block. When the data is received, the reverse takes place and the meaning is restored. The scrambling and descrambling requires a specific key, either hardware or software. Keys can be both public and private. As this text is introductory in nature, the reader is referred to any of the available works on this subject. We are more concerned here with how to employ encryption, not its technical characteristics.

In one approach, an encryption device is placed between the data terminal equipment (DTE) and the LAN. Every data bit that leaves the DTE is encrypted. A similar encryption device, with a matching key, is located near the device to be accessed by the user. This could be a file server, a host, or a print server. The data bits are then decoded to their original condition and fed into the device to be accessed. Normally, encryption devices are used only when transmission media leave an area not under the direct control of the organization supported by the LAN.

Another benefit of encryption is that it allows only authorized subscribers to have access to applications and data, and yet it allows the use of a personal computer with removable diskettes. What is accomplished when encrypting data for transmission, when plain data can be copied to a diskette and the diskette then taken from the building? When personal computers are in use, the data is encrypted before it is written to the diskette and then decrypted after it is read from the diskette for use by the applications resident on the personal computer.

Perhaps the only major problem with encryption, other than price, is the distribution of keys. Because encrypted data transmissions are subject to interception and analysis, the keys must be changed frequently. The Data Encryption Standard (DES) used by banks and financial organizations has a chance of 1×10^{72} of being "broken." Yet with computers running at speeds of millions of instructions per second, even this key can be broken if it is in use long enough. Some experts indicate that the time consumed in this "breaking" process can be measured in years.

A key can be distributed either physically or electronically. If the new key is transmitted in an encrypted data transmission and the old key was broken, the new key is compromised. If the new key is lost or stolen in physical movement, it is useless and users of encrypted services will be required to use an old, and perhaps previously compromised, key.

Encryption devices are perhaps the single most awkward method of providing LAN security available today. They are expensive and difficult to use. Key distribution for them is a problem. Furthermore subscribers who gain access to the LAN through encryption devices, are automatically assumed to be authorized subscribers and they can do anything they want while the connection is open. Despite all the drawbacks to encryption devices for data transmission, not only do banks and financial organizations use encryption, it is the method of choice for securing traffic for the various branches of the federal government.

Biological Measurements: The single most expensive means of providing security within the LAN is that of biological measurements. This may include retina prints, fingerprint analysis, and in some applications, voice analysis. Normally this is used as part of a layered approach to LAN security.

The biological devices "learn" what a given individual's biological measurements are. These measurements are then taken every time the individual wants to access the LAN, the devices that are part of it, or hosts attached to it. The measurements taken are compared to a digital "image" of previous measurements. If the two sets of measurements match, the LAN allows the subscriber access. If not, access is prohibited and alarms sound.

When dealing with both encryption and biological devices, the LAN Manager can develop a false sense of security. Both encryption devices and biological identification devices only prevent the casual attempts to breach LAN security. They are like a lock on a door—they will keep an honest person honest, but will not prevent a determined thief. We leave it to your imagination how to bypass biological measurement devices. Encryption keys have been sold in the past and will be sold in the future. Humans are corruptible; machines can be spoofed.

Dial Back: Some LANs are constructed in such a manner that persons remote from the LAN can connect via dial-up lines. Such methods are quite common where field agents need access to databases, or to place orders from a customer's location. When subscribers dial in, they identify themselves in some prearranged fashion. The file server/host connected to the LAN then breaks the connection and places a call through the public switched network to a predetermined telephone number. The drawbacks to this scheme should be obvious.

Calls can be placed only to preapproved locations. If the salesman is at a customer's location, this cannot be preprogrammed. He must place calls from a field office. This provides little security. If an agent is removed from the organization, and his dial-back number is not immediately removed, he can wreak revenge for his firing until the authorized dial-back number is removed or his password is changed.

Layered Security

A proper LAN security program may include some or all of the security methods just discussed, plus physical security of access points to the LAN. This is called the layered approach and is shown in Figure 7.1.

Physical Security: The first layer is that of physical security. This starts with securing the building(s) within which either communications devices or transmission media are housed. Most organizations of any size already have some type of physical security in place through guards and visible identification cards.

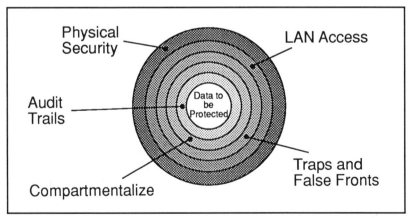

FIGURE 7.1

If transmission media transit unsecured areas, additional security is required. If wire or cable is the method of choice, such media should be buried or run through underground raceways or cable trenches. If the transmission media are emplaced on poles, the media should be alarmed. The alarm sounds when the transmission characteristics change suddenly. These sudden changes occur during surreptitious taps, or a cut-and-splice process. If free-space light or radio is used for transmission media, no genuine security against interception and "spoofing" can be guaranteed without recourse to additional hardware and software. Encryption is usually the method of choice in these instances.

LAN Access: The physical security layer prevents unauthorized persons from entering an area housing LAN hardware and transmission media. The next layer should be that of access to the LAN itself. This can be done with passwords or random number devices. The allegedly authorized subscriber is challenged by the LAN or by devices that are part of the LAN. Multiple challenges are not totally uncommon. Once access to the LAN and the attached devices has been granted, the apparently authorized subscriber may also be challenged again when she tries to access a host attached to the LAN. This challenge is under the control of the host administrator, not the LAN Manager.

Once security procedures have decided that the person in question is an authorized subscriber, the next layer is to in some way protect the data that flows through the LAN. Encryption is usually the approach of choice. Such encryption should be transparent to the authorized subscriber.

Compartmentalize Data: Continuing with the layered approach, certain highly sensitive information should not be on the same LAN as more common information. Yes, this does fly in the face of the purpose of a LAN, which is to share information. Yet, some data is too sensitive to share. The very sensitive data can be passed over another LAN, although the LAN will probably be of an order of magnitude smaller. In addition to the physical security present under normal circumstances, the sensitive information available via LAN access will be guarded with all the preceding procedures, plus others.

Access to devices that can move, modify, display, or reproduce this sensitive data must have some type of positive protection mechanisms. The biological methods discussed earlier are very good initial screening mechanisms. But if material is that sensitive, a two-person rule may be put into place. The two-person rule prohibits one person alone from accessing such sensitive data. That is, if someone who is authorized to know about Project X needs to access data concerning the project, this person must be escorted by another person who is also allowed to know about this project. The second person affirms that no unauthorized modifications, retrievals, or deletions took place. Of course, the problem then arises as to who vouches for the honesty of the second person. The ancient Romans knew of this problem: "Que custodiet custodiens?"

Traps and False Fronts: Another approach to LAN security is that of the false front. Assume that an unauthorized person manages to penetrate several layers of security and accesses the LAN. But, at perhaps the third or fourth layer, he fails a challenge and response. Instead of merely closing down, the LAN allows this person access to a false set of data, records, and correspondence. For those who are sufficiently devious, this can lead to many fun hours of planning. In all seriousness, once the unauthorized subscriber has broken into this false front, an alarm should sound and attempts be made to trace the source of such access.

Audit Trails: Previous sections of this text have discussed the idea of tracking the usage of bandwidth on the LAN. This bandwidth consumption can have security applications as well. Every time an authorized subscriber logs in to the LAN, a record should be made of this activity. If the subscriber accesses a particular host, this should also be noted. The amount of traffic between the host and the subscriber should be recorded. The time the subscriber breaks the connection with the host and logs off the LAN must also be included. This process is known as an audit trail.

By creating audit trails for each LAN or host connection, the LAN Manager can create subscriber profiles. If an allegedly authorized subscriber suddenly deviates from her usage profile, the LAN Manager may want to find out why this change took place. In all likelihood, this change is perfectly natural because of changing duties, promotion, or transfer. However, multiple attempts at passwords or attempts to enter many hosts within a short period of time should raise some type of alarm. The purpose of this alarm is to cause an investigation of why this activity has taken place. Once again, such activity could be perfectly harmless, or it could be an actual attempt at hacking.

Positive Aspects of Security Management

Security management provides three gains for the LAN Manager. These include prevention of sabotage/espionage, an increase in traffic loading, and prevention of infection.

Prevention of Sabotage or Espionage

Certain types of corporate information are the targets of covert action.

Proprietary Information: Consider what would happen if an organization's competitors were to find out that the organization was able to produce a product for 40 percent of the competitor's production cost. Alternatively, think what would happen if a disgruntled employee were able to tap into the payroll and print out every employee's wage or salary; or, even worse, to send a copy of data from the last payroll to everyone in the organization through the LAN.

One of the primary purposes of LAN security is to prevent sensitive material from being available to any who wish to look at it. However, just reading sensitive data is not as dangerous as modifying this data.

LAN security, if properly administered, can prevent such activities as corruption of corporate databases. If a particular casting were to cost $32.20 and 1000 of them were needed for a new product, the financial planning group would have to earmark $32,200 for a production run. If an unauthorized subscriber modified the cost of this item to $3.22, the same planning group would set aside $3220 for the same production run. This would lead to a shortfall of almost $29,000. The other side of this particular security problem is not quite as evident. What would happen if someone accessed the payroll files and gave himself an extra 2 percent raise every year?

Financial Information: Certain information under control of some organizations bears very close scrutiny. Assume a bank was in the process of evaluating a person for a loan. The person was found to be a poor credit risk. An unauthorized subscriber tapped into the bank's LAN and asked for a printout of those who have been identified as poor credit risks. This printout is then sold to various purchasers. What is the bank's liability? Could the person whose loan was turned down bring suit for breach of confidentiality or for defamation of character?

Confidential Information: "But," the LAN Manager says, "all we do is manufacture widgets. We do not keep that type of information on hand!" Those who keep personnel records have a special trust to maintain these records confidentially. Unauthorized release of information in personnel records, particularly derogatory information, may be grounds for a civil suit. If nothing else, at least one employee is going to be very irritated and may seek restitution or revenge.

Traffic Load Increase

Surprisingly enough, LAN security activities have little or no measurable impact on network loading. The amount of overhead data involved with challenge and response or with encryption of transmitted data is less than 1 percent of the entire throughput.

In secure LANs, the total quantity of traffic may rise a considerable percentage. The obvious question is why? The answer is equally obvious. Prior to having a secure LAN, much of the proprietary or sensitive data was moved via the "tape and tennis shoes net," that is, via courier. Once those who are charged with the usage of this type of information become confident of the security provided, they abandon the less flexible means of information interchange.

Of course, there are those who say that no LAN, or network for that matter, is ever secure. To them we offer the following evidence. The United States government routinely transmits data through its own networks. This data, if ever compromised, can lead to immediate and irreparable damage to the United States of America.

Preventing "Infection"

With today's threats of worms, viruses, Trojan horses, logic bombs, and trap doors, LAN security is even more important than ever. Worms seem to be this generation's answer to the "Kilroy was here" graffiti of a previous generation. The other forms of invasion are dangerous, destructive, and must be protected against. More than sufficient articles both popular and technically esoteric have been written about how to keep these destructive programs out of the computers attached to the LAN. Proper LAN security, aided by common sense, will help prevent unauthorized subscribers from sabotaging the LAN with these devices.

Negative Aspects of Security Management

Security management of the LAN is not without its price. This section discusses some of the negative points involved in LAN security management.

Additional Subscriber Actions

The single greatest negative point, at least from the subscriber's point of view, is that of slightly increased difficulty in accessing the LAN. Logging in to the LAN is delayed by the request for passwords. If passwords are to be layered, the subscriber needs one password to access the LAN, and its resources such as print servers. Another password is required to get to each file server in the LAN. Still another password is required to access the hosts connected to the LAN. One more password is required to access each application or file within the host. Yet another password is required to perform maintenance on network equipment. To go from a personal computer to the application on the host, the subscriber must remember no less than three passwords.

Audit Trails

Each time the subscriber logs in to or out of a part of the LAN requiring a password, an audit trail must be kept. This audit trail provides the date, time, and name of every person who attempts to use the LAN or some of its resources. Maintaining the audit trails and evaluating the information within them consumes time, corporate resources, and manpower. Who has a right to access what part of the LAN? Obtain data from which file server? Use the printer? Even if everyone is completely honest, use of LAN resources must be checked. The audit trails show who used these resources. Even if we know who used the resources, how do we know if that person has the authority to do so? Each usage requires validation by a disinterested party. Remember, someone is paying for every bit of data on the LAN, every CPU cycle in the hardware, and every sheet of paper in the printer.

Random Number Devices

If random number devices provide LAN security, someone must be assigned to issue, maintain, and retrieve them. It is all well and good to say that Joe Smith is authorized to use the random number device. Who sees to it that he gets the one he needs? Once the device is issued, who maintains records of such "assignments?" If, like other hardware, the random number device malfunctions, who repairs it? Such hardware simply cannot be sent out for repair like a bad terminal or modem. If the device is sent out for repair, the organization doing the repair can access the LAN and all the LAN resources that Joe had. In the meantime, what does Joe use to access the LAN and the attached resources?

Assume that Joe dies in an aircraft accident. Who goes to his widow's home to collect the company property? Or, what if Joe decides to quit, and refuses to return the random number device? These questions have no immediate answer, but the LAN Manager should be prepared to answer them.

Encryption Devices

Encryption devices require a new "key" every time an old key becomes unusable. Keys must be changed with depressing regularity. Some types of encryption devices encrypt the key and transmit it to all other encryption devices. But the first time the device is installed and every time a new encryption device is installed, someone must physically deliver the keying material. Loss of a key allows anyone who finds it to decrypt the transmitted data. So, every time a key is lost or compromised, someone must physically deliver a new key to every encryption device in the LAN. Failure to cancel the key when an encryption device is removed for maintenance is compromise of the key. If the person who has access to the keys leaves, new keys must be distributed. Oh, yes, records of all these actions must be maintained.

Biological Measuring Devices

Although biological measurement devices are available on the open market, there is not a large demand for such items. Lack of demand normally prevents lower prices in a free market; fewer companies will make the product, thus a lack of competition and higher prices. This is true for these devices. Without resorting to specialized trade literature or consulting services, the LAN Manager has very little information available about these devices.

Dial Back

If dial back is used to verify who is on the other end of a circuit, the authorized numbers must be updated quite regularly. Realize that every time a new field agent is hired or every time a field agent changes location, the dial-back number must be updated to reflect the change. Also, every time a field agent terminates employment, his authorized dial-back numbers must be removed.

There is no method by which LAN security can be created without making the LAN more difficult to use. As with the introduction of any new process or technology, training, particularly for the subscribers, is required. This training takes time, money, and manpower.

Security Loopholes: LAN security does provide some protection against unauthorized access to corporate data. Unfortunately, LAN security may, in the end, provide a false sense of security. Even if LAN security is technically sufficient, the best security cannot protect against human error and human frailty.

Human Error: The first of these areas is that of stupidity. Even with the most carefully thought-out plan of protection, every activity documented, all subscribers well trained, and every possible check made, one simple mistake can set all this effort to naught. What is the sense of having passwords, if the subscribers write their passwords on their calendars? Random number devices provide an excellent, and fairly simple, means of providing security—until they are lost. Encryption protects data from unauthorized interception; until a key is compromised. Biological evaluation devices can be "spoofed." The required methods are quite grisly, but it can be done. Dial-back numbers can be passed out to an assistant, and who knows what happens next?

Human Frailty: The second area of concern is that of the intentional release of data that was entrusted to an employee who was assumed to be a good "security risk." Assume, for the sake of discussion, that XYZ Holding Company wants to take over the supported organization in a distinctly unfriendly manner. How much easier would it be if the prospective buyer knew financial information about the organization it wanted to buy? If a senior person in finance knows a merger is in the works and wants to ensure a warm reception by the new owners, what would be the best way for her to curry favor? Alternatively, what would be the impact of someone opening a file on a corporate file server and finding the annual salary of every employee in this file?

Regardless of how close to the state of the art an organization's LAN security may be, it cannot prevent the disclosure of corporate data by someone who has authorized access to that data.

Implementing LAN Security Management

LAN security is similar to any other type of information security. This section discusses how to implement security in and on the LAN.

Identify Threats

The first step to such implementation is to identify the spectrum of threats. Some of these are obvious. What is to be protected is data. This data can take many forms and formats. Data can be on paper, on magnetic media, or in traffic that leaves the physical confines of the organization.

Controlling Nonelectronic Data: Paper-based data is treated like any type of document for security purposes. Such treatment includes identification of numbered copies, stamps for the classification of information, and accountability of each copy. Limit the distribution of copies only to those who need this information. If possible, extract only the required parts for that person.

The contents of magnetic media are a little more difficult to identify. Any magnetic media that leaves the physical location of the organization to which it belongs must be cleared by someone in authority. If this is the form that data is in when it is mailed to another location, someone other than the sender must authorize the release of the data. Data in magnetic media format should not be hand-carried by an employee unless no other realistic means are available. Data on magnetic media should not be brought into the organization unless its contents have been screened thoroughly by someone other than the courier. If data is mailed, seals should be intact. Any sign of tampering should be investigated before the data is read from the media into corporate hardware or software. Effectively, this means that someone's favorite batch file or menu structures for the file server are strictly forbidden until a knowledgeable person can verify that no worms, viruses, or Trojan horses are part of the data on that particular item.

Control of Traffic: Traffic that leaves or enters the physical confines of the organization through a WAN or VAN is almost impossible to track and verify for accuracy and presence of destructive code.

Implement Security Plan

Implementation of a security plan for the LAN must be approached in a step-by-step, thoughtful, and planned manner. The first order of business is to identify what type of threats the organization faces. Realistically, does the corporate data attract industrial espionage? Are the accounting practices so loose that someone can dip into various accounts without prior approval?

Identify Areas To Be Protected: The first step to securing the LAN is to identify what parts of the LAN, or of the hosts connected to it are targets for those who perform illegal acts. Obviously, the financial management aspects of data processing are a high-priority target. But what if an outsider does break in? What can he do? He probably does not know the accounting systems in use and what each account is for. Therefore, financial data is usually not a high priority for protection; at least from outsiders. Is R&D information important in the organization? Much depends on the industry under consideration. In a highly competitive field, perhaps some effort must be made to protect patent or copyright type information. Customer lists are worth a lot in some types of organizations. Perhaps these need extra protection. Although most legal information is sensitive, how much of it is of use to someone breaking into the LAN? Usually it is of very little use. Such a discussion could go on for many pages, but it would provide little additional information.

The result of this effort is a list of information that must be protected. The first item on the list is the most important one: the last item is the least important one. After identifying what must be protected, the next step is to identify what level of effort someone will make to get to this data. If the effort to reach protected data will be minimal, passwords alone may be sufficient. Alternatively, if the data is of high value, merger information, for instance, more than password protection is required. Random number devices or encryption may be necessary. If the information is very sensitive, you should seriously consider the option of actually removing that particular host or file server from the LAN. A simple physical switch can interrupt data flowing to or from this host or file server. If the switch is in a container with a lock, even more protection is afforded.

Threats To Protect Against: Three general types of attacks must be protected against: curiosity, theft, and modification.

Most hackers really do not want to get at the data. Out of curiosity perhaps, they are more interested in finding out what is there than in damaging the information. If damage is their goal, the damage is usually done to the operating system. If damage gets out of hand, the information can be destroyed. What would be the result of the destruction of the inventory information for the parts and raw material for the new product due out next month?

The second type of action to protect against is only marginally different. The theft of data and wiping out of all copies can be disastrous under certain circumstances.

The most insidious attack, and the most difficult to protect against, is that of modification of data either within the LAN or in hosts attached to the LAN. Consider the impact of dividing every person's paycheck by 10. This means that someone who was expecting a check for $350.00 this week gets a check for $35.00. Something like this is easy to spot. Yet, if the organization depended on mailings for part of their income, and the hacker just shifted each name, not address, one address over, the results could be devastating.

The LAN Manager can only do so much to protect the data that is stored in file servers or hosts attached to the LAN. The host administrator must work closely with the LAN Manager in defining the "how" and then implementing LAN security.

Recent studies indicate that the majority of "computer crime" is perpetrated by insiders. The "wily hacker" does not get into the corporate accounting system and transfer millions of dollars to a numbered account outside of the country. Too many checks and balances exist. No one outside a company really cares that the senior vice president makes three times his salary in stock options. Yet if that information were to be made public within the company, some rancor could develop.

Because of the threat of internal sabotage or espionage, the LAN Manager must work with others in the organization to educate them on the capabilities of the LAN in preventing unauthorized access. Supervisors whose subordinates have access to sensitive information must identify or characterize these subordinates into two categories. The first category is that of trustworthiness. If Joe has access to payroll information, can he be trusted not to make public the data he has available to him? Once those trustworthy persons have been identified, the next step is to decide exactly how trustworthy they are.

What are these people allowed to do with access to sensitive material? For instance, the technician who repairs the LAN may need to determine that a user can access a particular file server on the LAN. That file server contains patent information. Should the technician be allowed to read this information? Common sense says yes; after all, he must be able to log in to the file server for testing purposes. Security says no! A technician does not need to know that patents have been purchased or sold. Sensitive information on the file server can be password protected. Once the subscriber can log in on the file server, the technician is no longer required.

The limitations on what activities can be allowed to a specific person, or group of persons, and how these limitations are implemented depends on the hardware and software that make up the LAN. Some brands of software allow up to eight levels of file access. Some types of hardware only work with operating commands specific to themselves. Once again, no specific guidance can be offered on how to prevent or allow specific individuals specific privileges from the LAN. Yet, sooner or later, someone must decide whether or not Joe Smith can only read data from a datebase, not modify it, copy it, or erase it.

We have identified the types and seriousness of threats a LAN Manager must protect against. The actions that can be taken against protected data have been specified, and the personnel problem within network security has been addressed. What is left is to select the most cost-effective means of implementing the required protection.

This chapter began with the analogy of security and insurance, so we will end it in the same way. Some people do not object to paying $100 a month to insure a $15,000 automobile, yet they refuse to implement, at little cost, a password system for their LAN. A LAN carries data so sensitive that its release could result in losses that would be measured in millions. How much should be spent on the effort to secure the LAN and the data that can be accessed through it is a question each organization must answer for itself. The LAN Manager plays "You Bet Your Job" each day that no security is in place.

Summary

This chapter addressed the concept of LAN security through LAN access. By managing the access to the LAN, the file servers, and the hosts attached to the Lan, the LAN Manager is contributing to security. Some of the positive and negative aspects of LAN security were also mentioned. Finally, a brief plan for implementation of security management was outlined.

This chapter discussed many aspects of LAN security,

particularly the need for security management. The following topics were covered:

- Prevention of crimes against the organization, including
  — Loss of corporate resources
  — Fraud and theft
  — Unauthorized release of information

- Methods of denying access, including
  — Passwords
  — Random number devices
  — Encryption
  — Biological measurements
  — Dial-back procedures

- Layered security, including
  — Physical security
  — LAN access
  — Compartmentalize data
  — Traps and false fronts
  — Audit trails

- The positive aspects of LAN security management, including
  — Prevention against sabotage and/or espionage in various areas, including
    — Proprietary data
    — Financial data
    — Confidential information
    — Protection against electronic attacks despite increased traffic loading

- The negative aspects of LAN security, including
  — Additional subscriber actions
  — Required audit trails
  — Additional hardware, including
    — Random number devices
    — Encryption devices
    — Biological measuring devices
    — Dial-back equipment
  — Security loopholes, including
    — Human error
    — Human frailty

- Implementation of LAN security management, including
  - Identification of possible threats, including
    - Danger to nonelectronic data
    - Traffic interception
  - Implementation of the security plan, including
    - What types of protection to apply
    - What is to be protected
    - Where the protected item is located

Measurements of the LAN

Measure twice, cut once.
—*Tradesman's axiom*

This chapter provides information on the required measurements for LANs. It includes what is to be measured, what is needed to make measurements, and some of the more common benefits from these measurements. Before discussing the how such measurements are taken, let us address the "why" of measurements.

Why Measure the LAN?

In a nutshell, measurement of the LAN is the only true basis for present and future management activities that concern the LAN. This includes anything from adding one more subscriber to complete replacement of hardware, software, and transmission media.

Performance Management

Perhaps the single most important reason for measuring the LAN is performance management. Although this area of LAN management was the subject of Chapter 6, a brief review may be useful here. Performance management tells the LAN Manager and the supported organization whether the LAN is performing "as advertised." Does the equipment work in accordance with manufacturer's specifications? Is sufficient bandwidth available? Do subscribers suffer from numerous delays or excessive response times? Is the LAN suffering numerous inexplicable outages? Are subscribers being locked out of or kicked off a session with a host or file server? These types of questions can only be answered by evaluating the LAN's performance. Such evaluation requires measurements.

Fault Management

These same measurements aid LAN Managers and their staff in fault management. Many of the reported problems in a LAN are based on subscriber complaints. By making the appropriate measurements, the LAN Manager can tell if the subscriber complaint is legitimate or specious. Legitimate complaints can be traced to defective conditions in the LAN. A specious complaint can be traced to ignorance or lack of training on the part of the subscriber. Some engineers, many technicians, and not a few LAN Managers prefer to place the blame on the subscriber. This is dangerous for several reasons.

The first, last, and utmost thing LAN Managers must remember is that they are providing a service. They must ensure that a baseless subscriber complaint is truly a baseless complaint and not a LAN malfunction. This situation can only be ascertained by measuring LAN functionality. Such measurements are objective proof that the subscriber's complaint is not based in fact. Another reason that danger exists in ignoring subscriber complaints is that the subscriber may well have the ear of senior members of the organization. The LAN Manager must have documented evidence that the LAN was functioning properly and that the complaint was based in ignorance. This same type of proof can be the basis for requesting additional funds to train subscribers.

LAN Growth

In addition to performance and fault management, the measurement effort helps LAN Managers in their efforts concerning LAN growth. One of the major technical questions LAN Managers must be prepared to answer is that of response time. Response time may be one of the major points in driving the need for LAN redesign under organizational growth conditions. Does the LAN and the attached hardware provide sufficiently rapid response time? Previous discussions concerning performance management addressed that question. LAN Managers must have established baselines for performance on hand, before anyone asks about response time.

The only way to tell if response times are too long is by measurement. Depending on the pattern revealed by measurement and analysis of the results, there may truly be a need to let the LAN grow in response to reduced throughput. Alternatively, there may only be the need to shift several subscribers around a little or to put in a bridge or router.

It is important to remember that performance management, fault management, and LAN growth are the three legs of the tripod that supports the LAN Manager's career. Actions taken concerning these areas must be based in knowledge, not intuitive feelings. This knowledge is based solely on objective measurement of the LAN and the services provided. This does not mean that other managerial areas are not supported by, nor require, measurement.

Usage/Budget Data

One of the measurements the LAN Manager must make answers the question: How expensive is the LAN? Such expenses are not limited to salaries or to paper and pencils, but they involve such questions as: How many CPU cycles are required? How many modems were replaced this year? Why were they replaced? Is it cheaper to build, buy, or replace something? What is the impact of changing topologies at this point? How many subscribers will be out of communications if thus, such, and so happens?

None of these questions, including those about next year's budget, can be answered without measuring the LAN. How these measurements are taken is the content of following sections of this chapter. Analysis of the results of those measurements is not covered in depth in this text. These analyses provide LAN Managers with a base upon which to build their arguments for funding modifications and growth.

WAN/VAN Vendor Billing

The LAN Manager receives from WAN/VAN vendors a monthly bill for products and services rendered. Individuals know that if they are billed for a call on their phone during a time when no one was at their residence, it is an erroneous bill. How does the LAN Manager know that a charge on the bill is genuine or not?

The answer is that unless the usage of WAN/VAN-vendor–provided circuits is continually measured, the LAN Manager will have no idea whether the charges are correct or not.

Some vendors lease telecommunications equipment for a set fee. Assume, for example, that the LAN requires several leased modems for certain circuits. The organization supported by the LAN pays for these modems on a monthly or quarterly basis. The LAN Manager must be able to show where these modems are and that they are in use. Otherwise, the supported organization is paying for something it either does not have or does not use.

Vendor Hardware Claims

Measurement of the LAN provides the LAN Manager with objective proof of the claims of hardware and software vendors. Let us assume that the LAN Manager selected Vendor A's file server because the vendor claimed that the hard disk drive could store 600 megabytes of data and had an access time of 28 milliseconds. How can the LAN Manager prove or disprove this claim without resorting to outside testing laboratories? Without measurement, there is no way to prove or disprove the vendor's claim.

Measuring Transmission Media

This section discusses the steps taken to measure the quality of the transmission media used by the LAN. Once again, this does not explain "how to do it," but rather "what must be done."

Time Domain Reflectometer

The continuity or the ability to pass an electrical signal is easy to check with common TMDE such as an ohmmeter. This instrument determines whether metallic transmission media is continuous from end to end, or whether it is open or shorted. The time domain reflectometer tests the quality of the transmission media.

Quality checks are required to ascertain the electronic, not electrical, characteristics of the transmission media. Signals that travel over a LAN are subject to distortion from electromagnetic fields or from the propagation characteristics of the wire and cable. The time domain reflectometer helps eliminate the possibility of distortion by identifying portions of the transmission media that can induce distortion.

Signal-To-Noise Ratio

When transmission media pass through different geographic locations, they can be affected by various electromagnetic fields. These fields induce random noise on the transmission media. This noise can be of sufficient amplitude to override the signals that represent data bits going over the LAN. The higher the signal-to-noise ratio, the better the chance of receiving the correct signals.

Nonmetallic Transmission Media

There are two general types of nonmetallic transmission media, radio and light. Radio signals propagate through the atmosphere through distances as short as several hundred meters, up to halfway around the world. Measurement of these types of signals is a science unto itself and requires highly trained engineers and technicians with expensive and specialized TMDE. The LAN Manager must realize that LAN traffic that uses the radio transmission media may be subject to different types of interference. Unless qualified in propagation theory, the LAN Manager should leave this type of measurement to specialists. The key point though is that this type of transmission medium requires frequent measurement.

LAN traffic that utilizes free-space light must also be measured. Free-space light uses infrared beams to carry traffic in the tens of megabits per second range over short distances, normally less than 2 kilometers. Dust, snow, rain, haze, and fog can lessen the ability of this transmission media to carry traffic. Before measuring this transmission media for signal-to-noise ratio, the LAN Manager should refer to the vendor's installation and acceptance checks. The free-space light signal-to-noise ratio should not vary until the light-emitting diode used has lost luminescence. This should not happen under most conditions. Loss of signal-to-noise ratio is more likely to be caused by a shifting of the transmitter or receiver. A shift of less than 0.25 inches in the transmitter can have a major affect on receiver performance.

Fiber optic cable is normally trouble free. The only repetitive measurement the LAN Manager requires is that of received signal strength. The physical characteristics of fiber optic cable prevent interference from electromagnetic fields. However, fiber optic cable is subject to signal loss at improperly made junctions. Each time a fiber optic cable is mechanically connected, signal strength losses accrue. Specialized TMDE, for example, an optical time domain reflectometer, is required to evaluate the propagation characteristics of fiber optic cable.

All of the preceding measurements are required to show that the transmission media used in the LAN are capable of passing traffic. Once this capability is shown, the next step is to measure the consumption of the bandwidth provided by transmission media.

Measure Throughput

Throughput is the number of bits that can transit the LAN at any given time increment, normally per second. Throughput is measured in bits per second or multiples thereof. This measurement is called, logically enough, the bit rate. Telecommunications is always measured in bits, never in bytes.

Once the throughput is measured, what is to be done with such results? Somewhat like the dog who chased cars: What does he do with one when he catches it? The bit rate is a performance characteristic of the hardware and software that make up the LAN. This hardware and software were purchased based on, among other things, the bit rate. By knowing this bit rate, the LAN Manager can tell if the LAN is passing traffic at its specified throughput.

Many junior technicians or LAN Managers may be disturbed to find that a 4-Mbps token ring network will not pass traffic at 4 Mbps. They often question this finding. The nearest analogy to explain this is that of the top speed of a passenger vehicle. The vehicle may have a top speed of 125 mph but failure to read the fine print can disappoint the owner. This speed was only reached on the test track with special tires, a professional driver, a very recent tune-up and extra high test gasoline. If the ordinary run-of-the-mill LAN received the same type of tuning and attention, it may reach the 4-Mbps specification noted. Other than that, the LAN Manager should be satisfied with between 2–2½ Mbps. One other consideration when measuring the bit rate in the LAN is whether or not there is sufficient subscriber-generated traffic to stress the LAN. Without loading, the question is moot.

The next point concerning measurement of the bit rate is: How heavily or lightly loaded is the LAN? If the LAN is supporting an organization that maintains normal business hours, with one shift, the LAN will exhibit two daily usage peaks. One peak occurs somewhere between 9 and 11:30 AM; the second peak occurs somewhere between 1:30 and 4:00 PM. If the organization's product or service is cyclical or based on seasonal fluctuations, the peak may be higher in one cycle or season than the other. Therefore, when measuring throughput, the LAN Manager must know what peaks, and cycles of peaks, affect the supported organization.

This measurement activity produces objective data that the LAN Manager can use to support the argument for redesigning the LAN in order to provide subscribers with useful telecommunications services. Redesign does not always require the addition of new and expensive hardware and software. If the LAN is subdivided into subLANs, perhaps the subdivisions need to be reevaluated and some of the subscriber's taps moved to a less heavily loaded section. If the LAN is monolithic, an increase in certain parameters of subscriber equipment may increase the response speed noted by the subscribers.

One of the more common pieces of LAN hardware is a terminal server. Each subscriber connection to the terminal server may be set at different speeds in bits per second.

Another piece of common LAN hardware is the modem. Some modems have switches mounted on the inside or outside. These switches set the speed at which the modem operates. If the transmission media can accommodate the higher speeds, the LAN Manager should set the modems to this higher speed, decreasing the response time for the subscriber.

A word of caution is needed at this point. Transmission media, or some of the equipment attached to it is limited in throughput. The most common example is that of WAN/VAN-vendor–provided circuits. Without special preparation, most of these circuits can operate no faster than 2400 bps. If a modem can transmit and receive traffic at 9600 bps and is attached to one of these circuits, very little if any improvement will be noted. In fact, the subscriber may not even be able to communicate after the modem's speed is changed to the 9600-bps setting. Because of these limitations, the LAN Manager must have configuration management information handy. Configuration management was the subject matter of Chapter 4.

If these minor adjustments, tuning adjustments actually, do not solve throughput problems, they show that the LAN Manager has done everything possible before beginning the more expensive process of purchasing and installing new hardware and software required in support of increased traffic loading in the LAN. The strategy for procuring and installing new hardware and software is based on the politics of the supported organization. No specific guidance can be offered without a thorough knowledge of the organization, but certain general guidance is always applicable.

Traffic delays and subscriber dissatisfaction do not contribute to improved productivity in the supported organization. Therefore, anything that does increase such productivity has cleared the first hurdle. Any hardware or software procured that can reduce the total LAN equipment population may also be viewed in a favorable light. Fewer technicians and engineers may be required to support the new equipment. Any purchase that reduces costs for WAN/VAN-provided circuits should also be well received. If certain types of equipment fail with depressing regularity, creating reduced throughput, the LAN Manager should have records showing this constant failure. Perhaps such equipment should be replaced, increasing reliability, throughput, and subscriber satisfaction simultaneously.

Protocol Functions

Almost all LANs in use today use one or more protocols to ensure that accurate packetized data is being used for information interchange. Unfortunately these packets can still be transmitted or received in error. All packets should be evaluated randomly or periodically.

Evaluating these packets requires a protocol analyzer. This text is not a vehicle for discussing the pros and cons of various vendors' products in this field. A good protocol analyzer with all required functions should cost one-half of an engineer's annual salary.

One of the major purposes of a protocol analyzer is to identify defective packets. Defective packets are bad for the LAN for several reasons. Although it is highly unlikely that a destination will accept a defective packet, such circumstances are statistically possible. "Possible" in this instance means chances in excess of 1×10^{-7}. This does not mean that it cannot happen. What is the impact of a defective packet?

Consider the following information. Using Ethernet, packets can range in size from 60 through 1542 bits. If the bits in that packet contained information concerning a multimillion-dollar-profit order, information pertaining to stock offers, or electronic funds transfer, the impact on the supported organization could be nothing short of catastrophic.

Protocol analyzers can evaluate packets in speeds of up to 10 million bits per second. With the appropriate programming, these analyzers can find every defective packet that transits the LAN. Once the defective packets are found, the analyzer can electronically dissect the packet and find its origin. Some of the better quality protocol analyzers can even "decode" the contents of a packet.

Once the source of defective packets has been found, troubleshooting must be done. Assume, for the sake of discussion, that a terminal server is producing bad packets at random intervals. The LAN Manager must decide to either replace the device or troubleshoot it on the spot. Unless she thinks the restoration can be completed in less than two to three minutes, the LAN Manager is advised to replace the defective device with a spare and do the troubleshooting on a bench. The protocol analyzer can also be used to do this type of bench troubleshooting under certain circumstances. In some repair facilities, complete LANs are duplicated for no other purpose than to troubleshoot defective equipment.

The LAN Manager gains more than just returning a defective piece of equipment to service after the terminal server is repaired. Every time a defective packet is transmitted, the intended receiver requests a retransmission of a correct version of the defective packet. Assume that there were four terminal servers on one subLAN. Each terminal server produced 1 percent defective packets. Based on this data, the LAN is running at 4 percent less than optimum. But this is not all. For every defective packet that is retransmitted, a message must go to the originator of the packet, requesting retransmission. Therefore, the increased load on the LAN will be greater than the 4 percent generated by the terminal servers. An 8 percent increase in traffic is not unheard of under these circumstances. By reducing these unnecessary requests for retransmission, and the resulting repeat transmission of packets, the LAN Manager has increased the throughput of the LAN.

Measure Response Time

Response time is the time it takes for a user to get an action resulting from a file transfer or to log in to a host. Response time varies depending on, among other things, LAN traffic loading.

Response time can be measured three ways:

1 With a stopwatch
2 With an oscilloscope and/or protocol analyzer
3 With software built into some types of communications equipment

Since the third method is vendor dependent, it is not discussed in this text. Either of the first two methods may be employed, but the stopwatch approach is recommended for routine applications. Measuring response time with an oscilloscope is technological overkill unless a laboratory situation is encountered.

The simplest measurement that may be taken is that of logging into a host. Normally the subscriber must enter his name and password. The time measurement begins when the subscriber enters the last digit of the password, or presses the carriage return key. The more complicated measurement is that of file transfer. A test file of 100,000 bits or so should be prepared. The length of time it takes to transmit and/or receive this file from one source to a sink should be measured.

What is to be done with these measurements? As the LAN matures, or, as its configuration changes, traffic loading patterns change, and the subscriber load changes. The LAN Manager has no way of knowing the impact of these changes without constantly measuring the LAN for different characteristics. One of the more prominent of these is that of response time. By constantly measuring the response time as discussed earlier, the LAN Manager has a historical record of past performance. From this, the LAN Manager can extrapolate the degradation of future performance.

All this action has one goal: a more satisfied subscriber. If response times are adequate, the LAN Manager can spend more time on management and less time on answering complaints. This also gives the LAN Manager more time to plan future growth.

Measurement Supports Several Management Functions

LAN management supports three LAN Management functions: fault management, accounting management, and performance management.

Fault Management

In certain types of LANs, response time does have a linkage to the throughput of that network. Any fault that reduces throughput will increase response time. Why does this linkage exist? Assume there is a modem in the LAN that creates, under fault conditions, extra traffic. This is normally known as either a "streaming" or "screaming" modem. As long as the erroneous traffic from the modem is occupying and thereby consuming bandwidth, throughput is lessened from all other sources of traffic. As throughput goes down, response time increases.

In some types of packet-based LANs, packets can collide. When they do, the intended receiver cannot understand them. Therefore, the LAN Manager must have some way to measure the quality of the packets that are on the LAN. Occasionally a protocol analyzer is required to determine collisions.

In a packet-based LAN, defective packets can be created. The intended receiver cannot understand defective packets. Alternatively, packets that are created correctly can become garbled and distorted in transmission. This distortion process is common. When the quantity of distorted or defective packets exceeds a given percentage, troubleshooting must begin. As a rule of thumb, if more than 1 percent of packets are defective on receipt, someone should be investigating the cause(s). Once again, a protocol analyzer is required to determine the conditions of the packets on the LAN.

Measurement of the LAN in support of fault management

will also find defective circuits. One of the more common problems on a circuit is a low signal-to-noise ratio. This means that the noise on the circuit is loud enough to overcome the desired signal. Common causes of noise include motor brushes, fluorescent lamps, and electrical welding devices. Another somewhat prevalent type of "noise" is cross-talk from wires that carry other signals, yet are in very close physical proximity to the circuit under test. Other types of common defects found include circuits that are shorted, that is, two conductors are touching; or circuits that are open, that is, there is a break in one or more of the conductors.

Accounting Management

When you want to use the chargeback method to bill subscribers for their use of LAN services, you need a way to determine who uses how much of the available bandwidth. Measurement of how much bandwidth is in use as well as measurement of the sinks and sources of traffic that consume that bandwidth are required. Although how such measurements are made is not the subject of this text, it is sufficient to say that the topology and topography of each LAN determines the measurement process.

Performance Management

The relationship between throughput and response time was discussed earlier. What was not mentioned was the scope of the measurements required. When the performance of the entire LAN is being measured, more than one subscriber or more than one host must be part of the effort. The LAN Manager should have available the performance characteristics of each circuit within the LAN. These characteristics should show how much of the bandwidth is consumed on a routine basis and what peaks and valleys of usage exist. Why is this information required?

If one part of the LAN is working at an average of 12 percent of capacity, and another part is working at 66 percent of capacity, and both are carrying traffic from the same sources to the same sinks, would it not make sense to balance the loading of both parts equally? Yet how can the LAN Manager balance this traffic loading without measuring the bandwidth consumption? What the LAN Manager must do is to measure all of the LAN.

TMDE Type and Applications

Throughout this text the acronym TMDE has been used frequently. Test, Measurement, and Diagnostic Equipment is an extension of human senses. By putting a screwdriver across the terminals of a battery (dumb!), most people can tell if it is charged or not. But how much of a charge does hold? If enough money is available, the charge can be measured to six decimal places.

Time Domain Reflectometer

As was discussed earlier, the time domain reflectometer determines the quality of the transmission media. It does this by injecting a pulse of known frequency and amplitude into the transmission media and measuring the time it takes to receive the reflection of that pulse. A strong received pulse indicates a defect that is either major or close by in the transmission media. Conversely, a weak received pulse indicates a minor or distant defect.

As the pulse injected into the transmission media travels at a known speed, it is easy to compute the distance traveled by measuring the time from injection of the pulse to the time of reception of the pulse. This figure is then divided by the known speed of the pulse. The answer is the distance, in either feet or meters, to the fault. The same concept applies to optical time domain reflectometers that are used with fiber optic cable. When purchasing either type, the LAN Manager must ensure that a cathode ray tube display is selected. Usually, the higher the price paid, the better the quality of the time domain reflectometer.

Oscilloscopes

An oscilloscope is perhaps the most versatile piece of TMDE the LAN Manager can use. It can show wave shapes, the amplitude of transmitted or received bits, or the level of noise in the circuit. When determining which oscilloscope to buy, the prime consideration is the working bandwidth. Most nonfiber optic LANs do not need an oscilloscope with bandwidth of over 30 megahertz. Oscilloscopes with digital storage capability are very useful. They are also rather expensive.

Meters

The DMM (digital multimeter) can be used to measure voltage, current, and resistance. DMMs come in two "flavors," industrial and laboratory quality. The industrial flavor is used in field work, where a lack of accuracy does not hinder the user. The laboratory quality DMM is used where precision measurements are required. When purchasing the industrial flavor DMM, ruggedness is the most important parameter. Such a DMM should be able to withstand a 6-foot drop, to a concrete floor, without affecting either its physical integrity or functionality. The parameter of highest importance in a laboratory DMM is accuracy. A minimum accuracy for a laboratory DMM should be one part in one thousand.

Break-Out Boxes

The break-out box is used to test for the presence or absence of a certain signal at pin connectors on the various sizes of D connectors so prevalent in LAN equipment. This presence or absence of signal is noted by light-emitting diodes. If the diode is lit, the signal is present; if not, the signal is absent. The break-out box's functionality is almost directly related to price. The higher the price paid, the more useful the device.

Other TMDE

The LAN Manager should know about several other types of TMDE. If a broadband LAN is in use, a spectrum analyzer can show the presence, absence, and relative amplitude of the signals that are on the backbone cable. A frequency counter can be used to ascertain the frequencies of signals on the LAN. The frequency counter can also be used to check the timing signals that are required in some types of LAN equipment. A signal generator can be used to substitute for signals that are thought to be in error or missing altogether. When selecting these types of TMDE, accuracy and linearity are the prime factors to consider.

Protocol Analyzers

There is some discussion whether a protocol analyzer is a piece of TMDE or whether it is a computer. As a rule of thumb, if it must be calibrated, it is a piece of TMDE. The protocol analyzer is not, under normal circumstances, calibrated.

An in-depth explanation of the capabilities and applications of protocol analyzers requires the same depth of understanding of the protocols in use in the LAN. Therefore, only some of the functions of these devices will be discussed.

Packet Analysis: Packet analysis shows the user the condition of the captured packet. Is it of the correct size? Are all the control bits present? Is the checksum correct?

Traffic Capture: Traffic capture allows the user to capture all packets coming from a source or going to a sink. This is particularly useful when a host is thought to be transmitting defective packets. It can also be used to find the address of unknown traffic.

Traffic Generation: If the LAN Manager wants to determine the impact of heavy loads on the LAN, the protocol analyzer can be used to generate artificial traffic. The quantity of bandwidth consumed is adjustable as a percentage of the bandwidth available on the LAN. In the wrong hands, this traffic generation capability can bring the LAN to a crashing stop! Because of this danger, traffic generation should be used with great care.

The protocol analyzer can also be used to measure the amount of traffic that flows from one part of the LAN to another. This source-to-sink report is used to show what parts of the LAN are generating and receiving the most traffic at what time(s) of the day.

Calibration

Earlier in this section, we stated that TMDE was an extension of human senses. If this extension does not report accurately, it is less than useless. An inaccurate indication leads to misplaced troubleshooting efforts. Most manufacturers recommend cyclical calibration periods. The LAN Manager should plan to keep the TMDE calibrated in accordance with these recommendations. The calibration procedures and the standards used should be traceable to the National Institute for Science and Technology.

Summary

In discussing LAN measurements, this chapter covered the following topics:

- Why measurements must be taken

- What measurements are used for, including
  — Performance management
  — Fault management
  — LAN growth
  — Usage or budget data
  — WAN/VAN billing evaluation

- The measurement of transmission media, including
  — Applications of time domain reflectometers
  — Signal-to-noise ratios
  — Nonmetallic transmission media

- The measurement of throughput and the impact of such measurements

- The impact of protocol functions with the LAN

- The measurement of response time

- How measurement supports LAN management, including
  — Accounting management
  — Fault management
  — Performance management

- Types of TMDE, including
  — Time domain reflectometer
  — Oscilloscopes
  — Digital multimeters
  — Break out boxes
  — Protocol analyzers

Case Study

Section 1: Factual Data

The firm involved is a small manufacturing firm with one plant in a medium-sized town in the northeastern part of the United

States. Their product line is not consumer oriented; almost all sales are to other manufacturers. Their LAN was a small one, less than 30 subscribers on a CSMA/CD (Ethernet) topology. As certain industries grew, the demand for this firm's product increased proportionately. This in turn led to a demand for people, and, of course, more connections to the LAN. Some subscribers, noticeably in the engineering department, complained of increased delay times when accessing another host in the organization. The original LAN had been sold to this firm by a vendor who was no longer in business. The operations manager contacted a consultant and asked him to evaluate the LAN in light of increased traffic loading.

Section 2: What Happened

The consultant came in, looked around, talked to everyone, took a lot of notes, and went away. Shortly thereafter, he returned with a report listing what he thought the problems were and how they could be eliminated. And, by the way, he could offer the firm a very good price on just the hardware necessary to fix the problem. The operations manager must have been around this track before. She took the consultant's plans to another person who was also technically astute. This person's opinion was that the consultant could not have come to this conclusion without some type of traffic analysis, and that he would like to see the consultants' notes and findings. In the end, the consultant was paid for his report and no more. Someone else modified LAN by using routers to route traffic to where it belonged, reducing the delay time noted by the engineering department.

Section 3: Losses

Once again, big financial losses were not involved in this case. The firm continued to operate, it made a profit, and the problems were not so bad that people voluntarily resigned. But no matter how small or insignificant the losses were, this firm was in a reactive mode.

Section 4: Lessons Learned

Someone should have been measuring the traffic loading. Growth of the organization will, in most cases, cause increases in LAN traffic. These increases, unless planned for in advance, will have a negative effect on the firm. Even in a firm this small, someone should have been tracking the increased traffic loading and been prepared to modify the LAN to support such increased traffic.

9 *Standards*

standard Anything recognized as correct by common consent, by approved custom, or by those most competent to decide; a model; a type; a pattern; a criterion.

—Webster's New Twentieth-Century Dictionary

Standards, like goals, are things that, if achieved, make everyone a success and create good feelings among all who are affected. But, like goals, standards are not always achieved and they can mean different things to different people. This chapter discusses

- Philosophy concerning data communications standards
- Types of data communications standards that exist
- What standards are applied to LANs
- Impact of standards on the LAN Manager's functions.

There also will be a short discursion into the area of LAN management standards and their impact on the LAN Manager.

Philosophy of Standards

Data communications standards are inherently a set of commonly agreed-to rules concerning the methods by which two or more subscribers transmit and receive data. When promulgating standards, the standards-making bodies are torn between two goals that are constantly in tension. The first goal is to provide a commonly acceptable set of rules for everyone to use. Yet once these rules have been accepted, such acceptance has a tendency to freeze the growth of the future development of technology. The second goal is to create a standard that does not freeze future development. The standard must be capable of modification. Once modified, it can still be perceived as a standard.

Types of Standards

There are two levels of LAN standards: international and vendor specific. LAN standards (standards hereafter) are created by two types of bodies, those with legal standing (that is, based on international treaty) and those that are advisory. Those with legal standing are discussed first.

International Standards

Two bodies establish the international telecommunications standards:

- International Telecommunications Union (ITU)
- Consultative Committee International Telephone and Telegraph (CCITT)

The CCITT is subordinate to and part of the ITU. Other parts of the ITU concern themselves with movement of mail or postage rates for international mail. Both bodies are legally recognized by the United Nations. Each member nation of the CCITT provides technical input to the CCITT concerning telecommunications standards. This input comes from organizations that have parity with the United States Department of State. Other groups that provide technical input include the ministers of post, telephone, and telegraph (PTTs) and regional private telecommunications operating agencies (RPOA). In the United States, RPOAs include inter- and intra-LATA (Local Access Transport Areas) common carriers such as AT&T or MCI.

The CCITT receives input from nontreaty recognized organizations as well. This input is funneled through the International Standards Organization (ISO). The ISO is a manufacturer's organization. Each national member of the ISO receives guidance from organizations within his own country. In the United States, such guidance is presented by the American National Standards Institute (ANSI). ANSI, in turn, receives guidance from different sources. Guidance comes from organizations such as the Electronics Industry Association (EIA) or the International Association of Electrical and Electronics Engineers (IEEE). Other input derives from organizations such as the Department of Defense or the National Institute of Standards and Technology (NIST). NIST used to be known as the National Bureau of Standards (NBS).

Two of the most common standards with which LAN Managers should be familiar are IEEE 802.3 and IEEE 802.5. This is not the ISO nomenclature for these standards. Refer to Appendix A for more information on ISO standard nomenclature.

The IEEE 802.3 standard is sometimes known as Ethernet. Although they are similar, they are not the same. A LAN that operates in strict conformance with IEEE 802.3 cannot communicate with a LAN that strictly conforms to Ethernet standards. Therefore, the LAN Manager must be careful not to mix these standards without some type of gateway to do the appropriate signaling conversions. The same situation does not apply to token ring standards. The IEEE 802.5 standard describes the specifications of a token ring LAN. Reportedly the largest vendor of token ring LANs is International Business Machines (IBM). An IEEE 802.5 token ring LAN can communicate with an IBM token ring LAN. One standard that LAN Managers should also be aware of is that of X.25 (packet switched) data communications. This standard is used by many VAN vendors for their commercial offerings. The X.25 standard is also used by the United States Department of Defense. The X.25 standard has been accepted by the CCITT and was made an official international telecommunications standard.

Vendor-Specific Standards

Many organizations create LAN standards for the most basic reason, to make a profit. They assume that if someone buys their equipment, this buyer will be locked into brand loyalty. One of the more common vendor specific standards is that of Ethernet. This standard was created by the Xerox Corporation for its own market. Many other vendors copied Ethernet for the purpose of selling their specific equipment to Xerox's customer base. Ethernet is so widespread that a user can buy hardware and software to allow IBM's products to use Xerox's communications standard. Datapoint's ARCNET claims to have the largest installed base of LAN communications hardware and software.

The OSI Model

The International Standards Organization has created a seven-layer data communications model known as the Open Systems Interconnect (OSI) model. Each layer in the model performs one or more specific data communications functions or has specific descriptions for these functions. Each layer in the model is either a client or a server for the layer above it or below it, respectively. Figure 9.1 shows the relationship between the layers of the OSI model schematically.

It is all well and good to know what the OSI model is, and how it is created. The next obvious step in this process is to define the elements, the layers, and very briefly discuss what each layer does. Each of the seven layers performs one or more specific data communications functions in the form of services and protocols.

Physical Layer (Layer 1)

The physical layer identifies the electromechanical connectivity between the subscriber's equipment and the network to which it is attached. Mechanical identification includes such parameters as pin layout and cable connector sizes and forms. The electronic identification includes parameters such as voltage and current levels or modulation techniques in use. Many people associate the V series of modem identifications with the Physical Level.

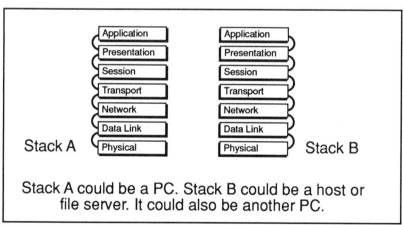

Stack A could be a PC. Stack B could be a host or file server. It could also be another PC.

FIGURE 9.1

Data Link (Layer 2)

The Data Link Layer specifications have control over the procedures used to format frames and packets of data for transmission. If frames are too large, they are divided into multiple smaller frames for transmission. Frame and packet receipt mechanisms are also present in the Data Link Layer. A representative standard for this layer may be IEEE 802.3 CSMA/CD media access.

Network Layer (Layer 3)

The Network Layer ensures that packets that have been inserted into the network are routed to the appropriate destinations. This may also include routing and relaying between networks. The X.25 standard at the packet level is representative of Layer 3.

Transport (Layer 4)

The Transport Layer defines four functions: how to address the physical devices on the network, how to guarantee delivery of packets, how to set up and tear down connections, and finally how to internetwork packets. TCP/IP is an important part of the Transport Layer.

Session Layer (Layer 5)

The Session Layer is the lowest layer that is not directly concerned with data transport. It can be thought of as a conceptual boundary between the computation being performed and the network that is being used to access the computational capabalities. Name-to-address conversion takes place in the Session Layer. ISO standard 8327 represents some of the functionality within this layer of the Open Systems Interconnect model.

Presentation Layer (Layer 6)

The Presentation Layer provides data translation. Encryption can also take place at this level. The Presentation Layer takes data from the computer and presents it to the Session Layer or vice versa. CCITT X.410 is one of the protocols associated with the Presentation Layer.

Application Layer (Layer 7)

The Application Layer is almost totally computer oriented. It is used to define and control access to file servers, hosts, or other like devices. Electronic mail (E-Mail) is one of the more well known Application Layer functions. VTAM is one of the more well known protocols in the Application Layer.

Review

Remember that the model is just that, a model. All hardware or software vendors must build their products to this model. In addition to specifying the functions within each layer, the model specifies the format of the signals (I/O) that flow across the boundaries of each layer. Vendors are free to build inside each layer the hardware and software that they think are the most cost effective and technically elegant. The basis for the entire concept is that vendors whose products are totally compliant with the ISO model can be assured that their products will interoperate with any other vendors' products that meet the same specifications. This can have a major impact on the LAN Manager's decisions affecting the specification, purchase, installation, operation, maintenance, and management of LAN hardware and software.

Impact of Standards on the LAN Manager

Part of the LAN Manager's functions include specification, evaluation, procurement, installation, operation, and maintenance of the hardware and software that make up the LAN.

LAN hardware and software vendors will, at times, make claims that seem to imply that their hardware and software are totally in compliance with certain standards. It is the LAN Manager's responsibility to ensure that these vendors' claims are true and not just sales puffery. A vendor who claims his bus interface unit (BIU) operates within the constraints of such-and-such a standard should not hesitate to demonstrate such operations within the supported organization's LAN.

The LAN Manager with the good fortune to be working with a totally homogeneous LAN will have minimal standards problems. A totally homogeneous LAN could be one that is provided by a single vendor or one that complies to a specific standard: IEEE 802.3 or IEEE 802.5 for example. This usually is not the case; the LAN Manager must work within a heterogeneous LAN with mixed hardware and software standards.

The LAN Manager should, wherever possible, bring the LAN

to one set of common standards. These need not be the OSI model nor those of a particular vendor. These standards should be easily implemented, provide high-speed traffic (high throughput), and be reasonably robust. The selected standard should not be so esoteric that hardware and software do not exist to support it. The selected standard should be popular enough that a pool of available engineers and technicians are available for installation, operation, and maintenance. The standard should be transparent to subscribers; they should not have to memorize strange and exotic commands to use the hardware and software selected to implement this standard.

When selecting a standard for the LAN, the LAN Manager should be aware of the end points of the spectrum of possibilities. A vendor-specific standard such as Digital Equipment Corporation's DECNET is one end of such a spectrum. The other end of the spectrum is that of the International Standards Organization's Open Systems Interconnect (OSI) model. In general, the more heterogeneous the LAN, the less vendor-specific the selected standard should be. In a heterogeneous LAN, national or international standards should be used as the guiding principle in the purchase of new or additional hardware and software. If, on the other hand, a LAN is composed of one vendor's product line, that vendor's standard should be used for further procurement.

LAN Management Standards

As there are standards for the operation of the LAN, there are standards for its management as well. Chapter 2 discussed the five general areas of LAN Management. Any LAN Management standard must include all five of these functions. As with LAN standards, there are two types of LAN management standards, international and vendor-specific. The same comments made earlier concerning LAN standards apply to LAN management standards. This text addresses only the international LAN management standards, those promulgated by the International Standards Organization.

The following discussion touches very briefly on the five OSI Specific Management Functional Areas (SMFAs) and the functions performed within each area.

Accounting Management

There are two functions within accounting management, communications instance accounting and accessing accounting. These two functions are concerned with determination and assignment of operating costs.

Configuration Management

This includes object management, relationship management, and state management. Configuration management provides operational control over network hardware and software. It allows for the changing of operational parameters. Status information and association of names to managed objects takes place within the configuration management SMFA.

Fault Management

This includes two functions, error reporting/information retrieval and confidence and diagnostic testing. These two functions are self-defining. Error reporting concerns troubles on the LAN. Information retrieval is concerned with information pertinent to such errors. Confidence testing is a periodic evaluation of the LAN's functionality. Diagnostic testing applies to error conditions thought to be the cause of problems.

Performance Management

Four functions are performed within this SMFA: confidence and diagnostic testing, workload monitoring, response time monitoring; and statistical analysis. Confidence and diagnostic testing are somewhat the same as in the fault management SMFA. Workload monitoring is essentially concerned with LAN throughput. Response time monitoring is self-explanatory. Statistical analysis includes gathering and logging data.

Security Management

There are four functions within this SMFA: the audit trail, security alarm reporting, auditing and alarm reporting management, and security object and attribute management. The audit trail is a list of who did what and when. Security alarm reporting is what the name suggests, a report that indicates the triggering of some preset security parameter. Auditing and alarm reporting management is concerned with how such alarms are reported and followed up. Security object and attribute management is a type of configuration management for security devices and procedures.

One very important caveat should be made at this point. When this text was written, only four of the functions were at draft stage. These four were the error reporting/information retrieval, object management, relationship management, and state management. All other functions in the five SMFAs were at a lesser stage of readiness. Therefore, the final functionality may be quite different from what is discussed here.

Summary

This chapter touched very briefly on what standards are and how they affect the LAN and the LAN Manager's functions and duties. Many highly detailed texts, some of which are mentioned in Appendix A, are recommended for those who wish more knowledge in this area. This chapter covered the following topics:

- The philosophy of standards and why they are necessary.
- The two general types of standards
  — International
  — Vendor specific

- The Open Systems Interconnect (OSI) model
- The impact of standards on the LAN Manager's functions
- An early view of LAN management standards

10 Personnel in Network Management

We have met the enemy and he is us.
—*Pogo*

In addition to the technical aspects of LAN management, the LAN Manager must also be reasonably well grounded in the selection, training, motivation, guidance, and retention of people to staff the effort of LAN installation, operation, and maintenance. This chapter touches on three general areas of personnel management applied to those who make up the technical staff. These three areas are

1 Selection
2 Training
3 Prevention of personnel turnover

Selection of Personnel

Where does the LAN Manager get people when they are required? What procedures should be followed? What problems exist in this activity? The following section answers these questions.

Selection

Selection of new personnel does not necessarily begin outside of the current staff. Selection from within may help to retain those who are currently assigned. Perhaps the analyst who has been watching over the technician's shoulder may need just a little more formal, on-the-job training to be able to hold down the technician's position. If on-the-job training is not enough, perhaps vendor-specific training could fill in the few rough spots. Perhaps both of these, combined with a few additional college courses, would be sufficient. The answer depends on the individual, the organization, and the LAN in use.

Does the job description for a LAN Engineer really require a Bachelor's degree? Or perhaps, only a few college courses plus some vendor-specific training will qualify a technician for the title of LAN Engineer.

When will the senior LAN Engineer be ready to perform the functions of the assistant LAN Manager? What additional training in management areas are required? Does the senior LAN Engineer aspire to the position of assistant LAN Manager? The LAN Manager must be able to rely on one or more persons to fill in for him during scheduled or unscheduled absences.

Costs of New Employees

Like every other part of any business, the selection of LAN staff must be looked at for excessive costs. Pity the poor personnel manager. In boom times, the personnel manager cannot find people to fill a position at any price. When businesses are in a recession or depression, there is no need to hire additional people. The personnel manager loses under both conditions. The LAN Manager must look to the personnel manager to obtain likely candidates to fill vacancies on the LAN staff.

How much does it cost to fill a position on the LAN staff? Assume there are no advertising costs for the position. That is, someone told a friend that a vacancy exists and several applicants show up to apply for it. The time spent in reviewing resumes, performing interviews, screening the applicants' forms, and negotiations with suitable applicants can take hours. All of these hours are paid for by the supported firm. Now, if advertising is necessary, additional costs are incurred by placing the vacancy announcement in one or more publications. If potential applicants come from far away, the supported organization may have to pay transportation and lodging costs for the purpose of the interview.

If vacancy announcements are not successful in finding acceptable applicants, the supported organization must resort to placement agencies. These firms will provide anything from a handful of résumés to carefully screened lists of potential employees. The more work the placement agency performs before the applicant is interviewed, the more that service may cost. As a minimum, the supported organization may have to pay such agencies the equivalent of one to two months of the new employee's salary. Even then, there is no guarantee that the new employee will be any more satisfactory than someone who walks in off the street. As a rule of thumb, the cost of one new hire can be as high as one-third to one-half of that person's annual salary.

Interviews

The LAN Manager must remember several points when beginning the interview and screening process for a new hire.

Legalities

Certain questions may not be asked of an applicant for a given position. Questions concerning race, creed, color, religious preference, or physical condition are not allowed unless they can clearly be shown to be related to the tasks to be performed. The following examples are just that, examples. They are not specific guidance for any interviews for any LAN staff position.

An applicant's age cannot be directly questioned, but it is acceptable to ask "Are you between 18 and 70?" An acceptable question pertaining to national origin would be "Are you a U.S. citizen?" Questions pertinent to fluency in other languages should be used only if the applicant will be required to speak that language on the job. Questions about physical disabilities should be phrased somewhat like: "Do you have any physical, medical, or mental disabilities that would prohibit you from performing the job of LAN technician?" Questions about financial conditions should be limited to: "Where are you living now?" "Do you have reliable transportation to and from work?" "Where can you be reached in an emergency?" Questions concerning marital status or children can be very touchy to some people. Perhaps the best single way to phrase such questions is "Do you have any other responsibilities that will interfere with your ability to be a prompt, regular employee?" Questions concerning a criminal record can be covered with "Have you ever been convicted of a crime? If so, please give details." Some applicants belong to the military reserve or National Guard. One way to find out about such activities is to ask, "Do you have any continuing military obligations that will interfere with your job performance?" Any question asked must be in some way job related, yet not attributable to any type of prejudice or even hint of prejudice. The LAN Manager should work very closely with the personnel manager when developing questions for interviews.

Testing

Avoid testing. If, after much thought, the LAN Manager feels a test is necessary, the test must be very carefully written. Each part or question on a test for applicants must be directly related to the job performed. The following examples should be evaluated very carefully before being used.

The various types of LAN hardware use different color lamps or light-emitting diodes to indicate operational status. Therefore, it may be legitimate to test potential LAN staff members for color perception. Which members of the LAN staff will be required to read blueprints and schematics? Tests for the ability to identify the symbols and figures used on blueprints and schematics could be shown to be job related. Should mathematical abilities be tested? Only if the applicant will be required to perform those same computations. Some typical mathematical functions may include computation of power budgets, gain or loss in decibels, or conversion from English to metric and vice versa. Reading comprehension is very difficult to justify for some LAN staff applicants.

Any test questions should be keyed to the job description. If a test is required, the LAN Manager should get very close cooperation from the personnel and legal department in creating such tests. Most courts have held that if the test pertains solely to work performed, it is acceptable. However, very few employers want to take the time and money necessary to have a court, or series of courts, review such tests. In conclusion, do not test unless absolutely necessary.

References

Most résumés have two types of references, personal and professional. Both sets of references must be checked as closely as time and monetary restrictions allow. Professional references are probably the easiest to check. Further, the LAN Manager can get a good "feel" for an applicant from these. One word of caution on checking professional references: many of these references are the applicant's current employer or fellow worker(s). Before contacting these people, the LAN Manager should obtain the applicant's specific permission to do so. This is particularly true if one or more of the references are the applicant's supervisor(s).

Once the decision has been made to check the professional references, the check must be as thorough as possible. Although it is easy to call the telephone numbers given, the LAN Manager may wish to ensure that such numbers correspond to the person or firm listed as a professional reference. The same guidance can be applied to membership in professional societies, publications, and schools. The applicant may claim a Bachelor's degree from a school on the East Coast. However a West Coast LAN Manager may not know the reputation of that particular school. The school may be real or it may be a mail box in some small town. Regional scholastic accreditation bodies can also assist in this type of reference checking. There may actually be such a school that offers a Bachelor's program, but is the school or program accredited? While on the subject of scholastic achievement, the LAN Manager may also wish a copy of the applicant's grade transcript. Two points should be made concerning transcripts. They cost the applicant money, and they are not reliable if the raised seal or notarized certificate of authenticity is absent. Because the applicant must spend money to get such a transcript, the LAN Manager should offer to reimburse the applicant for out-of-pocket expenses involved in such documentation.

If the applicant indicates several publications to his or her credit, the LAN Manager may wish to ask for copies of them for review. This serves two purposes: to verify the accuracy of the claim, and to evaluate the applicant's depth of technical knowledge or communications skills. Membership in professional societies can be verified by membership cards or correspondence with the societies in question.

Personal references should be used to evaluate the applicant's ability to mesh with the rest of the LAN Manager's staff. If the applicant for the position is a four-season athlete, and the rest of the staff think that sweat is a dirty word, friction may result. If the applicant is a "workaholic" and the rest of the staff is quite "laid back," the result may be a dissatisfied employee. A word of caution should be given on the subject of personal references. Many personal references should be taken with a large grain of salt. Personal references are often thought to be the friends of the applicant. This is not always the case. It is amazing how little money it will take to motivate some types of people to lie, cheat, and steal.

Security

There are security aspects to be aware of when selecting new personnel for the LAN Manager's staff. Was the applicant's previous employer a competitor of the potential new employee? Anyone who works with the LAN can, under certain conditions, have access to proprietary or confidential information. If this information is leaked to a competitor, what would the result be? Caution is advised under these circumstances.

An alternative set of conditions could apply. A competitor could approach someone, an engineer for example, and offer him two jobs for the time spent in one. The engineer would be employed by a given employer, working on that employer's LAN. At the same time he could be performing industrial espionage for his employer's competition and drawing a good salary for his efforts. One of the problems with using such people is that they can never be trusted not to sell out to the competition, or not to work for even another competitor at the same time.

Those potential employees who have been convicted of crimes of moral turpitude are not always suitable for some positions on the LAN Manager's staff. People who fit in this category can fill positions that do not have access to proprietary or confidential data. A technician does not have to be able to log in to a database on a file server to check the operation of that file server. The technician can accept the approval of a subscriber for whatever repair or restoration was performed. Those who have been convicted of a crime of moral turpitude can fill an engineering position that is concerned with LAN design or equipment evaluation.

When evaluating his or her staff, the LAN Manager may wish to consider two types of protection: commercial bonding and life insurance.

Bonding

Commercial bonding provides financial compensation to the supported organization if the bonded individual does something to harm that organization. Some bonding agencies do in-depth background investigations on the person(s) to be bonded. This does not necessarily mean that the applicant is to be trusted, but it does mean that there is no obvious reason not to trust the applicant. Once again, this is a business decision. How much does it cost to obtain bonding for an employee? Will the amount of the bond compensate the supported organization if the employee turns bad? Is the cost of the bond greater than the potential loss? If so, what is the sense of getting the bond?

Life Insurance

Life insurance should be considered for the person(s) the LAN Manager considers indispensable. Such policies are paid for by the supported organization, and that organization is the beneficiary of the policy. The aim of such policies is to cover any potential losses that may occur between time of the insured's death and the time a replacement is fully functional.

One final comment on bonding and insurance. Very, very few organizations find the need to bond or insure LAN staff. These people are not key to the continuing function of the supported organization, and they can normally be replaced by temporary workers with some degree of facility. Bonding and insurance is an expense most LAN Managers will never have to budget for.

Training for LAN Staff

Training is different from education. Education is general in nature and does not apply to a given piece of hardware or software. Training, on the other hand, is directed solely to one objective. A textbook definition of training is "to create a measurable change in behavior." Such training is usually directed toward specific components of the LAN or TMDE that supports the LAN. Two types of LAN staff require a formal training program: newly hired engineers and technicians.

Engineer Training

Someone who has completed at least a Bachelor's degree in electrical engineering, computer science, or telecommunications has very little need for further general education to become a productive member of the LAN staff. However, the engineer may need training in the vendor-specific equipment. Most engineers know quite well how a multiplexer works, but may not know how to program, install, operate, or troubleshoot the particular model in use within the LAN. Vendor-specific training can bring this engineer to a higher level of productivity. The engineer should have some exposure to the device before attending such training and the opportunity to practice the newly acquired skills afterwards.

Engineers also need additional training in supervisory functions. Perhaps the most common supervisory function includes assigning work to those present who have the capabilities to perform it. Another supervisory function is the ability to be a problem solver for those who need such assistance. Evaluating the performance of subordinates is still a third supervisory activity that is not always taught in engineering schools. One of the more important training topics for newly hired engineers is an understanding of the organization that the LAN supports. In most organizations, newly hired engineers are expected to understand the organization through osmosis. This is the same as trial-and-error learning. It is expensive, and accidents can happen.

Those who have responsibility for directing the actions of others or for controlling corporate resources fall into three distinct levels. The lowest is that of supervisor; the next higher is that of manager. A manager has all the responsibilities of a supervisor, plus control over real assets. The third and highest level is that of leadership. Fortunately, or unfortunately, leadership can show up in every level of the organization. The LAN Manager who is blessed with supervisory engineers who also exhibit the finest traits of leadership is very lucky. Otherwise, the LAN Manager must learn, develop and practice leadership for all of the LAN staff.

Technician Training

Technicians, even inexperienced ones, may not need training on all types of hardware and software in the LAN. Yet, certain vendor-specific training can be as useful to the technician as it is to the engineer. Many technicians are capable of doing more than just installation, troubleshooting, and replacement of defective equipment. The LAN Manager must evaluate the technicians for additional abilities.

One of the jobs a technician may be able to perform with additional training is statistical analysis of LAN performance characteristics. Such analyses include Mean Time To Repair (MTTR), Mean Time Between Failure (MTBF), and bandwidth consumption. Much of this type of training can be given by those who work in the firm or by local colleges and universities.

A very important type of training for technicians is that of subscriber relations. For most subscribers, the technician is the LAN Manager's most visible representative. The LAN Manager must ensure that the technicians can project a professional, concerned image while they are going about their assigned duties. On the other hand, the technicians cannot allow themselves to be bullied or distracted from their tasks because of other immediate problems. To be able to discern the difference between assigned duties and ad hoc assistance may require very specific training and direct guidance from the LAN Manager.

Part of keeping the subscriber satisfied is ensuring that the problem the technician was called to fix has been fixed to the subscriber's satisfaction. The technician, engineer, or LAN Manager can perform such activities by providing appropriate quality control measures. The methods used for such quality control will vary from organization to organization. The LAN Manager is best qualified to determine the proper approach for the organization.

The technician may also need training in how to keep appropriate records of LAN performance, maintenance activities, and costs of repair functions. LAN performance includes things such as response time, throughput, or outages. Maintenance activities can include handling trouble tickets, installing and removing hardware and software, and testing transmission media. Costs include man-hours expended, the cost of repair parts or external repair actions, and calibration procedures for TMDE. Training in these areas should be built around the supported organization's internal procedures for accounting and bookkeeping.

Other Professional Training

Both the engineers and the technicians assigned to the LAN staff need constant professional retraining and updates on new technology as it applies to the LAN. Some of this can come from reading trade literature, vendor's literature, and professional journals. This is not enough in most cases. Engineers and technicians should attend at least one trade show or professional society meeting each year. This not only allows for cross-pollination of ideas, but also exposure to new technology and practices. Oh, yes, the LAN Manager should do the same thing. By encouraging the LAN staff to prepare articles for trade journals or society publications, the LAN Manager is encouraging the LAN staff to learn new skills and keep abreast of current and future technologies.

Nonprofessional Training

Those who are neither engineers nor technicians, yet are members of the LAN staff, need training as well. The major drawback to providing formal training for these people is that they do not have the base of knowledge for training to build on. A well-thought-out and carefully applied formal program of on-the-job training may begin to build such a base. These people should be encouraged to attend local trade schools, colleges, and universities to build a base of knowledge that formal training and daily experience will be able to convert into useful capabilities.

Preventing Turnover

Those who are well versed in personnel management know that it is cheaper to retain present employees than it is to hire new ones. This section discusses actions the LAN Manager should take to prevent voluntary termination of well-qualified LAN staff.

Challenging Work

A recent survey of the types of people who would be working on the LAN staff indicates that the single biggest reason for voluntary termination is a lack of congruency between work performed and work desired. The LAN Manager is responsible to ensure that the LAN staff is assigned work that is personally and professionally challenging.

Engineers are perhaps the most difficult members of the LAN staff to offer work to that is technically challenging. By the time the engineer has learned all the hardware and software within the LAN, most of his efforts will consist of minor LAN redesign activities. If the engineer is competent in hardware, the LAN Manager may wish to offer the engineer a chance to become more proficient in the software that is part of the LAN. The opposite is also true. If the engineer is strong in software skills, a chance to build strengths in hardware skills should be offered.

Technicians are somewhat easier to offer work that is technically challenging. Technicians, as a group, do not have the depth of technical expertise that is found in engineers. By offering technicians the challenge of learning engineering-level skills, the LAN Manager gives the technicians the chance to stretch themselves and by doing so learn the boundaries of their abilities.

Analysts who lack sufficient technical skills to benefit from such technically challenging work provide the LAN Manager with another type of problem. How can a person with little technical knowledge be offered work that is not boring, but also not beyond this person's ability to learn from?

One way in which all members of the LAN staff can be offered technically challenging work is to form them into teams. Control and direction of the team will rotate among team members for the duration of a given project or activity. After completion of the activity or project, each team member offers constructive criticism of the actions of the rest of the team members. This type of activity is dangerous. If one team member is rated by another team member in the annual review process, constructive criticisms may not be quite as frank as they should be.

No matter which method(s) are chosen to ensure that the staff is offered technically challenging work, the LAN Manager must realize that certain people have limitations, either inherent or self-limited. We have known those who were superb technicians, but when placed in a supervisory position, turned out to be totally inept. Perhaps an engineer is content doing nothing more than programming, and the technician is perfectly satisfied doing bench work. LAN Managers are responsible for knowing their staff's limitations, desires, and goals. Only by applying this knowledge can LAN Managers offer them technically challenging work.

Personal And Professional Growth

If members of the LAN staff are not satisfied with their current position and working conditions, the LAN Manager must provide them with a clear path to better positions and working conditions. That path should not lead through the front or back door. The first step in this path of professional growth is an evaluation of the person's abilities and liabilities.

Evaluation

Most organizations require the LAN Manager and supervisory members of the LAN staff to provide a formal, written evaluation of the performance of their subordinates during the past year. We believe that such evaluations are pro forma at best, and useless at worst. Anyone who has raised children or trained dogs knows that reward or punishment must take place almost immediately after the noticeable action. If an engineer designs and installs a device that reduces troubleshooting time, he should be rewarded then, not six months later when he gets his evaluation. If a technician develops sloppy work habits, she should be corrected immediately, not during her next review. How does the LAN Manager do this? Experience has shown that one of the best ways to accomplish this goal is to ask three simple questions and be prepared to provide rapid actions to the answers given. These questions are as follows:

What Are You Doing? This question brings to light the LAN staff's past, present, and future activities. Responses include recently completed projects and the success or failure of those projects. Present activities include not only the operationally immediate projects such as restoration and installation, but also ongoing projects such as network analysis, evaluation, and redesign. Future activities may include the evaluation of new hardware or software for inclusion in the LAN, the rerouting of existing circuits in support of new offices or opportunities, or plans for more training or education.

How Is It Going? Many projects or activities fizzle out early because of problems their sponsors do not know how to fix. The sponsors may not feel as if their activities are worthwhile, and they let projects languish. Personal problems may also interfere with the ability to complete assigned tasks. It is difficult to concentrate on a given action if the worker is concerned with tax or medical problems. Although LAN Managers should not try to practice tax law or medicine, they certainly should be able to direct staff members to the appropriate practitioner.

What Do You Need? LAN staff members often need certain types of hardware or software to successfully complete their assigned tasks. If the LAN is large enough, the LAN Manager may not be aware of day-to-day activities. By questioning the needs of subordinates, the LAN Manager accomplishes two goals. First, the actions taken in support of the LAN are completed faster, easier, or cheaper. Second, and perhaps more important, the LAN Manager shows concern for what the LAN staff is doing and how they feel about the job.

In asking these three questions, the LAN Manager must also do what many people cannot do effectively, and that is to listen. If the LAN Manager comes in some morning and finds a letter of resignation from a staff member, the letter really says, among other things, that he was not listening correctly. Sudden voluntary terminations are one sure sign of dissatisfied employees. The LAN Manager must be aware of dissatisfaction and actively seek to eliminate it.

Promotions

Evaluating the LAN staff is not, in and of itself, sufficient to prevent turnover. Regardless of how much technically challenging work a person can receive, sooner or later he expects a promotion for his efforts. Unlike raises, promotions are publicly visible actions. A promotion should not be considered a reward for past activities; rather it should be considered as a demonstration of the LAN Manager's opinion of the person's future capabilities and responsibilities. On some occasions, the LAN Manager is forced to decide whether to promote a person who is not totally ready or to bring in someone from outside to fill a senior position. It is generally better to promote from within and help the person grow into the job rather than to bring in a complete stranger.

By promoting from within, the LAN Manger sends two messages to the staff. First, there is room at the top for those who work hard, improve themselves, and show that they care about what they are doing. Second, the organization cares for its people, and wants them to succeed. Those who do not agree with this philosophy point out the dangers in promoting someone who is not ready for the position. The obvious counter to such an argument is that if the person is not ready, it is easy enough to demote him and then try someone else than it is to explain why he was not selected for promotion in the first place. Many employees have been known to grow into a more responsible position almost overnight.

While we are on the subject of promotions, LAN Managers must also be thinking of who to groom to take their position when they get promoted to another position in the firm. LAN Managers must realize two very important points. First, they are not irreplaceable. They can die, become invalids, or in some other manner become unable to continue work. What chaos will result if no one is ready to step into their shoes? Second, LAN Managers must realize that their chances for promotion are slim if they do not have a capable replacement. Who would move a successful person to another position without a suitable replacement? By showing upper management that a replacement is on hand, the LAN Manager is also saying "I am ready for promotion when you find a place for me."

Transfers

By evaluating the members of the LAN staff, training them, and grooming them for promotion, the LAN Manager has created another problem: Once a person is ready for promotion, what happens if no vacancy is available? This raises the issue of transfers.

By the time a person is ready for promotion, she and the LAN Manager plus others who supervise her directly have a large emotional investment in this effort. What happens now? If the LAN Manager is serious about this person's professional growth, he may realize that he must turn this person loose and let her find another position within or without the supported organization.

Such actions are fraught with peril. How does the LAN Manager tell a subordinate that he has gone as far as he can and now must wait for a long period of time? What rewards can be given to overcome the employee's bitterness of seeing much effort appear to go to waste? It may seem to be heresy to release a competent person, but if that is what is necessary for personal and professional growth, the LAN Manager really has no choice but to do so.

Other Activities to Prevent Turnover

Salary does not prevent turnover. Too many writers on the subject of turnover have shown that salary is very low on the scale of reasons to quit. When money is the subject in question, other benefits act to retain an employee. Some of these other benefits include Employee Stock Option Plans (ESOP), medical and dental benefits if members of the employee's family become ill, and a retirement plan.

Pride in a job well done helps to retain an employee. Being appreciated by fellow employees also acts as a retention factor. One of the best ways to ensure that this takes place is to develop a sense of teamwork within all members of the LAN staff. Almost all people respond well to public notice of their positive actions. If one of the LAN staff did a particularly good job, a letter of commendation may be posted in the work area and entered in the employee's permanent records. (In counterpoint, the author has seen one organization where the individual who made the most mistakes in a given period of time was also awarded!) The "Toilet Seat" award was not something people looked forward to receiving. Some LAN Managers seem to forget the old adage about how to catch more flies with honey than with vinegar. A simple "Thanks, well done" does more to prevent turnover than most people realize.

Aside from personal and professional development and the chance for promotion, one of the most valuable retention tools the LAN Manager can apply is that of loyalty. One of the problems with this tool is that the LAN Manager may think that loyalty comes with the annual salary. Nothing could be further from the truth. Like respect, loyalty must be earned. Further, loyalty is like a tire on a car. It wears out and must be replaced from time to time. Replacing loyalty can only be accomplished by giving loyalty in return. Loyalty, like respect, flows both ways. Failure to realize this and act on such realization can prevent the LAN Manager from being able to rely on his or her staff's loyalty in times of stress.

Summary

This chapter has addressed the subject of managing the people who make up the LAN staff. Instead of the routine form of summary used in previous chapters, this summary simply lists things that should be done and other things that the LAN Manager should refrain from doing.

Should Do	*Should Refrain From Doing*
Selection Process	
Evaluate those inside for promotion from within.	Immediately advertise outside.
Read the resume; evaluate the experience.	Rely only on education and degrees.
Keep hiring costs low.	Use placement agencies.

Should Do	Should Refrain From Doing
Interviews	
Ask job-related questions.	Ask personal or prejudicial questions.
Refrain from testing; ask searching technical questions.	Give unqualified, or inapplicable and indefensible written tests.
Check references thoroughly.	Ignore references.
Evaluate the person's "fit."	Disregard corporate culture.
Training	
Provide training to fit the individual.	Provide the same training for everyone, regardless of background and current skills.
Provide growth-oriented training.	Provide only technically oriented training.
Prevention of Turnover	
Provide technically challenging work.	Assign work on an ad hoc basis.
Provide clear growth paths.	Promote without concern for appearances.
Comment on significant actions when they happen.	Comment only during annual reviews.
Talk to the LAN staff on a regular, but not scheduled, basis.	Talk only during the organization functions.
Promote from within.	Hire senior persons outside.
Provide rewards other than financially based ones.	Ignore exceptional behavior.
Actively develop loyalty.	Expect loyalty.

11 *Required Reports*

Report!
—*US Army Field Manual FM 22–5; "Drill and Ceremony"*

The preceding command elicits a response from subordinates to superiors concerning the status of personnel from the units under review. The same concept applies to LAN management. The LAN Manager must know the status of the hardware, software, and transmission media he or she manages. Obtaining this information requires a constant flow of reports and updates. This chapter addresses some of the required reports and the questions that these reports answer.

Previous chapters of this text were generic; they did not apply to a specific type of LAN. This chapter follows the same format. The reports that follow must be augmented by reports specific to the LAN(s) being managed. If, for instance, the LAN is based on IEEE 802.3 (Ethernet), the LAN Manager must know how many collisions are occurring during a specific timeframe. If the LAN is an IEEE 802.5 (token ring), the LAN Manager must know how often the token is being regenerated.

Some types of LAN hardware and software provide additional information beyond that minimum required for the following reports. This additional information should not be ignored. Instead, it should be used to supplement the required reports.

Address

All telecommunications equipment that is part of a packet-type LAN and has even rudimentary electronic intelligence may have an address. Each address must be unique. The address report answers such questions as

- What addresses have been assigned?
- To what piece of equipment has address such-and-such been assigned?
- Are there duplicate addresses? (Duplications cause loss of traffic or confusion between those with the same address.)
- What is the maximum number of addresses that can be assigned to a specific LAN or subLAN?
- If a name-to-address conversion table has been created for subscribers' ease of use, who assigns host or resource names?
- Is there any security over addresses and name-to-address conversion tables? (If a hacker already knows the name and/or address of a host or resource, breaking in is much easier.)
- Has an address been changed? If an address is changed, the same change must take place in every name to address conversion table within the entire LAN.
- What is the relationship (if any) between the old and new address? Does this relationship create a breach of security? Are subscribers brought up to date on changes? Do they need to be?

Some of these questions can be answered if the LAN Manager has access to a report like the one shown in Table 11.1.

Add/Drop Subscribers

As the organization supported by the LAN changes, the LAN must reflect these changes. One of the more common changes that takes place is the change in state of LAN subscribers. There are three possible changes for each subscriber: adding a new subscriber, moving an active subscriber: and dropping a subscriber from service. Questions to be answered about these functions are as follows.

Table 11.1: Address Report

Address	Sequence Number	Equipment Type	"NAME"	Changed Date	Records Updated	By Whom
123ABC4D	1/1024	File Serv	Newton	None	Not Rqd	N/A
124ABC4D	2/1024	PersComp	None	1/12/90	1/13/90	IMD
⋮						
243NDS5A	212/1024	TermServ	R&D	5/18/90	5/21/90	IMD

Notes:
1. In the first address, no change has ever been made. Therefore, no updates to the report are required.
2. In the other two records, the address has been changed, and the record of the change made by the person with the initials "IMD."
3. Address "124ABC4D" is the second address out of a possible field of 1,024 addresses for the topology of this LAN.

- Who is the new subscriber? Where will he be located? What LAN-provided services does he need?

- Who has authorized this subscriber access to which hosts or services? Is there a need to document this authorization? If so, who has the paperwork? Have all the appropriate signatures been gathered?

- Has the new subscriber been given (or created) the required passwords?

- If the new subscriber needs training on the LAN and its associated resources, has he received it, or is it scheduled?

- Does the new subscriber know who to call if he has problems?

Fortunately when the subscriber moves, the list of questions becomes much shorter:

- Does the new connection exist, or must it be installed?
- If it exists, does it work?
- Can the subscriber access all his authorized services? Does he need new hardware or software in his terminal or personal computer?

When the subscriber is dropped from the LAN, other questions arise:

- Is the subscriber's authorization removed from all hosts and resources?

- Have the subscriber's passwords been changed back to the common password? By assigning a common password, the LAN Manager or his designated representative can "clean up" after the removal of the subscriber. This is particularly true when multiple file servers are attached to the LAN. The dropped subscriber may have files on all or any of these file servers.

- Has the address of the equipment assigned to the dropped subscriber been removed from name-to-address conversion tables and held for reassignment as required?

- If key diskettes are in use within the LAN, have they been recovered?

- Has all other assigned software been recovered?

- Are there any trouble tickets still open that name the dropped subscriber as the point of contact?

- Has the dropped subscriber turned in physical or electronic keys for the encryption equipment to which he had access? Did the subscriber have any LAN remote access devices? If so, were they turned in?

These questions, or others like them are easier to answer if the LAN Manager has access to information that is formatted like the report shown in Table 11.2.

Alarm Conditions

Alarms sound when one or more parts of the LAN exceed predefined parameters. When an alarm sounds, the LAN Manager must have answers to the following questions:

- What piece of equipment caused the alarm to sound? An alarm does not always mean a piece of equipment has failed; merely that it has exceeded some predefined criteria.

- What time did the alarm sound?

Table 11.2: Add/Move/Drop Subscriber Report

Add New Subscriber	
Name	Joe Jones
Address	183FNB2A
Internal extension	27013
Authorized by	Mary Smith
Password created	2/12/90
Training completed	1/15/90
Move Subscriber	
Date of last move	6/30/90
New tap available	yes
New tap functional	yes
Move authorized by	Mary Smith
HW/SW functional	yes
Dropped Subscriber	
Authorization canceled by	Mary Smith
Password(s) reset	6/15/91
Address removed	6/15/91
H/W and S/W recovered	yes
Reviewed trouble tickets	no
Keys recovered	yes
LAN Manager's review	OK, IMD

- Did anything else that could influence the hardware happen at the same time? For example, a lightning strike, movement of hardware within the LAN, or installation of new hardware and software?

- What are the preliminary symptoms? Loss of signal? Loss of timing? High signal-to-noise ratio?

- How many times has this same alarm sounded in the past? What was done to correct the condition then?

- Is the equipment that is sounding the alarm under guarantee?

- Who is working on the problem now?

- What is the priority of the circuit or trunk to which the alarmed equipment is connected?

- Where is the allegedly defective equipment located?

- Do spares exist? If so, where are they?

- Do alternate routing capabilities exist? If so, have they been used?

Questions such as these can be answered by the type of data that is shown in Table 11.3.

Table 11.3: Alarm Condition Report

Equipment Originating Alarm	Time of Alarm	Symptoms	Trouble Ticket Required	Location	Ckt Prio
2400BPS Mod MOD–24/103	10:33	Loss of Cxr Detect	No, transient	Training Dept	3C
File Server FS–Nov/02	19:33	Garbled Packets	Yes 88-1245	Gary, Indiana	1A

Notes:
1. The organization creates equipment identifiers such as MOD–24/103. In this case, MOD stands for modem; 24 is the throughput of this device, 2400BPS; and the /103 indicates that it is the 103rd such device purchased.
2. Time should be in 24-hour format. This precludes confusion between AM and PM.
3. Under "Trouble Ticket Required," 88-1245 indicates that this is the 1245 consecutive trouble ticket in 1988.

Bandwidth Availability

This report is simple, straightforward, and can be massive if the LAN is large. The report answers one question: What is the designed bandwidth for each circuit and trunk in the LAN? A typical report is shown in Table 11.4.

Bandwidth Changes

The bandwidth change report is historical in nature. It is concerned solely with modifications of bandwidths within the LAN.

Table 11.4: Bandwidth Availability

Trunk #	Circuit #	Bandwidth
	33-4A55B6	4.8Kbps
A-125		4Mbps
A-126		4Mbps
A-127		16Mbps
	29-A43219V-0	19.2Kbps

It documents circuit and trunk bandwidths by answering the following types of questions:

- What bandwidth changes have been completed during the last reporting period?
- Have new circuits or trunks been installed? If so, when was the work finished?
- Have old circuits or trunks been removed? If so, is the supported organization still paying for them?
- Has bandwidth increased or decreased as a whole?
- Who authorized bandwidth modification?
- Does this increase or decrease the LAN operating budget? If so, by how much in any given quarter?

Table 11.5 is one manner in which this type of information may be presented to the LAN Manager.

Bandwidth Consumption

The LAN Manager provides subscribers with a service, that of available bandwidth. To manage this service effectively, the LAN Manager must know how much of the bandwidth is being consumed at any given instant. Reports on this consumption can provide answers to questions like those that follow:

- How much of the total available bandwidth was consumed at 1:37 PM on January 10?
- What are the daily, weekly, monthly, and annual peaks of bandwidth consumption?

Table 11.5: Bandwidth Change

Ckt or Trunk #	New?	Add, Mod, or Del	Date Completed	Trouble Ticket #	Author- ization	Increase Decrease
A-129	Y	A		89-003	IMD	+4Mb
21-4456A3	N	D	3/31/90	89-121	IMD	−2.4Km
1945-BY3	N	M	4/01/90	89-129	IMD	+9.6Kb
⋮						
34-AB44	Y	M		89-356	IMD	+2.5Mb

Date of this report	06/30/90
Date of last report:	12/31/89
Change since last report:	4.007200Mb
Increase/Decrease:	Increase
Percentage	2.3409%

Note:
Circuit number 34-AB44 was not included in this report because the completion date was not entered into the appropriate logs or data base.

- What are the daily, weekly, monthly, and annual valleys of bandwidth consumption?
- What percentage of the bandwidth available is assigned to the R&D section? What is their average consumption of this bandwidth? Do they need more, less, or is this amount sufficient?
- How much bandwidth nonavailability is attributed to faults, and how much to events?
- What is the cost on a per-bit basis for leased and dial-up circuits and trunks?
- Are sufficient leased and dial-up circuits available? If not, how much more is needed?
- How much will this cost?
- Is there too much bandwidth in the current leased and dial-up circuits? Will a reduced bandwidth affect throughput?
- How much of a cost saving is foreseen by reduction of leased and dial-up circuit usage?

Information shown in Table 11.6 provides some assistance to the LAN Manager in answering these questions and others like them.

Table 11.6: Bandwidth Consumption Report

Time	Circuit # 33-4A55B6	Circuit # 21-4456A3	Trunk # A-128
⋮			
08:22	0.00	88.31	12.21
08:24	0.00	89.72	10.31
08:26	0.00	44.14	33.89
08:28	0.00	31.44	76.78
⋮			
10.22	21.33	0.00	98.35

Notes:
1. This covers only three circuits/trunks. In a real-life situation, a column would exist for all circuits and trunks within the organization.
2. The times noted here are at two-minute intervals. In some cases, arguments can be made for taking such readings at 10-microsecond intervals.
3. The figures shown are consumption of bandwidth by percentage, not by throughput in bits.
4. This report covers only one part of one day.
5. In real life, this report would be graphic in nature, showing peaks and valleys of usage on a bar chart.

Circuit Status

The circuit status report lists the status of both circuits and trunks. (Status is listed in the glossary.) The report may or may not differentiate between circuits and trunks. That is the LAN Manager's decision. Regardless of which method is used, the report answers the following types of questions. See Table 11.7.

- Which circuits hold what status now?
- When was the last time circuit 12345AB67 changed status?
- What is the trouble ticket number for defective trunk ABCD12EF?
- When was the last time the standby circuit 2345CD67 was activated?
- How many circuits whose bandwidth is greater than 56 Kbps suffered an outage in the past reporting period?
- When did the new trunk between points A and B change to "in use" status?

Table 11.7: Circuit Status

Circuit Trunk #	Last Effected Date	Band Width	Vendor Code	Number of Outages w/in 30 days	Media Used
12345AB67	12/12/89	4.8 Kbps	12	None	Tw/Pr
2345CD67	01/10/90	19.2 Kbps	None	2	Tw/Pr
21-4456A3	02/18/90	9.6 Kbps	09	4	Tw/Pr
A-102	02/20/90	10 Mbps	None	1	Radio

Notes:
1. Tw/Pr is an abbreviation for twisted pair wiring
2. Radio indicates a wide-band radio link between two locations.

- Which circuits or trunks are provided by vendor V?
- Which circuits or trunks suffer from the most frequent outages?
- Which subscribers use which type of transmission media?
- Do propagation conditions affect radio or free-space light transmission media? If so, can such propagation conditions be correlated to time of day, season, or weather conditions?

Designed Capacity Limitations

Within configuration management lies information about the designed capacity of the LAN. The LAN Manager must be aware of these capacities and be knowledgeable of conditions that indicate any traffic loading that approaches these limitations. The report on design capacity limitations is not specifically concerned with individual pieces of hardware or software, but rather with the LAN as a whole. (A typical format for such a report is shown in Table 11.8.) Such a report answers the following types of questions:

- How many new subscribers can be attached to the LAN before exceeding the maximum number allowable?
- Has the backbone cable been extended to its maximum length? Are propagation times in excess of specified limits?
- Do alternate routing capabilities exist? Is traffic loading balanced across all subLANs?
- Does the installation of power and signal cables meet local, state, and federal safety and fire codes?

Table 11.8: Design Capacity Limitations for LAN (id) or sub (LAN (id)

Subscriber Limitations		Backbone Length		Alt Routing	Bandwidth Percentage	TT/WO Status
Now	Max	Now	Max			
21	200	434M	500M	N	12	Open

Notes:
1. This LAN (or subLAN) is very lightly loaded with few subscribers and only 12 percent of bandwidth being consumed.
2. One or more trouble tickets (TT) or work orders (WO) are open on this LAN (or subLAN).
3. The "Backbone Length" noted here is for a one segment LAN using either Ethernet, or some other IEEE 802.3 compliant standard. 434M indicates that the current length of the cable is 434 meters.

- Does specialized TMDE support the hardware on the LAN?
- What is the worst signal-to-noise ratio anywhere in the LAN? If such a ratio is excessive, what is being done to correct it?
- What and where are the single point(s) of failure in the LAN? What is being done to ensure that these do not fail in a catastrophic manner and bring down the entire LAN?
- What percentage of the maximum available bandwidth is being used? This last question intentionally duplicates the same question in the bandwidth consumption report.

Equipment Capacity

The organization supported by the LAN may or may not require accountability by the LAN Manager for each piece of hardware that makes up the LAN. Regardless, the LAN Manager must know where each piece of hardware and transmission media is located as well as the physical and geographical relationships among all pieces of equipment. This type of knowledge is gained by answering the following types of questions:

- Where is the 2400-bps modem, SN 123456, manufactured by Vendor A located? Is this modem in a given building? If so, at what floor, room, rack, or office?
- What is the modem connected to?
- What subscribers make use of this modem? Where are the transmission media concentration points? If they are in a locked wiring closet, who has the key to the closet?

- Where are the taps, joins, and drops for each branch of the transmission media? Where do WAN/VAN circuits connect to the LAN?
- Where is all spare equipment of each type located?
- If radio or free-space light is used, where are the antennas, transmitters, and receivers? Are they physically secure?

Although the information in Table 11.9 does not answer all these questions, it answers some of them. This type of information may be best presented as a map of the entire LAN.

Table 11.9: Equipment Capacity

Device Id	Bldg Name	Floor Number	Room Number	Subscriber (If using)	Address	Bit Rate
BIU__3c/12	R&D	1	22	Joe Jones	123ABC4D	10Mbps
MUX__T56/1	R&D	1	Base	None	None	56Kbps
FS__Nov/02	Gary	5	108	Mary Jones	128ABC4E	10Mbps

Equipment Status

The equipment in the LAN can have only one status at any given instant. A report on equipment status can answer many of the following questions for the LAN Manager.

- What pieces of equipment have the status of defective (D), in use (I), operational (O), and standby (S)?
- How long has a given multiplexer had the status of "in use"?
- What is the number of the open trouble ticket that applies to the defective terminal server that was in the personnel division?
- What pieces of LAN hardware have been sent out for external repair? When are these pieces of hardware scheduled to be returned?
- What pieces of hardware have been defective for the longest period? For the shortest period?
- Which piece of equipment is in standby status?
- Why is a given terminal server operational, but not in use?
- When is the next scheduled calibration period for a given piece of TMDE?

As each organization is different, the report format shown in Table 11.10 may not apply to every organization. However, it is a good base on which the LAN Manager may wish to build.

Table 11.10: Equipment Status

Equipment Identifier	Status	Date of Status Change	Trouble Ticket Number	External Repair Required
FS__Nov/02	I	12/22/90	N/A	No
MOD__24/103	S	01/03/91	N/A	No
MUX__T56/1	D	04/12/91	89–123	Yes
BIU__NE2/12	O	01/04/91	N/A	No

Equipment Upgrade

From time to time, equipment within the LAN, and under certain conditions the LAN itself, needs to be upgraded. The LAN Manager must know the upgrade status of all LAN equipment at any given time. To keep this information handy, the LAN Manager must be able to answer the following questions. Although the report shown in Table 11.11 may not be sufficient for every organization, it may be a good place to start.

- Which pieces of equipment within the LAN require upgrade actions?
- Where is this equipment located?
- What is the cost of the upgrade? What benefit is derived from the upgrade?
- If an upgrade is required, who initiates the process of requesting the upgrade?
- When does the actual upgrade begin?
- What is the impact of this upgrade on the LAN and its subscribers?
- What percentage of the upgrade is completed to date? What is the scheduled upgrade completion date? When was the upgrade actually completed?

Table 11.11: Equipment Update

Equipment Identifier	Location			Requested By	Authorized By	Estimated Date		Actual Date		Costs	
	Bldg	Floor	Room			Begin	End	Begin	End	Estimated	Actual
FS_Nov/02	Gary	5	212	Nancy Brown	IMD	10/01/90	10/10/90	10/12/90	10/14/90	$ 1,251.43	1,334.80
subLAN_04	Memphis	All	All	Pres. Jones	IMD	11/30/90	01/30/91	11/30/91	01/30/91	$12,350.00	14,721.09
CC_Bridge/01	Boston	Base	1222	IMD	IMD	02/01/91	02/05/91	02/08/91	02/09/91	$11,000.00	11,000.00
Modem Pool	Boston	Base	1221	IMD	IMD	06/01/91				$ 8,450.00	

- What was the relationship between budgeted and actual costs for the finished upgrade?
- Does the upgraded equipment perform as promised?

Key Changes

If encryption is used in the LAN, the "keys" for the encryption process must be distributed to all authorized users. The report on key change procedures is very sensitive. Rigid fail-safe procedures should be created and applied to ensure keying material and key change reports do not get into the wrong hands. Table 11.12 shows one form of such a report. The key change report answers some or all the following questions:

- What is the frequency of key changes?
- Are key changes manual or automatic?
- How many complete key changes are in stock, ready to be issued to subscribers?
- How soon does another order for more keying material need to be placed?
- Who has access to keying material? Is this person trustworthy?
- If keying material is moved by courier, is there a trail of receipts?
- Are out-of-date keying materials destroyed?
- When encryption devices are sent out for repair, are keying materials removed?
- Does keying material require two-person control?

Table 11.12: Key Changes

Key Identity	Change Period	Manual or Auto	# of Days Stockage	Reorder Date	2 Man Control?
A5	12 Hours	Auto	10	01/01/90	N
B33	Daily	Manual	30	01/20/90	N
C12	Weekly	Manual	30	02/01/90	N
C22	Hourly	Auto	5	01/05/90	Y

LAN Access Count

The LAN Manager knows how much bandwidth is available from the bandwidth availability report. He knows how much is used from the bandwidth consumption report. What these two reports do not reveal is who is using this bandwidth. The report shown in Table 11.13 shows one possible report configuration. The LAN access count report does provide this information by answering the following types of questions:

- Who logged on to what LAN resource or host?
- When did this happen?
- What application or file was used?
- How long was the connection open?
- When did the subscriber log off?
- How many bits of traffic passed between the host or resource and the subscriber during this period?
- What host or resource received or transmitted traffic over the LAN?
- What was the source address of traffic sent to the draft quality printer on the second floor?
- What is the total number of subscribers logged in to the LAN at any given moment?
- How many times a day does such-and-such a subscriber open a connection, and how long is that connection kept open?

Table 11.13: LAN Access Count 12/12/90

Subscriber ID	Log On	Log Off	Total Time	Total Bits	Application Used (VER)
Jones, Joe	08:55	11:48	173 Min	1.23Mb	PWP 5.3
Green, Mary	09:03	09:21	018 Min	0.22Mb	BKP 1–2–3
Smith, Frank	09:04	09:05	002 Min	0.00Mb	??
Smith, Frank	09:05	09:10	005 Min	0.02Mb	Drawl 2.02

Lease/Dial Circuit Cost

Many small LANs or subLans can be interconnected through WAN/VAN provided circuits. The LAN Manager must know how much these circuits cost. A report, somewhat like the one shown in Table 11.14 can answer questions such as those that follow:

- How many leased circuits are used to support the LAN?
- Where are the originating and terminating points for these leased circuits?
- How much does each leased circuit cost?
- How many leased circuits are being charged for that are actually in use?
- What is the total cost for all dial-up circuits?
- What percentage of these costs can be attributed to the LAN?
- Are there many repeat calls to the same location? If so, would a leased circuit be less expensive?
- Is the PBX performing the least cost routing on dial-up circuits? Does it need new programming or new trunking? Do alternative WAN/VAN vendors offer equal quality of service at a lower price?
- Does the WAN/VAN vendor have a special tariff (schedule of charges) that the supported organization is qualified for?
- Do several leased, low-bandwidth circuits go to the same location? If so, is it less expensive to procure one higher bandwidth circuit and multiplex several subscribers on it?

Table 11.14: Leased/Dial Circuit Costs For the Month of January, 1990

Sequence #	Circuit Number	Originate	Terminate	Lease/Dial	Cost
1.	21-4456A3	Boston	Gary	L	$243.12
2.	33-4155B6	Boston	Detroit	L	$222.35
3.	12345ABC	Boston		D	$ 89.17
⋮					
108.	23456FG8	Detroit		D	$ 21.12
	Total				$24,789.33

Lease/Dial Circuit Status

The glossary lists four definitions of status that a piece of hardware or circuit could hold at any given instant. The same criteria apply to lease/dial-up circuits. A report on this subject, as shown in Table 11.15, should answer the following questions:

- What circuits hold what status now?
- When was the last time a circuit changed status?
- Does any leased or dial-up circuit have open trouble tickets?
- How many leased or dial-up circuits can pass traffic at speeds in excess of 56 Kps?
- What is the total nonavailable time for all leased circuits?
- When is the last time leased circuits were tested for quality in accordance with the WAN/VAN vendor's contract terms? Are there records of previous tests? If so, where are they located?
- What is the WAN/VAN vendor's circuit number for each leased or dial-up circuit? What is the WAN/VAN vendor's trouble reporting numbers? (Yes, we mean plural.) Are those numbers manned continually?
- Are alternate routing circuits tested randomly?
- What circuits are being charged for that are defective?

Table 11.15: Lease/Dial Circuit Status

Circuit Number	Status	Date Status Change	Open TT #	Band Width	Nonavail Time	Last Test Date	Vendor Code
21-4456A3	I	12/18/89	None	2.4Kbps	028M	06/05/90	12
21-4457A3	D	06/14/90	88-234	9.6Kbps	284M		09
21-8834J0	S	None	None	2.4Kbps	000M	06/18/90	12
A-126	O	06/12/90	None	1.5Mbps	000M	06/20/90	09

Loss/Slippage of Timing

Many pieces of equipment within the LAN require very precise timing signals. These signals can come from the WAN/VAN vendor's network clock or an internal (LAN) clock. The LAN Manager must be aware of the accuracies of these clocks. Although the reports shown in Table 11.16 may not be correct for all organizations, it is a starting point for the customization process. A report on timing signals answers the following questions:

- Who is providing the clock signal?
- What is its guaranteed accuracy? Is it that accurate? How is the accuracy measured? Is the measuring instrument accurate enough by itself?
- Are records of timing signal errors kept? Where are these records located?
- Who is to be called if timing signals become defective?
- How great a percentage of slip of timing signals is allowed?
- What pieces of LAN equipment depend on the timing signals? Where are they located?
- What are the symptoms of loss or slippage of the timing signal?

Password Data

Passwords are an inexpensive form of security for the LAN and the resources attached to it. The LAN Manager needs to establish procedures for creation, use, and protection of passwords. A report, somewhat like the one shown in Table 11.17, may answer the following types of questions.

- What is the longest a password may be kept in use?
- Are passwords being recycled?
- Are project or customer names being used as passwords?

Table 11.16: Loss/Slippage of Timing

Vendor Code: 09
Point Of Contact: Charlene Wiggins, 800-111-1234

Date of Loss/Slip	Time	Circuit Number	Guaranteed Accuracy	Actual Accuracy	Measured With
12/02/90	19:22	A-121	$1 \times 10 (-3)$	$1 \times 10 (-2)$	HP 9944
12/03/90	00:42	A-121	$1 \times 10 (-3)$	$1 \times 10 (+2)$	HP 9944
12/20/90	06:21	A-201	$1 \times 10 (-6)$	$1 \times 10 (-2)$	HP 9944
⋮					
08/12/91	10:21	A-193	$1 \times 10 (-6)$	No signal	TX1000

- Are dates used as passwords?
- Are passwords kept in open view? What procedures are in place to bypass password protection? This may be required if a subscriber is not available to use his password.
- What is the impact of compromised passwords? Are duplicate passwords in use?
- What procedures are in place to ensure password protection is being utilized?

Table 11.17: Password Data

Subscriber Identity	# of Passwords in Use	Last Changed	Change Due	Password Holder	Updated
Jones, Joe	1	12/01/89	02/01/90	Frank Smith	Y
Green, Bill	3	12/15/89	02/15/90	Frank Smith	Y
IMD	8	12/31/89	02/15/90	Nancy White	Y
White, Nancy	8	12/31/89	02/15/90	IMD	Y

Private Branch Exchange (PBX) Data

In some organizations, the LAN is connected to the PBX to provide connectivity outside the immediate geographical area. In many of these organizations, the LAN Manager is responsible for the PBX. To successfully manage this component of the LAN, the LAN Manager must have certain reports about the PBX. No report format is available because such reports normally depend on the PBX vendor's engineering decisions. These reports answer the following types of questions:

- How many subscribers does the PBX support in a nonblocking mode of operation?
- How much redundancy is available within the PBX in case of component failure?
- What is the highest bit rate the PBX will support? Does the PBX have the ability to expand? How many unused ports (subscriber connections) are available on the PBX now?
- What is the maintenance history of the PBX?

- Who is capable of programming the PBX and modifying existing programs?
- What usage data is available from the Station Message Detail Report (SMDR) port on the PBX?
- How is this usage data used in management of corporate tele-communications activities?

Subscriber Authorization

To maximize use of limited resources, or provide security for proprietary information, some subscribers are authorized only limited access to the LAN, its resources, or the hosts attached to the LAN. The LAN Manager must be aware of which subscribers have access to the LAN. A subscriber authorization report, such as shown in Table 11.18, will provide the LAN Manager answers to the following types of questions:

- Where is sensitive or proprietary data stored in the LAN?
- Who is allowed access to such storage facilities?
- Who can authorize a given subscriber access to this data?
- If someone is authorized access, what level of access is it? Is the subscriber allowed to only read data, can he change data, or even remove data?
- How often must a given level of authorization be updated?
- Is there some indicator that shows levels of authorization?
- What mechanisms are in place to delete authorization of access?
- What positive actions are taken to ensure that the allegedly authorized subscriber is really the person at the keyboard?
- What records of authorization exist?
- Where are they?

Subscriber Location

The subscriber is the person who benefits from some of the services provided by the LAN Manager. When the subscriber has a problem, the LAN Manager must know, among other things, where to send help. Table 11.19 shows one possible format of such a report. The subscriber location report will give that information and other useful data by answering the following questions:

Table 11.18: Subscriber Authorization

Subscriber Identity	Auth By Whom	Date Granted	Date Reviewed	Levels of Access	Authority Deleted
White, N	Huff, W	02/20/88	02/20/90	RWAPMXDCO	
Jones, J	Huff, W	04/15/89	04/15/90	RWAP	
Smith, F	Huff, W	04/15/89	04/15/90	RWAP	
Balke, N	Huff, W	05/18/89	05/15/90	RWAPCO	06/20/90

R = Read   W = Write   A = Change   P = Print
M = Make Directory   X = Remove Directory   D = Delete
C = Copy   O = Off Net Traffic

Table 11.19: Subscriber Location

Name: Huff, Wilhelmina
Internal Extension: 72013

LAN Connection Type:	Fiber Optic
LAN Connection Location:	See subscriber location below
Hardware/Software:	SUN Workstation, "C," UNIX
Shared/Direct Connection:	Direct

City/State	Building	Floor	Room
Boston, MA	Hancock	28	28-133

- What is the physical location of the subscriber? What building, floor, room, or corridor is the subscriber located in?
- What type of LAN connection is in use?
- Where is the subscriber's connection to the LAN?
- What type of hardware and software does the subscriber normally use?
- What is the subscriber's telephone number and extension?
- Does the subscriber share common equipment such as a multiplexer or terminal server?

Test, Measurement, and Diagnostic Equipment (TMDE)

Management of the LAN requires measurement of its electronic functionality. TMDE is used to make these measurements. The

LAN Manager must know the condition and capabilities of the TMDE used by the engineers and technicians. One possible format for this report is shown in Table 11.20. A report on TMDE will answer the following questions:

- What is the highest speed data that current TMDE can evaluate with satisfactory accuracy?
- Is there enough TMDE to provide rapid restoration when circuits or hardware become defective?
- Does every engineer and technician know how to use all the TMDE on hand to its fullest capabilities?
- Is every piece of TMDE calibrated within its recommended cycle times?
- Is there enough different TMDE to test each piece of hardware in the LAN?

Table 11.20: Test, Measurement, and Diagnostic Equipment

Equipment Type	Training Completed	Calibration Date Due	Location	Bit Rate
HP 9742	No	None	Boston	1.544 Mbps
HP 2231	Yes	None	Boston	19.2 Kbps
TEK 4491	Yes	12/15/90	Detroit	N/A
TEK 4491	Yes	12/15/90	Gary	N/A
TEK 4491	Yes	12/15/90	Atlanta	N/A
"Sniffer"	No	None	Detroit	10 Mbps

Trouble Ticket Data

Trouble tickets are a formal means of tracking problems that affect the LAN. The LAN Manager must have at his fingertips the present condition of all open trouble tickets. This type of data can come from a report; one potential form of such report is shown in Table 11.21. Such a report can answer the following questions:

- How many trouble tickets are still open?
- What hardware or transmission media are included in these open trouble tickets?

- What is the oldest open trouble ticket?
- Which person is assigned to work which trouble ticket?
- Which trouble ticket has the lowest (highest) priority?

Table 11.21: Trouble Ticket Data

TT #	Priority	Date Open	Date Closed	Labor Costs	Parts Costs	Outside Repair	Total $ Cost
88-123	3A	03/12/90	03/18/90	12.00	0.43	0.00	12.43
88-124	4D	03/12/90	03/12/90	12.00	0.00	0.00	12.00
⋮							
88-345	2C	06/03/90	08/04/90	0.00	0.00	98.63	98.63
88-346	1A	06/03/90	06/03/90	48.00	29.35	0.00	77.35

Summary

This chapter listed many questions the LAN Manager must be able to answer in order to effectively manage the hardware, software, and transmission media that make up the LAN. It has listed some, but by no means all, of the reports the LAN Manager must have available. Potential formats of these reports have been shown. These reports are based on data that is gathered either automatically or manually.

Before leaving this chapter, a few more questions about the data and the reports themselves may be required. What mechanisms are in place to create these reports? Who gathers the data, who analyzes it, and who generates the reports? Once the reports are created, how are they stored? Would a commercially available database be sufficient? Are they available to anyone? Are they protected from public view? Where are reports kept? What protection should be applied?

The reports are a record of previous LAN functionality. This is important information. Do backup copies of the reports exist? Where are these kept? Would a common disaster destroy both original and backup copies? Are three copies enough, or may four be needed? Five perhaps?

After answering all these questions, the LAN Manager must ask one more question: "Are you sure?!"

APPENDIX:
A Subscriber's
Guide to the
Corporate LAN

Common is to sense as thundering is to silence.
—Oxymorons

Introduction

Several groups of people should find this appendix useful:

- LAN Manager
- LAN Manager's supervisor
- Corporate training department
- Subscribers.

The LAN Manager

Many times the LAN Manager has the responsibility to provide subscribers with practical guidance on daily LAN usage and operations. Therefore, he should have some formalized collection of organization-specific LAN knowledge to help him discharge these responsibilities. This appendix describes the format, and to a limited extent, the content of that "formalized collection."

The LAN Manager's Immediate Supervisor

The LAN Manager's immediate supervisor needs the information in this appendix to provide him with an understanding of the LAN Manager's responsibilities. Perhaps the single most important responsibility (within the framework of this appendix) is to ensure that the subscriber makes maximum use of the productivity inherent in the LAN.

Training Department

In most organizations, those in the training department do not have the technical expertise necessary to present productive training on the use of the LAN. The trainers must look to vendors or the LAN Manager's staff to provide the necessary technical expertise. This appendix provides the training department with a framework on which they can build the program of instruction for students who will, when finished with the training, make maximum use of the productivity inherent in the LAN.

The Subscribers

The subscriber needs this appendix to ensure he or she can use the LAN to its fullest extent. Using the LAN in this manner is beneficial to several groups.

All Subscribers: By maximizing the use of the LAN, the subscriber can ensure that his efforts are completed on time and with a minimum of effort. For example, instead of a secretary typing a draft document, reproducing it, and making internal distribution, the author of the document can type it on a word processing package, allow others to review an electronic version of the document, and then present the secretary with a final draft for creation of a finished product.

The Organization: When subscribers use the LAN, the organization gains as well. By exchanging information via electronic means the speed and accuracy of such exchange is increased. Greater numbers of subscribers use expensive resources. This spreads the cost of these resources over more profit centers. The organization has also positioned itself to make use of new or upcoming technologies in this area.

Required Subscriber Information

The subscriber needs two types of information about the LAN, a subscriber handbook and a map of the LAN itself.

Subscriber Handbook: The subscriber handbook must explain several points to ensure proper subscriber interaction with other subscribers, the LAN Manager (or his staff), and the training department.

- Technical Characteristics—This is generalized information about the makeup of the LAN: What topology is in use, what is the topography of the LAN, and what are its limitations.

- Error Reporting—This error-reporting section of the handbook could be no more than a list of names and telephone numbers, or internal extensions, to be used to report perceived error conditions. As a minimum, this list includes:

  — LAN Manager
  — Help desk
  — Technical control

- Software Assistance—Many organizations separate the responsibility of telecommunications and management information services. When this approach is used, the subscriber's handbook should list the name(s) and telephone number, or internal extension of the person(s) to contact when assistance is needed with one or more software applications.

- Training Department—Subscribers may need to contact the training department to answer specific questions or for refresher training. Therefore, the appropriate name(s), telephone numbers, or internal extensions should be listed in the handbook.

- Other Documents—If the firm is large enough, or sufficiently organized, the subscriber's handbook may be an integral part of the Employee's Handbook.

Map of the LAN: The subscriber needs a map of the LAN—at a high level —to determine if the LAN extends to a given location. If a subscriber needs to pass a file to a field location, what is the routing that the file must take? Does the LAN extend to the required location? What other elements of the organization are connected to the LAN?

Training Department

The training department of the organization benefits from this appendix in two ways.

Outline: This appendix assists the training department in the creation of an outline for a program of instruction for new employees, or for employees who do not have knowledge of the LAN and its capabilities.

Performance Objectives: In addition to providing an outline for a program of instruction, this appendix provides a limited number of performance objectives.

Demarcation Point

In keeping with the rest of this text, this appendix does *not* offer LAN specific guidance. This appendix does *not*

- Show how to use

  — Bus, ring, or star topography LAN
  — Specific print or file server
  — Given vendor's telecommunications hardware and software

- Discuss the benefits of one vendor's products over another's.

Rather, this appendix does allow the transition from a general LAN configuration to organization specific LAN features and benefits.

Review and Preview

This section has provided an overview of the appendix and who can either use it or benefit from it. The remainder of the appendix discusses various aspects of LAN usage and operations. There are six of these areas:

- What the LAN is
- Who pays for the LAN
- LAN operations
- Telecommunications failures
- What to do if response time is slow
- Information security

Each of these areas is discussed from the subscriber's point of view. Following each discussion is a list of performance objectives for the training department's use. Where appropriate, supporting objectives are also noted.

The LAN Defined

Definition

The organization's LAN is a cost-effective means of information interchange within the organization in support of the organization's missions and goals.

Performance Objective

From a list of definitions of LANs, the student will be able to correctly select the definition that applies to the LAN in use by his organization. This selection is made without recourse to reference material. The selection will be made within two minutes.

Goals

There are several sets of goals to keep in mind concerning LAN usage.

Individual Goals: Each worker has certain individual goals that are set by either his immediate supervisor or himself. These may include completion of projects or products on time and within budget. Achievement of some of these goals may be supported by the LAN.

Performance Objective: The student will be able to correctly identify those individual goals that have been set by or for him. From all of these, he will be able to select those goals whose successful completion is supported by the LAN. The selection will be made within five minutes and with recourse to personal notes and any other reference material supplied by the training department or his immediate supervisor.

Corporate Goals: The LAN supports certain corporate goals. These may be the manufacture of products such as appliances and clothing, or providing services such as banking or telecommunications. The subscriber uses the LAN in successful completion of these corporate goals.

Performance Objective: Given a list of corporate goals the student will, from memory, within a period of three minutes, select those goals whose successful achievement is supported by the LAN.

Makeup of the LAN

The LAN is made up of three general types of components: hardware, software, and transmission media.

Hardware: The hardware in the LAN performs many functions.

- Terminals accept keyboard input and provide screen (CRT) output.
- Personal computers perform the same functions as terminals, plus they store input and output and provide computation capability.
- Printers and plotters provide output of the computation process. Such output could be text, graphics, or a mixture of both.
- Bus or network interface units connect various types of hardware to the transmission media.
- Repeaters extend the length of the transmission media to general design limits.
- Bridges connect two or more LANs.
- Routers separate traffic on multiple LANs based on addresses.
- Gateways pass traffic to and from dissimilar LANs; or from LANs to commercial communications media and vice versa.
- Terminal servers connect the terminals to transmission media.
- Print servers "share" one printer among many subscribers.
- File servers and/or hosts store and manipulate data used by the subscribers. These devices also provide computational capability.

Performance Objective: Given a list of hardware titles and descriptions, the student will be able to match the correct definition to the device(s) described. Such matching will be performed without recourse to notes or other written material.

Software: There are two types of software in any LAN.

- Application specific software performs such tasks as word processing, drawing, financial calculations, or general/specialized mathematical functions.

- Communications software is that software that is used to ensure the LAN functions as a telecommunications device. This can include file server/host operating systems, terminal emulation, and modem control software, to name three types.

Performance Objective: Given a list of software that runs in or on a LAN, the student will be able to specify if the software is application specific or telecommunications oriented. The specification process will be made without reference to notes or written material of any type.

Transmission Media: Transmission media is required to interconnect various types of hardware. In some LANs, transmission media types may be mixed. Transmission media include:

- Twisted pair wiring
- Coaxial cable
- Fiber optic cable
- Radio waves
- Free-space light

Performance Objective: After being shown the types of transmission media in use in the organization's LAN, the student will, from memory, and within two minutes, be able to identify the transmission media that is being used to connect his equipment to the LAN.

The LAN In Concept

Conceptually the LAN is nothing more that a very large computer with peripherals attached to it. If the subscriber understands personal computers, no further explanation is necessary. If not, the subscriber must realize that the file server is a place to store his information (data) and application specific software. The subscriber "owns" a portion of the storage and computational capabilities to be used in support of personal and corporate goals. He shares the peripherals with other subscribers on an as-needed basis.

How To Use the LAN

As has been mentioned, the LAN is a means of information interchange. Exactly how is this activity performed? Precise methods vary from LAN to LAN as the hardware and software are different on each LAN. Remember, this text is not written for a specific type of LAN, but for LANs in general. However, many functions are vendor independent and common to most LANs.

Sharing Resources: It was noted earlier that the subscriber owns storage capacity and computational capabilities. To access and use these devices, several steps take place:

1 From the terminal or personal computer, the subscriber notifies the file server/host that he is ready to perform some action.

2 The file server/host acknowledges this request and tells the subscriber to identify himself.

3 After giving proper identification, the subscriber begins his tasks using the software and data that he owns in the file server/host.

4 If some type of hard-copy output is required, the subscriber directs the file server/host or print server to produce this hard copy on the printer or plotter of the subscriber's choice.

5 If the subscriber has a personal computer, he can perform the calculations or processes on the personal computer and send the completed product to the print server to create the hard copy on the output device of the subscriber's choice.

Performance Objective: Several performance objectives are associated with subscriber usage of the LAN. Unless otherwise noted, each of the following performance objectives must be completed in no more than 90 seconds, and the student may refer to personal notes or vendor's manuals.

1 The student will be able to turn on and set up the terminal or the personal computer assigned to him.

2 The student will be able to invoke telecommunications software that allows him to open a link to the file server/host, a printing device, or both, depending on the type of hardware in the LAN.

3 Without recourse to written materials, and within 20 seconds of opening a link to the file server/host, the student will be able to log in and select the data or applications specific software of his choice.

4 The student will be able to produce a hard copy of his finished product by selecting the appropriate printer or plotter and directing the output to that device.

5 If the student is using a personal computer, he will be able to produce a hard copy of his work on the printer or plotter of his choice that is attached to the LAN via a print server.

Supporting Objectives: Several supporting objectives must be completed before the student can complete the performance objectives noted immediately above. These include:

1 Select from a list of software, that particular software that is required for communications or computation. Such selection is made from memory and within 20 seconds.

2 When given a list of file servers/hosts, printers, plotters, or other shared devices, the student will identify those that he is authorized to use. Such identification will take no more than ten seconds per device. No reference to written materials is allowed.

3 From memory alone, describe either orally, or in writing, the procedures used to log on to authorized file servers and/or hosts.

File Transfers: Many times a subscriber will send an electronic form of his work, a file, to another subscriber or location for further manipulation. This process is called a file transfer. There are two electronic ways to accomplish this.

1 Find the name or electronic address that corresponds to the destination of the file. Open a connection to that location and command the LAN to transmit the file.

2 Put the file in a common area of the file server/host and notify the other person(s) that the file is ready for their use.

Performance Objective: Two separate performance objectives exist. The student must have access to a list which contains genuine and dummy names and addresses provided by the organization.

1 With recourse to the list, the student will be able to identify, from memory, and within one minute, all genuine names or addresses usable for file transfers.

2 Without recourse to anything other than personal notes, the student will be able to perform a file transfer to a common area of the file server/host for other's use.

Backups: All LANs that are properly managed are backed up often; some on a daily basis. The subscriber has certain responsibilities in this area.

The subscriber should ensure that data and software applications in "his" storage area are in use and current. Old, superseded, or useless data should be transferred to a personal floppy disk if available, or an archived tape. Application specific software that has been superseded by newer revisions, or is no longer in use should be either removed or destroyed.

Performance Objective: Without recourse to notes or references, the student will be able to differentiate between old and current data and software. He will be able to archive old data on floppy disks or magnetic tape. With recourse to organization policy the student will be able to specify procedures which deal with old or unused application specific software.

Who Pays For Use of the LAN?

All assets in the organization have costs associated with them. These costs include purchase, usage, and maintenance costs. All three costs are applied to the LAN. We will discuss how the subscriber can keep LAN costs to a minimum.

Usage Costs

These are the costs deriving from daily LAN operation.

Transmission Media: Once the LAN hardware and software have been purchased and installed they cost very little to run. The major costs involved are those of traffic passing over commercial carrier provided circuits. To keep these costs to a minimum the subscriber must make certain decisions.

1 Does the file transfer have to take place now? Should I wait until transmission rates are lower?

2 Would it be cheaper to send the data on paper, floppy disk, or tape instead of electronic means? Note this is normally not the case.

3 Would it be cheaper to use facsimile instead of file transfer? Facsimile may be more expensive.

Performance Objective: The student will be able to select the cheapest means of information interchange. The selection process will be aided by recourse to all available information. The selection will be completed within three minutes.

Supporting Objective: The student will be able to list all possible routes that he may select for transmission. Further, the student will be able to list the good and bad points of his selection(s). Such listing can be done by recourse to any type of written or printed material.

Maintenance: As the subscriber uses the LAN on a daily basis, he is the one best qualified to note error conditions when they arise. Where possible, the subscriber should also be able to prevent error conditions. Such activities include:

- Ensuring that the file server/host or other hardware that he connects to is the one that he is authorized to use, and the one he has selected to use.
- Choosing and using the appropriate telecommunications software.

- Identifying loose or missing cables connected to the hardware where he works.
- Identifying the symptoms of improper operation.

Performance Objective: Two performance objectives are required here.

1 Given a complete suite of hardware, manuals, and notes, the student will be able to interconnect all the hardware so that it will function properly when power is applied and software is loaded.

2 Given a defective suite of hardware and software, the student will be able to correctly describe the symptoms of failure.

Cost Reduction

Because the subscriber uses the LAN daily, he is in the best position to note ways to decrease LAN operations costs. He should, from time to time, ask himself and other users, is there another way to achieve the same goals, personal and corporate, by changing practices and procedures. One possible way to do this is by asking three questions. Can the same activity be done better, faster, or cheaper?

Better: What is being done now in a manual mode that could be automated, or if not automated, done in such a manner that it is less manually intensive? For example:

If the subscriber needs to do a file transfer to a file server/host at a distant location, and he does not know the name or address of that device, how does he find the name or address? If he has to go to the help desk then he wastes time and effort. It would be better if the subscriber has a listing of host names and addresses available to him.

Faster: Faster does not mean greater throughput on the LAN. That is an engineering decision that the majority of the subscribers are not well enough educated to make. Rather it means quicker completion of a process. For example, when a subscriber opens a connection to another device on the LAN he must enter certain keystrokes. Could this process be done with a batch file, or by allowing the subscriber to select the device by means of pointing to an icon with a mouse?

Cheaper: Many times subscribers can be aware of hardware and software vendors who offer quality products at reduced prices. The subscribers should be encouraged to spread the word about these vendors.

Faster is not always cheaper however. A modem that operates at 9600Bps is eight times faster than one that operates at 1200Bps, right? This is not always the case. If the transmission media between two 9600Bps modems is noisy, the modem will automatically (in some cases) drop in speed to accommodate the degraded conditions. Therefore increasing potential throughput is not always a cheaper way to go.

LAN Operation

LAN operation, in this context, is from the subscriber's point of view. The following will discuss some of the daily operational problems, and their solutions, that the subscriber may encounter.

Physical Parameters

There are two physical parameters that the subscriber must be aware of, safety and ergonomics.

Safety: Although LANs and their associated equipment pose very few safety problems, some problems do exist and the subscriber must be aware of them.

1 High voltages exist in almost any component that uses 110-volt power. The subscriber must use caution when connecting LAN equipment to power outlets.

2 The screen (CRT) on terminals and personal computers can have extremely high voltages present on the inside of the case. Under no conditions should the subscriber remove the case or cover from the CRT.

3 Connecting cables may be too long and coil up around the equipment or on the floor. These cables can cause the subscribers or their coworkers to trip and fall. Alternatively, if the cable

is pulled by a foot or a drawer, it can jerk equipment off the desk or table, causing damage to people and equipment.

4 Transmission media are sometimes installed in false ceilings. Under no conditions should a subscriber attempt to enter the ceiling to make or check connections.

Performance Objective: Without recourse to any written material, the subscriber will be able to:

1 Identify all major safety hazards in and around his suite of equipment.

2 State or demonstrate the appropriate corrective actions to be taken when unsafe conditions are noted.

3 List the person(s) to contact when an unsafe act or condition is perceived.

Ergonomics: Ergonomics is concerned with how difficult or easy it is for a human to use a piece of equipment. With LAN equipment, the subscriber is predominantly concerned with two specific pieces of equipment, the CRT and the keyboard.

1 The CRT must be situated so that there is a minimum of light falling on the screen causing glare. The CRT should be easily viewed without eye or neck strain.

2 The keyboard should be placed so that the subscribers' fingers and hands fall into contact with the keys in a natural manner. The subscriber should note no muscle strain in wrists, arms, and shoulders.

Performance Objective: Given a complete suite of equipment at his desk, the student will be able to properly site the equipment in a way that is ergonomically sound.

Unauthorized Modifications

Much effort has gone into the selection, design, installation, and management of the LAN. An unauthorized modification to the hardware or software in the LAN by the subscriber can destroy all this effort. This does not mean that the subscriber should be dissuaded from looking for other ways to use what is available, or from suggesting modifications. Rather, the subscriber must know who should be contacted to evaluate such suggestions. From the subscribers' point of view there are two general approaches to LAN modifications: the individual and user groups.

Individual: This approach was discussed earlier in the section dealing with better, faster, and cheaper.

User Groups: Many times several people do the same tasks repetitively. These types of jobs and the people who do them are prime areas for sources of modifications. The workers should be encouraged to form user groups to determine what may need changes. Once the changes have been discussed, they should be sent forward as formal suggestions.

Performance Objective: The student has these objectives.

1 The student will be able to identify areas of the LAN subject to modifications after more than six months' exposure to the LAN.
2 The student must, from memory, list any user groups that may be in existence.
3 With recourse to policy and procedure manuals, the student will be able to complete and forward through appropriate channels a formal suggestion for a modification to the LAN.

Addresses

Just as mail cannot be sent to a person without knowing that person's address, information cannot be interchanged on the LAN without the subscriber's knowledge of the addresses of the recipients.

It is easy to say that this file should go to Mark Jones in Engineering, but the LAN does not know how to translate "Mark Jones in Engineering" to an electronic address. The subscriber must be able to provide the LAN with the address of transmitted data.

Normally an address is nothing more than a series of digits arranged in a specific format. This format depends on the topology of the LAN. Some types of hardware and software allow for a cross-reference between name and address.

For example, the file server in the Engineering Department has an address that, if shown in numbers, would be written as

100.023.024.129. For ease of use, this file server has the name of "Newton." In this instance, when the subscriber wants to send data to Engineering, he opens a connection through the LAN to "Newton," not to 100.023.024.129.

Performance Objective

Given a list of dummy and genuine names and addresses with the LAN the student will be able to:

1 Separate the dummy names from the genuine.
2 Correspond the name or address with the element of the organization that device serves.

Such actions will be performed without recourse to written materials. Each selection should take no more than ten seconds.

Telecommunications Failure

Although the following statement is sometimes made in jest, it is not appropriate for LAN subscribers:

> When in trouble or in doubt,
> Run in circles, scream and shout!

This is not the type of activity for a subscriber to engage in when the LAN actually fails. There are several things the subscriber should be doing:

- Inform the correct people of the trouble.
- Pay attention to what has happened.
- Provide assistance as requested.
- Report trouble accurately.

Inform the Correct People

Not only must the failure of the LAN be reported, but it must be reported to the correct people. Depending on the size of the organization, the initial report must be made to either the help desk or technical control office. After notifying the correct persons, the subscriber must report the failure to his immediate supervisor. If the help desk or technical control do not exist, and the subscriber's supervisor cannot help, the subscriber must contact the LAN Manager's office directly. If notification of the trouble was by telephone, the subscriber should note the name and telephone number of the person who took the trouble call.

Performance Objective

The student will be able to list the necessary persons or office to contact when he notes a telecommunications failure. This list will be constructed in the correct contact sequence with primary and, where available, alternate telephone numbers.

Pay Attention To What Has Happened

Many times the problem experienced by the subscriber has bothered other subscribers simultaneously. Those charged with the responsibility to correct errors may recognize that this is just another affected subscriber rather than a new problem.

Some problems can be corrected from a remote location without an engineer or technician traveling to the subscriber's location. Such travel is costly in terms of time and corporate resources. Many times the subscriber can correct the problem under remote guidance from the engineer or technician. In either of these cases, a detailed description of the symptoms of the error will speed the restoration process.

In addition to noting the symptoms, the subscriber should also provide other information when he reports a telecommunications failure. This information should be as specific as possible.

Location: Location in this context means the location of the equipment the subscriber was using when the failure was noted. Simply saying "in the personnel department" is normally not enough. Give the floor and office number. If cubicles are in use, describe the location by referring to a door, window, or other fixture. The subscriber must also report his full telephone number or extension as appropriate.

Type of Equipment: The final part of the reporting process is to list the type of equipment experiencing the failure. Is the defective device a terminal, a personal computer? A printer? A modem? If known, the model number, serial number, or any other unique identifier will assist the restoration process.

Performance Objective

Trouble reporting requires three separate types of knowledge. The student must be able to convey this knowledge to others. Therefore, without recourse to written materials the student will be able to:

1 Identify the specific symptoms shown by the defective piece of equipment.
2 Give directions so that maintenance personnel can get to his location as quickly as possible.
3 List the name(s) and model number(s) of equipment in use at his location.

Assistance

When engineers or technicians remotely troubleshoot a defective condition, they may need subscriber assistance. If this is the case, the subscriber should be available to perform whatever actions are requested. If the subscriber cannot be available to assist the troubleshooting procedures, the subscriber's immediate supervisor must find a substitute.

Accuracy in Reporting

Describing error conditions requires attention to detail. Simply reporting "my terminal doesn't work" is not enough. What are the symptoms? Does it turn on? Are the screen characters normal? Can a connection be opened to one address, but not another? When did this occur? Time of failure can be very important in the restoration effort.

Many organizations use a specific form, normally called a trouble ticket, for reporting and tracking error conditions. Subscribers should know exactly what information must be entered on the trouble ticket.

One very important point should be made here. If the subscriber sees smoke rising from his equipment his first action is to disconnect the equipment from the wall plug(s). His next step is to get a fire extinguisher while directing a coworker to warn others and call the fire department.

Performance Objective

The student will, with the assistance of appropriate forms, notes, manuals, and related documents evaluate a defective piece of equipment and prepare a detailed and accurate trouble report within five minutes.

Slow Response Time

From time to time, perhaps even during a given day the subscriber may notice a long delay in a transaction going across the LAN. This means that many people are using the LAN and its services. Patience is the only cure for this type of delay. Two points should be brought forward for the subscribers' consideration: subjective evaluation and realistic alternatives.

Subjective Evaluation

When people are in a hurry to finish a task, anything that delays that task is an irritant. When the cause of delay cannot be corrected, some people's judgment skews and minor problems assume major proportions. Subscribers and LANs fall into this category.

Time-Critical Information: If the information interchange is truly time critical, approaches other than the LAN are suggested. But in counterpoint, we offer this. Nothing the subscriber normally has available to him travels faster than electricity. Use the LAN; as slow as it may appear to be, it is faster than almost anything else.

Complaints: After some exposure to the LAN, the subscriber sees a pattern of periods of slow response. He may formally notify the LAN Manager of this pattern of slow response periods. In all likelihood the LAN Manager is aware of the problem, but it never hurts to remind him.

Performance Objective

After six to nine months of exposure to the operating characteristics of the LAN, the student will be able to identify patterns of slow response time and plan his use of the LAN accordingly.

Information Security

By virtue of his job, the subscriber has access to information that is important to his employer. That same information may be more important to his employer's competitors. Therefore, the subscriber must be knowledgeable of information security procedures.

Passwords

The use of passwords is the first line of defense for information security. The subscriber must be able to use passwords effectively.

Controlling Passwords: The subscriber must keep his password(s) confidential. He should not write them on a piece of paper that is left on his desk or in a drawer. The subscriber must treat passwords as he would his own money, the keys to his house and car, or his credit card(s). The subscriber should never tell anyone else his password. Passwords should not be easy to guess. The subscribers' name, address, telephone number, or license plate number should not be used for passwords. Passwords should not be fewer than six letters/numbers long, nor more than eight. Random letter/number combinations are the best, but they are also the hardest to remember.

Changing Passwords: Passwords should be changed regularly. The change should occur sometime between 60 and 90 days. The date of change should be varied. Do not always change passwords after 65 days. Previous passwords should not be recycled. If the subscriber's previous password was "jewels" and the new password is "lumber," the next time the password changes, "jewels" should not be reused.

Performance Objective

1 The student will, from memory, recite corporate policy on the selection and use of passwords.
2 The student will, using notes and manuals, demonstrate the ability to change his password without coaching.

Corporate Data

Information and data that organizations handle fall into three categories:

- Proprietary
- Confidential
- Secret

Without getting into legal definitions, proprietary information is that information on which the organization creates profits and jobs. Confidential information is that information concerning money and people. This includes corporate stock information, manufacturing costs, and medical or salary information about employees. Secret information is proprietary or confidential information that has been entrusted to the organization by an outside organization or individual.

Another item of interest should be brought to the subscriber's attention. The addresses of file servers/hosts are of prime importance to those engaged in electronic espionage. The names and/or addresses of such file servers and/or hosts should not be available to the casual passerby. Discussion of telecommunications capabilities should not extend beyond the confines of the organization without specific prior permission from both the LAN Manager and the security department.

Performance Objective

From memory, the student will be able to define the different types of corporate data and recite the procedures used to actively prevent the loss or compromise of such data.

Software

Software is subject to unauthorized modifications, which in turn damage or destroy corporate data and applications. The subscriber, either knowingly or unknowingly, can introduce infected software into the corporation through the LAN. Therefore, he should be warned, in plain and simple terms, that no software is to be installed in the LAN, or equipment attached to the LAN, without specific written permission from the LAN Manager.

Performance Objective

Without recourse to any written materials, the student will be able to recite current corporate policy regarding the inclusion of personal software on the LAN.

GLOSSARY

Address, the electronic location of a specific piece of hardware within the LAN.

Application, the software package that the subscriber wishes to use; for example, a word processing program, a spreadsheet, or a database.

Availability, a measure, in percentage, of the time the LAN is capable of passing traffic.

Bandwidth, a unit of measurement of the LAN's capacity; bandwidths are normally expressed in bits per second (bps) or multiples thereof.

Baseband, a method by which multiple communications are carried over transmission media sequentially; Usually applies to trunks only.

Bridge, a piece of hardware used to connect LANs of similar topography. Also see repeaters, routers, and gateways.

Broadband, a method by which multiple communications are carried over transmission media simultaneously; usually applies to trunks only.

Bit, Binary Digit; the smallest quanta of data communications.

Circuit, transmission media that can be used by only one subscriber at a time. (*See also* TRUNK.)

Checksum, the term is normally used for a mathematical representation of the data within a packet; used to ensure that a packet is not corrupted in transmission.

CSMA, Carrier Sensing Multiple Address; a random access topography LAN. When the CSMA is followed by /CD, it means Collision Detection. When followed by /CA, it means Collision Avoidance. CSMA LANs are some of the most common in existence. Also known as IEEE 802.3.

CPU, Central Processing Unit; the part of the computer that actually performs the data manipulation.

DCE, Data Communications Equipment; any part of the LAN that is not transmission media or DTE. Some of the more common DCE include modems, terminal servers, or multiplexers.

DTE, Data Terminal Equipment; the last piece of electronics hardware on the subscriber's end of a circuit or trunk; Usually a computer, a printer, or a terminal.

E-Mail, a software application that allows subscribers to send information to other subscribers over the LAN; usually very informal, almost like a bulletin board.

Encryption, the process of electronically "scrambling" traffic so that it is intelligible only by the intended recipient.

Ethernet, a telecommunications protocol developed by Xerox Corporation; most commonly used in conjunction with CSMA-type LANs.

File Server, a computer with one or more very large, high-speed disks which act as storage space for multiple subscribers.

Gateway, a specific piece of hardware and software used to link dissimilar LANs.

Kilo (or K), a prefix meaning one thousand (1000).

LATA, Local Access Transport Area; the geographic area within a telephone company's area code.

Location, the geographical nexus of a piece of hardware or software; usually given as building, floor, room, and so on.

Line, as in "leased line," a circuit or trunk provided by a VAN/WAN vendor.

LAN, Local Area Network; a self-supporting infrastructure of hardware, software, and transmission media dedicated to information interchange in support of a single organization.

Matrix Switch, a specialized type of telecommunications equipment used to switch data communications traffic at very high speed; somewhat akin to a private branch exchange. Sometimes known as an automated switch or an XY switch.

Metallic Pair, wire or nonoptic cable used to carry LAN traffic.

MODEM, Modulator/Demodulator; a piece of hardware used to converts bits from the terminal or computer into tones for transmission over WAN/VAN provided circuits. The process is reversed at the distant end.

Multiplexer, an electronic device that combines many circuits or trunks into a larger trunk. The process is reversed on the distant end.

Mega, (or M), a prefix meaning one million (1,000,000).

Micro, a prefix meaning one one-millionth (0.000001).

Milli, a prefix meaning one one-thousandth (0.001).

MTBF, Mean Time Between Failure(s), a statistically derived failure rate of LAN hardware; used for planning purposes in computing failure rates and spare equipment stockage levels.

MTTR, Mean Time To Repair, the statistical average length of time it takes to facilitate the repair of a given piece of LAN hardware.

Packet, a highly defined structure of bits used to ensure accurate delivery of data through the LAN.

Password, a short, usually 6–8 letters, numbers, or a combination thereof, word that provides some limited security to the LAN or hosts attached to the LAN.

Print Server, one or more printers, with some electronic "intelligence" attached to the LAN for certain authorized subscribers' use.

Propagation, the physical process of transmission of traffic through the LAN. Propagation characteristics are the electronic characteristics of the transmission media.

Protocol, a commonly agreed upon set of rules defining the methods used for data communications sessions.

PBX, Private Branch eXchange; a switchboard that is normally computerized. When used to switch only data communications, it can be identified as an XY switch.

Router, a piece of hardware used to send traffic to the correct subLAN, thereby reducing the traffic loading.

Sink, the destination of traffic on the LAN.

Source, the origin of traffic on the LAN.

Status, hardware, software, and transmission media can hold one of four different types of status at any given instant:
a. Defective—error condition(s) exist; cannot be used without restoration effort.
b. In use—passing traffic at this time.
c. Operational—capable of passing traffic, but not in use at this time; normally applies to "hot" spare.
d. Standby—ready to be made operational.

Subscriber, the person who is authorized to use the LAN; may or may not be authorized to use all resources connected to the LAN.

TMDE, Test, Measurement, and Diagnostic Equipment; hardware used to measure or evaluate the performance of the LAN.

Terminal, a combination keyboard and display device with no processing power; requires the LAN to provide connection to a computer located elsewhere; sometimes known as a dumb terminal or glass teletype.

Terminal Server, a piece of hardware used to connect many terminals to the transmission media at lower cost; provides limited "intelligence" but no computational power to the terminals.

Throughput, a measure of the ability of the LAN to pass a given amount of traffic in a specified time limit; can also mean the total number of bits passed, less protocols, retransmissions, and defective transmissions. The appropriate meaning is taken from context.

Timing, the pulses necessary to synchronize certain types of hardware. Such pulses must be of very high accuracy.

Token Ring, a very common, IBM-supported LAN topography that is also known as IEEE 802.5.

Topography, the conceptual (versus physical) design of the LAN that can include bus, ring, or star. These can be mixed. Theoretically, for instance, a ring topology LAN can be a series of interconnected stars.

Topology, the physical distribution of all components in a LAN. If represented in a drawing, the spatial relationships between components are shown.

Transmission Media, Wire, cable, radio, or free-space light methods used to carry traffic from one location in the LAN to another.

Trouble Ticket, a formal means of tracking the conditions of the restoration efforts put forth by LAN engineers and technicians.

Trunk, transmission media that can be used by many subscribers. (*See also* CIRCUIT.) Sometimes known as backbone.

Twisted Pair Wiring, common telephone wiring.

TCP/IP, Transmission Control Protocol/Internet Protocol; a widely implemented data communications standard.

VAN, Value Added Network; the product of a firm which buys local and long distance service from vendors of bandwith, and modifies this bandwidth in some fashion. The modified bandwidth is then resold to consumers.

WAN, Wide Area Network; bandwidth sold by local and long-distance telephone companies to consumers or VAN vendors.

Recommended Additional Reading

Ellis, Robert L. *Designing Data Networks*. Englewood Cliffs, N.J.: Prentice-Hall, 1986.

Folts, Harold C. *Data Communications Standards*, Vols. I–III. New York: McGraw-Hill Information Systems Co., 1986.

Halsall, Fred. *Introduction to Data Communications and Computer Networks*. Great Britain: Addison-Wesley Publications Limited. 1985.

Hammond, J. G. and O'Reilly, P. J. *Performance Analysis of Local Computing Networks*. Reading, Mass.: Addison-Wesley, 1986.

Held, Gilbert. *Data Communications Procurement Manual*. New York: McGraw-Hill, 1980

IEEE. "CSMA/CD Access Method." ANSI/IEEE Std 802.3–1985. New York: IEEE Standards Board, 1985.

IEEE. "Token Passing Bus Access Method." ANSI/IEEE Std 802.4–1985. New York: IEEE Standards Board, 1985.

IEEE. "Token Ring Access Method." ANSI/IEEE Std 802.5–1985. New York: IEEE Standards Board, 1985.

Kreager Paul S. *Practical Aspects of Data Communications*. New York: McGraw-Hill, 1983.

Kuo, Franklin F. (ed.). *Protocols and Techniques for Data Communications Networks*. Englewood Cliffs, N.J.: Prentice-Hall, 1981.

Lenk, John D. *Handbook of Data Communications*. Englewood Cliffs, N.J.: Prentice-Hall, 1984.

Marotta, Robert E. (ed.). *The Digital Dictionary*. Bedford, Mass.: Digital Equipment Corporation, 1986.

McNamara, John E. *Technical Aspects of Data Communication*. (2d ed.) Bedford, Mass.: Digital Equipment Corporation, 1982.

Peck, Richard J. (ed.). *Datapro Reports on PC Communications*. Vols. I–III. Delran, N.J.: Datapro Research Corp, 1988.

Personick, Stewart D. *Optical Fiber Transmission Systems.* New York: Plenum Press, 1981.

Rosner, Roy D. (ed.). "Satellites, Packets, And Distributed Telecommunications." Belmont, Calif.: Lifetime Learning Publications, 1983.

Stallings, William. *Local Networks.* (2d ed.) New York: Macmillan Publishing, 1987.

Stallings, William. *Handbook of Computer Communications Standards.* Vols. I–III. New York: Macmillan Publishing, 1987.

Tanenbaum, Andrew. *Computer Networks.* Englewood Cliffs, N.J.: Prentice-Hall, 1981.

Index

Access count report, 222, 223
Access methods of LANs, 20–23
  deterministic, 20, 21–22
  heuristic, 20, 22–23
Accounting management, 35–55
  case study, 53–55
  history of, 36
  implementation of, 46–49
  measurements of LANs and, 175
  methods of, 36–38
  negative aspects of, 43–46
  organizational growth and, 49–52
  OSI standards for, 189
  positive aspects of, 39–42
  summary, 52–53
Address of network devices
  reports on, 209, 210
  security and, 145–46
  subscriber's guide to, 246–47
Advanced Research Project Agency
  (ARPA or ARPAnet), 25
Alarm conditions, reports on, 211–13
ALOHA network, 13, 22
American National Standards Institute
  (ANSI), 183
Analysts and fault management, 96–97
ARCNET, 184
Audit trails, 151–52
  negative aspects of, 154–55

Authority/responsibility in technical
  control centers, 99
Automation and LANs, 138–39
Availability
  equation for calculating, 113
  objective standards for, 113–16
  subjective standards for, 117

Backups, 27, 241
Bandwidth, 12
  efficiently allocating use of, 67
  identifying consumers of, 39
  measurements of, 175
  report on availability of, 212, 213
  report on change in, 213–14, 215
Bandwidth consumption
  calculating, 47–48
  charging by, 38
  report on, 214–16
Beacon messages, 48
Biological measurements for security,
  148
  negative aspects of, 156
Bits. *See also* Throughput
  charging by number of, 37
  data, 47
  overhead, 47
  per second, 57
Bonding new employees, 197

Break-out box, 177
Bridges, 38, 50, 51, 131–32
Budget(s)
  commonality/standardization of
    equipment and, 65–66
  manager's responsibilities for, 2–3
  measurements of LANs and, 166
  supervisor's responsibilities for, 5–6
Bus networks, 13–14, 19–20
  access methods of, 22
  diagram of, 19
  point of failures in, 87
  strengths of, 19–20
  weaknesses of, 20

Carterfone ruling on data communica-
    tions, 14–15
Case studies, 6–7
Central processing unit (CPU), 12
Central vs. distributed computing, 24–
    26
Checksums, 127, 128
Circuits in LANs, 23–24
  dial-up, 79, 80
  inventory of, 79–81
  leased (see Leased circuits)
  operation capability of, 60
  report on, 216, 217
  report on costs of, 223, 224
  report on status of, 225
  speed of, 120
  use of non-LAN, 60
Clerical personnel and fault manage-
    ment, 96
Coaxial cable, 87
Cold spare equipment, 90, 98
Collision detection, 22
Commonality (standardization) of
    equipment/functions, 64–66, 70–
    72, 76–77
  performance management and, 137
Common carrier vendors
  charging for usage based on infor-
    mation from, 36–37, 38
  performance management and, 137
Configuration management, 56–84
  basic knowledge required in, 56–59
  case study, 82–84
  control of LAN assets in, 59–61
  implementing, 75–82
  negative aspects of, 70–75
  OSI standards for, 189

positive aspects of, 62–70
  summary, 82
Connection, 57
Connectivity in LANs, 23–24
Consultative Committee International
    Telephone and Telegraph (CCITT),
    183
Contract maintenance of LANs, 101–3
Corporate culture and LANs, 24–33
  central vs. distributed computing
    and, 24–26
  LAN Manager's viewpoint and, 27–
    28
  MIS departments and, 26
  organizational information move-
    ment and, 28–29
  organizational information needs
    and, 29–31
  PC user's viewport and, 26–27
  subscriber satisfaction and, 32–33
Corporate espionage, 94, 196, 252
  prevention of, through security
    management, 152–54
Corporate mergers/acquisitions, 31
Costs of information exchange, 3–4, 31
Costs of new employees, 192–93
Costs of LANs, 31
  budgetary considerations and, 2, 5–6
  configuration management results
    and, 81
  efficient allocation of, through ac-
    counting management, 40
  forecasting 65, 81–82
  hardware/software, for accounting
    management, 43–44
  leased circuits, 66–67
  maintenance, 242–43
  personnel, 43, 68
  subscriber's guide to reducing, 243–
    44
  usage, 36–37, 38, 242
CSMA/CA (Carrier Sense Multiple Ac-
    cess with Collision Avoidance),
    13, 22
CSMA/CD (Carrier Sense Multiple Ac-
    cess with Collision Detection), 13–
    14, 22
Customer Premise Equipment (CPE),
    36–37

Data. See also Information
  compartmentalized, 150–51

Data (*cont.*)
  controlling non-electronic, 157–58
  preventing infection of, 154
  subscriber's guide to security of, 252
Data communications, Carterfone rul-
  ing on, 14–15
Data Communications Equipment
  (DCE), 58
Data interchange, organizational, 28
Data processing equipment required in
  performance management, 124
Data Terminal Equipment (DTE), 147
Data Termination Equipment (DTE), 58
DECNET, 188
Department of Defense, 184
Designed capacity limitations, report
  on, 217, *218*
Deterministic access methods, 21–22
Dial-back security, 148–49
  negative aspects of, 156–57
Dial-up circuits
  inventories of, 79, 80
  report on costs of, 223, 224
  report on status of, *225*
Digital multimeter (DMM), 177
Disaster recovery, 103–4
Distributed vs. central computing, 24–
  26
Dumb terminals, 16, 71

Ease of use and subscriber satisfaction,
  118, 122
Electronic Order Interchange (EOI),
  28–29
Electronics Industry Association (EIA),
  183
Encryption devices, 100, 146–48, 150
  keys to, 147–48, 155–56, 222
  negative aspects of, 155–56
  report on changes in, 222
Engineers
  fault management and, 97
  providing challenges to, 201
  training for, 198–99
Ergonomics, 245
Ethernet LAN, 57, 172, 184, 208
Evaluation of personnel, 202–3
Events vs. faults in fault management,
  95
Expert systems, impact of, on fault
  management, 107

False fronts, 151
Fault management, 85–110
  case study, 108–10
  faults vs. events in, 95
  identifying recurring performance
    failures in, 133–34
  impact of expert systems on, 107
  implementation of, 98–104
  measurements of LAN and, 165,
    174–75
  negative aspects of, 96–98
  organizational growth and, 104–7
  OSI standards for, 189
  positive aspects of, 93–95
  proactive techniques of, 85–89
  evaluating performance and, 86–87
  developing alternative routing and,
    87–88
  monitoring transient disruptions
    and, 88–89
  reactive techniques of, 89–93
  contingency planning and, 91–92
  hot sites to avoid failures and, 90–91
  restoration after failures and, 68–69,
    89–90
  scenario building/effort prioritizing
    and, 92–93
  summary, 107–8
Federal Communications Commission,
  46
Fiber optic cable, 168–69
File server, 43
  point of failure at, 87
  security considerations and, 100, 142
File transfers
  subscriber's guide to, 240–41
  time required for, 128–29
Financial records, security management of, 153
Forecasting costs, 65, 81–82
Frames, 127
Fraud and theft, security for preventing, 143
Free-space light as transmission media,
  168–69

Gateways, 38
General and Administrative (G&A)
  costs, reduction of, through accounting management, 40
Growth of LANs
  measurements of LANs and, 165–66

multiple networks and, 106–7
single network and, 104–6

Hardware. *See also* Circuits in LANs;
    Transmission media
alternative routing of, 87–88
color perception in personnel work-
    ing on, 194
commonality/standardization of, 64–
    66, 70–72, 76–77, 137
costs of, for accounting manage-
    ment, 43–44
evaluating reliability of, 122–23
functions of, 58–59
impact of new, on performance
    management, 135
inventory of, 57–58, 62–63
maintenance history of, 63
measurements of LANs as proof
    against claims from vendors of,
    167
operating status of, 59–60
report on capacity of, 218, *219*
report on upgrade of, 220, *221*
saving on unused, 67
shipment of, 137
spare, 89–90, 98
status report on, 219, *220*
subscriber's guide to, 237–38
supervisor's responsibilities for per-
    formance of, 4–5
updates of, 61
Headers, 127
Help desk at technical control center,
    100–101
Heuristic access methods, 22–23
Host or server CPU cycle, charging by,
    37–38
Hot sites, 90–91, 103
Hot spare equipment, 89, 90, 98, 103

IBM (International Business Machines),
    184
IEEE 802.5 standard, 184
Information. *See also* Data
flow of, within organizations, 28–29
identifying security-threatened, 158–
    59
needs for, within organizations, 29–
    31

security management of corporate,
    143–44, 152–53, 252
Interconnected LANs, accounting
    management for, 51–52
Inter-LATA usage, 36
International Association of Electrical
    and Electronics Engineers (IEEE),
    183–84
International standards for LAN oper-
    ation, 183–84
International Standards Organization
    (ISO), 11, 183–84. *See also* Appen-
    dix A
International Telecommunications
    Union (ITU), 183
Interviews of potential LAN person-
    nel, 193–95
legalities affecting, 193–94
testing during, 194–95
Intra-LATA usage, 36
Inventory of LAN contents and config-
    uration management, 57–58
circuits and, 79–81
format for, 59(table)
security considerations of, 78–79

Keys to encryption devices, 147–48,
    155–56
report on changes in, *222*
Kilobits per second (Kbps), 57

LAN. *See* Local area networks (LANs)
Layered security
access to LAN, 150
audit trails and, 151–52
compartmentalized data and, 150–51
diagram of, *149*
passwords and, 145
physical security and, 149–50
traps and false fronts and, 151
Leased circuits, 12
inventory of, 79–80
report on costs of, 223, *224*
report on status of, *225*
saving costs on, 66–67
Life insurance for employees, 197
Light signals as transmission media,
    168–69
Line replaceable units (LRUs), 69–70
Local Area Networks (LANs), 8–34
access methods of, 20–23
case study, 34

Local Area Networks (*cont.*)
  components of, 11
  configuring (*see* Configuration management)
  connectivity of, 23–24
  defective conditions in (*see* Fault management)
  description of this text and, 8–9
  diagram of, *10*
  goal of, 2, 236–37
  history of private networks and, 9–15
  impact of, on corporate culture, 23–33
  map of, for subscribers, 234
  paying for (*see* Accounting management)
  report on designed capacity limitations of, 217, *218*
  summary, 33
  topologies of, 15–20
  unauthorized modifications to, 245–46
Local Area Transport Area (LATA), 36
Local Exchange Carrier (LEC), 11
Logical circuits, 23, 24
Logic bombs, 154

Maintenance of LANs, 27
  contracted from outside the organization, 101–3
  history of, 63
Management Information Systems (MIS), 24–25
  relationship to LANs of, 26, 27
Management paradigm, 2
Managers of LANs, 1–4, 232
  abilities required by, 3–4
  challenges to, 4
  delegation of authority by, 104–5
  impact of standards on, 187–88
  reports required of (*see* Report(s))
  responsibilities of, 2–3
  viewpoint of, within the corporation, 27–28
Matrix switch, 87
Mean Time Between Failures (MTBF), 73, 122, 130–31, 199
Mean Time To Repair (MTTR), 73, 122, 130, 199
Measurements of LANs, 164–81. *See also* Performance management

case study, 179–81
protocol functions and, 171–73
reasons for, 164–67
response time and, 173
scope of, and performance management, 175
support of management functions with, 174–75
throughput and, 169–71
TMDE type and applications and, 176–78
transmission media and, 167–69
summary, 179
usage, 36–38, 47–48, 166
Megabits (Mbps), 57
Meters, role of, in LAN measurements, 177
Modems, 70
  resource maximization of, 119–21
  streaming/screaming, 174
  throughput and, 170
Multiple LANs and organizational growth
  accounting management in, 50–51
  fault management in, 106–7
Multiplexers, 70–71, 90

National Institute of Standards and Technology (NIST), 184
Network analyzer, 43, 44, 89
  equipment commonality and, 64–65
  needed in multiple network growth, 106
Nonmetallic transmission media, 168–69

Ohmmeter, 167
Open Systems Interconnect (OSI) model, 185–87, 188
  diagram of, *185*
  layers 2 through 7 of, 186–87
  physical layer (layer 1) of, 185
  specific management functional areas (SMFA) of, 188–90
Operating status of hardware/software, 59–60
Organizational change, impact on performance management of, 125–26, 135–38
Organizational dissention
  caused by accounting management, 44–45

caused by configuration management, 72–74
consensus building to avoid, 74, 77–79
Organizational goals, configuration mmanagement and, 75–79, 81
Organizational growth
accounting management and, 49–52
commonality/standardization as factor in frozen, 70–72
creation of more LANs to facilitate, 50–51
fault management and, 104–7
increasing size of LANs to facilitiate, 50
performance management and, 134–39
Organizational information flow, 28–29
Organizational information needs, 29–31
current, 29–30
future activities and, 30–31
Oscilloscopes, 176

Packet analysis, 178
Packet-format networks, 12, 47, 126–27, 128, 174. *See also* Protocol functions, measuring
Passwords, 100, 144–46, 150
reports on, 226, 227
subscriber's guide to, 251
Patch panel, 87
Performance degradation, predicting, 121–23
Performance evaluation in LAN fault management, 85–89
developing alternative traffic routing, 87–88
monitoring service in, 88–89
quality of service in, 86
single point of failure in, 86–87
stress points in, 86
Performance management, 111–41
case study, 140–41
components of, 111–19
object standards for, 112–16
subject standards for, 116–19
implementation of, 126–34
improved, through accounting management, 40

measurements of LANs and, 164–65, 175
negative aspects of, 124–26
organizational growth and, 134–39
OSI standards for, 189
positive aspects of, 119–23
summary, 139
Performance tuning, 119, 171
Personal computer (PC) users, relationship to LANs of, 26, 27–28
Personnel, 191–207. *See also* Subscribers
bonding of, 197
configuration management, savings in manpower, and, 68
costs of, 43, 68, 192–93
errors of, as security problems, 157
evaluation of, 202–3
fault management and costs of, 96–97
interviews for hiring, 193–94
life insurance for indispensable, 197
opposition to configuration management by individual, 73–74
opposition to configuration management by physical plant, 73–74
performance management and costs of, 123–24
prevention of turnover among, 201–4
promotions for, 204–6
references for potential, 195–96
security considerations and, 157, 160–61, 196–99
selection of, 191–93
summary, 206–7
testing of potential, 194–95
training of, 92–93, 198–200
Personnel records, security management of, 1553
Physical circuits, 23, 24
Physical relocation of LANs, 30, 60–61
performance management and, 135–38
Point-of-sale terminals, 86
Post, telephone, and telegraph (PTTs), standards for, 183
Print server, security and 142–43
Private Branch Exchange (PBX), 37, 38
reports on, 227–28
Productivity, increased, through shared resources, 95

Promotions for personnel, 204–6
Protocol analyzer, 171–72, 174, 177–78
Protocol functions, measuring, 171–73
Protocol-required data, 127–28

Quality control, 199–200. *See also* Fault
management; Personnel

Radio signals as transmission media,
168–69
Random number generators, 146, 150
negative aspects of, 155
Reactive fault management, 89–93
Records of LAN conditions/history
role in configuration management
of, 62–63
in technical control center, 99–100
Redesign of LANs, 131–32
financial impact of, 132–33
measurements of throughput and,
170
References of potential personnel, 195–
96
Regional Private Operating Agency
(RPOA), 11, 183
Regulations on internal telecommunications organizations, 46
Remote terminals, 12–13
Remotely located LANs, manned vs.
unmanned, 105, 106–7
Report(s), 208–31
add/move/drop subscribers, 209–11,
212
alarm conditions, 211–13
bandwidth availability, 213, 214
bandwidth changes, 213–14, 215
bandwidth consumption, 214–16
circuit status, 216, 217
designed capacity limitations, 217,
218
electronic address, 209, 210
encryption key changes, 222
equipment capacity, 218, 219
equipment status, 219, 220
equipment upgrade, 220, 221, 222
LAN access count, 222, 223
lease/dial circuit cost, 223, 224
lease/dial circuit status, 225
loss/slippage of timing signals, 225,
226
password data, 226, 227

Private Branch Exchange (PBX) data,
227–28
subscriber authorization, 228, 229
subscriber location, 228, 229
subscriber's guide to accuracy in,
249–50
summary, 231
TMDE (test, measurement, and diagnostic equipment), 229, 230
trouble ticket data, 230, 231
Reservation services, 13, 21
Resources
increased productivity through
shared, 95
maximization of, through performance management, 119–21
preventing unauthorized loss of, 143
subscriber's guide to sharing, 239–41
Response time
contract maintenance and, 102
measurements of, 165, 173
objective standards for, 112–13
subject standards for, 117–18
subscriber's guide to slow, 250
Restoration of failed LANs, 68–69, 89–
90
decreased time devoted to, through
fault management, 93–95
disaster recovery and, 103–4
at technical control centers, 99
Ring networks, 13, 17–19
access methods of, 21–22
diagram of, *18*
strengths of, 17–18
weaknesses of, 18–19
Robotics and LANs, 138
Routers, 38, 50, *51*, 131

Safety considerations for subscribers,
244–45
Security management, 27, 142–63
configuration management and, 78–
79
considerations of, when restoring
failures, 94
contract maintenance and, 102–3
hiring new employees and, 196–97
implementing, 157–61
identifying threatened areas in, 158–
59
identifying types of threats in, 157–
58, 159–61

layered security and, 149–52
methods of denying access in, 144–49
biological measurements and, 148
encryption and, 146–48
dial back and, 148–49
passwords and, 144–46
random number generators and, 146
negative aspects of, 154–57
OSI standards for, 189–90
positive aspects of, 152–54
reasons for instituting, 142–44
subscriber's guide to, 251–53
summary, 161–63
technical control center and, 100
Signal-to-noise ratio, 168, 175
Single LANs and organizational growth
accounting management in, 50
fault management in, 104–6
Slotted rings, 13
Software, LAN
commonality/standardization of, 67–68, 71, 76–77
costs of, for accounting management, 43–44
evaluating usefulness of, 122
knowing functions of, for configuration management, 58–59
operating status of, 59–60
site licenses for, 67–68, 117
subscriber's guide to, 238, 252–53
updates of, 61
Spare equipment, 89–90, 98, 103
Standards, 182–90
impact of operational, on LAN managers, 187–88
for management of LANs, 188–90
Open Systems Interconnect (OSI) model for, 185–87
philosophy of operational, 182–83
types of operational, 183–84
Star networks, 15–17
access methods of, 20
diagram of, 16
strengths of, 15–16
weaknesses of, 16–17
Station Message Detail Report (SMDR), 36, 37, 38
Stress points in LANs, evaluating, 86
Students of LANs, 6

Subnetworks (subLANs), 4, 131
Subscribers, 233
determining problems experienced by, 118–19
growth in number of, 134
handbook for, 234
LAN ease of use for, 118, 123
methods of charging, 36–38
opposition to configuration management by, 72
preventing complaints by, 123
report on added/moved/dropped, 209–11, 212
report on authorization for, 228, 229
report on location of, 228, 229
security requirements of, 154
Subscriber satisfaction, 32–33, 94
moving LANs and, 137
subjective performance standards and, 116–19
Subscriber's guide to LANs, 232–53
introduction/overview of, 232–36
LAN definitions in, 236–41
LAN operation in, 244–27 44
payment for use of LANs in, 241–
response time in, 250
security of information in, 251–53
telecommunications failures in, 247–50
Supervisors of LANs, 4–6, 232–33
responsibilities for budgets, 5–6
responsibilities for hardware, 4–5
Support equipment for LANs, 64–65

Tap(s), 57, 94
Technical control center for large LANs, 98–101
Technicians
fault management and, 97
providing challenges to, 201
responsibilities of, 2–3
security issues and, 100
training for, 199–200
Telecommunications
Carterfone ruling on, 14–15
creating a separate internal organization for, 40–42, 45–46
subscriber's guide to failure of, 247–50
Terminal server, throughput and, 170

Test, Measurement, and Diagnostic
Equipment (TMDE), 64, 70, 89, 97,
112
calibration of, 178
measurements of LANs using, 167–68
network growth and purchase of,
105
in performance management, 124
reports on, 229, 230
type and applications of, 176–78
Test file, performance management using, 112–13, 122, 129
Throughput, 57
impact of performance-management
implementation on, 126–28
measurements of, 169–71
objective standards for, 112
Time, charging for transmission, 37
Time domain reflectometer, 176
Timing signals, report on, 225, 226
Token ring, 13
access methods of, 21
Topography, LAN, and configuration
management, 57, 62
Topologies, LAN, 15–20
configuration management and, 56–57
growth of LANs and, 106–7
Traffic
capture of, and LAN measurement,
178
generation of, and LAN measurement, 178
security management and, 153, 158
Trailers, 127
Training for LAN personnel, 198–200
for engineers, 198–99
professional and nonprofessional,
200
subscriber's guide to, 233, 235
for technicians, 199–200
Training for LAN users, 65

Transient conditions in LANs, monitoring, 88–89
Transmission media, 11
alternative routing of, 87–88
measuring, 167–69
nonmetallic (radio and light), 168–69
performance degradation due to,
121–22
subscriber's guide to, 238
throughput and, 170–71
Trap doors, 154
Traps, 151
Trojan horses, 154
Trouble-ticket data, report on, 230–31
Two-person security rule, 151

Value Added Network (VAN), 12
billing customers of, 51–52
circuits, 60
growth of LANs and vendors of, 106
measurements of LANs and bills
from vendors of, 166–67
Vendors
charging for usage based on information from, 36–37, 38
performance management and, 137,
187
standards specific to, 184
Virtual circuits, 23, 24
Viruses, 154

Wide Area Networks (WANs), 11–12
billing customers of, 51–52
circuits, 60
diagram of, 10
growth of LANs and vendors of, 106
measurements of LANs and bills
from vendors of, 166–67
Worms, 154

X.25 data communications standard,
184
XY switch, 87